BOY REPUBLIC

PATRICK PEARSE AND RADICAL EDUCATION

BOY REPUBLIC

PATRICK PEARSE AND RADICAL EDUCATION

BRENDAN WALSH

The
History
Press
Ireland

First published 2013

The History Press Ireland
50 City Quay
Dublin 2
Ireland
www.thehistorypress.ie

© Brendan Walsh, 2013

The right of Brendan Walsh to be identified as the Author
of this work has been asserted in accordance with the
Copyrights, Designs and Patents Act 1988.

British Library Cataloguing in Publication Data.
A catalogue record for this book is available from the British Library.

ISBN 978 1 84588 796 4

Typesetting and origination by The History Press

Contents

Foreword by Declan Kiberd

Brendan Walsh has given us an open, honest and persuasive portrait of Patrick Pearse as teacher, headmaster and educational theorist.

Pearse left few notes on the preparation of his classes, yet the colonial authorities, whose pedagogic 'murder machine' he denounced, pronounced him a fine and effectual teacher. He believed in a child-centred approach and hated the idea of a rigid curriculum imposed on student and teacher alike by the system known as public examinations. He repeatedly argued that teachers and schools should not be assessed and rewarded according to results achieved in these tests. Yet, for all that, he was pragmatic enough to permit boys from his own college, St Enda's, to take the Intermediate Examination if their parents wished it.

In this book, Walsh demonstrates that administrations in the later nineteenth century took a more child-centred approach than either Pearse or posterity has given them credit for. If that makes some of Pearse's ideas a little less original than they might have seemed, it also shows that they had their practical, up-to-date side. He believed in teaching business methods as well as science, reflecting the widespread Victorian and Edwardian desire to give students useful skills, but he also insisted that school should be a free zone, a utopian space in which people could be freed of the constraints of the material world.

I had long thought that Pearse was a disciple of Maria Montessori but Walsh has located just one reference, mildly laudatory, in his writings which go on to question her notion of the teacher as servant rather than master. Convinced of the charism which touches all great teachers, he felt that they were entrusted with a priest-like office. Whereas Montessori believed that the teacher should stand back to centralise the activities of free-bonding children, Pearse felt that the true educator brings 'not a set of ready-made opinions but an inspiration and an example'. This was both his strength and his weakness for, placing such a premium on emotion, Pearse has left a much less developed set of educational theories than did Montessori or Pestalozzi or Froebel.

Walsh demonstrates that he was a consummate liberal, even a libertarian. He saw St Enda's not just as an answer to Anglicised public schools in which those Gaelic elements, spurned by colonial thinkers might be centralised, but also as a democratic zone in which future citizens could learn the art of self-government. So he devolved a remarkable number of decisions about the running of St Enda's to a School Council administered by the boys themselves – St Enda's really was a republic of childhood. We read here that in 1913, when a senior boy named James Rowan proposed that cricket be adopted as a summer sport, there was a spirited debate. Rowan's nationalist credentials were not in doubt, as he had just published a lament for the slaughtered rebels of 1798 in the school magazine, *An Scolaire*. However, another boy, D.P. O'Connor, opposed what he called 'this pernicious proposal'. During the prolonged controversy, tennis was suggested as a possible compromise before the majority finally voted for hurling. It is an interesting moment – one can hardly imagine the boys of Clongowes Wood or Blackrock College in 1913 being encouraged to debate a similar proposition to replace, say, rugby with hurling.

Far from being a recruiting camp for physical-force nationalism, St Enda's emerges in the following pages as an early version of such alternative, democratic schools as Summerhill, Dartington Hall or Beacon Hill. As few as twelve past pupils took part in the Easter Rising. Four of these were sworn-in members of the Irish Republican Brotherhood well before Pearse himself had joined, which suggests that they were more likely influenced by family tradition or some other factor. The appeal of St Enda's reached well beyond nationalist insurgents – Jim Larkin sent his son there, as did Eoin MacNeill. The list of monthly guest-speakers in the college is a roll-call of the Irish revival – Yeats, Hyde, Casement, Markievicz, and Gonne to name but a few.

Its teachers included the witty and gifted Thomas MacDonagh, who became a lecturer at University College Dublin. If Cúchulainn was, in the words of Desmond Ryan, 'An important if invisible member of staff', he was there not just as Celtic warrior but as English public schoolboy in drag; one whose example appealed to a combination of athleticism and aestheticism, of muscular Christian self-sacrifice, such as would have been espoused at Thomas Arnold's Rugby. Pearse and MacDonagh might have opposed colonial theory but they were genuine admirers of the English tradition of lyric poetry, from Thomas Campion to William Wordsworth.

In a period when corporal punishment was still widely used – and would be for another fifty years – Pearse saw little need for it. Accepting that boys, if trusted, would tell the truth, he adopted the Fiannaiocht code of '*glaineinargcroi, neartinarlamh, is beart de reirarmbria-thar*', and it generally worked – so much for the fang-toothed martinet of revisionist lore.

In the end, says Brendan Walsh, there was nothing really new in Pearse's pedagogy. What was new was his placement of the child-centred tradition within a culture of schooling that was dissenting. Pearse saw education in much the same way as Joyce saw the English language – as a weapon of empire which might nonetheless be captured, remodelled and turned back upon its authors by a dissident intellectual. Brendan Walsh has in this book done full justice to Pearse's ideas and to his practice, and by admitting the limitations of both he has redoubled our sense of the importance of what Pearse achieved.

Declan Kiberd, Dublin
January 2013

Introduction

This book is about Patrick Pearse's work as the founder of two schools, the work he did as a headmaster and teacher, and how he foreshadowed modern ideas about the use of schools for ideological ends – how learning should happen in them and why what happens in the classroom is politically important. For many it will come as a surprise to learn that Pearse dedicated his adult life to education, and to some it will appear far less interesting than the glamour of his final few years as member of the Irish Republican Brotherhood and executed rebel. However, the two cannot be separated and this book demonstrates that Pearse's work at St Enda's and St Ita's was deeply political in nature. Pedagogically it was forward-looking but not innovative, rather that its importance lay in the creation of a model of schooling that was a direct challenge to the type prevailing at the time: intensely competitive and examination driven, the content of which was very much influenced by English culture. The extent to which Dublin was an 'English city' in early twentieth-century Ireland is easily forgotten (*see* Chapter Five). C.S. Andrews recalled in 1979 that, before he was enrolled as a pupil at St Enda's, he had 'never heard of Fionn or Cúchulainn', something which would strike any Irish schoolchild today as extraordinary.

It was this omission that Pearse sought to address, in a way that was as emphatic as it was dismissive. Writing in 1906 he stated the case simply: the British had no right to interfere in schooling in

Ireland because they were British, not Irish. They were, therefore, 'no more entitled to dictate what should be taught to children in Connemara than they were to dictate what should be taught to children in Yokohama' (*see* Chapter Three).

Pearse's dedication to Irish nationalism is well know and widely documented. But much less is known about his educational work, which represents a gap in our historical knowledge. By his own admission, Pearse dedicated his adult life to schooling, but until now no book has appeared that deals exclusively with that work. Given that 104 years have elapsed since he founded St Enda's, the silence is remarkable. In the Dublin of the early twentieth century Pearse was known as a head-master, and this is how W.B. Yeats defined him for all time – the man who 'kept a school' – and this is how Pearse would like to have been remembered. He wrote in *The Murder Machine* that he had 'dedicated the greater part of [his] life' to education (*see* Chapter Five), and this book reveals how many of his friends and associates remembered him, primarily, as a teacher.

The lives of teachers is seldom the subject of history, although a growing body of international and American work has started to preserve the narratives of school teachers, finding in them stories that intersect with feminist and labour histories in particular. In the case of Pearse and St Enda's, this is particularly so. Four staff members were executed for their part in the Easter Rising, others were impris-oned. Frank Burke, its last headmaster, was in Croke Park on Bloody Sunday, when the Black and Tans shot fourteen civilians during an inter-county football match. The great luminaries of Irish Ireland visited the school, addressed the pupils, helped fund it and sent their children to be educated there. For a brief period it was the brightest and most lauded adventure of the cultural nationalist movement and, as we see in Chapter Six, it spawned a number of imitators. Like any school it had good and bad teachers, pupils who liked and disliked it, its everyday routine was humdrum in the way schooldays usually are but, in several fundamental ways, it was very different. St Enda's was to be a training ground for boys, not in republican militancy as so often thought (*see* Chapter Four), but in democratic nationalism. It was, as such, an experiment, and like so many similar experiments it ultimately failed and closed in 1935. Yet, as this book demonstrates, what Pearse achieved there predated, by many decades, the work of better-known radical educationalists whose theories now inform much of the western world's educational practice. This book seeks to address this omission and in doing so to accord to Pearse the place he deserves as one of Ireland's foremost radical educational thinkers. It was Pearse who first articulated the now widely understood use of schooling as a colonial tool and he was among the very first, in turn, to use education as a means of undermining that colonial dominance.

Brendan Walsh, Dublin City University
January 2013

One

Who was
Patrick Pearse?

AT HOME AND AT SCHOOL

Patrick Pearse was the first son of James Pearse (1839–1900) and Margaret Brady (1887–1932). They had four children, Margaret (1878–1968), Patrick (1879–1916), William (1881–1916), and Mary Brigid (1884–1947). Patrick Pearse began attending Westland Row Christian Brothers School in 1891, and between 1893 and 1896 sat four Intermediate Examinations. He enjoyed school and remembered that he 'learned quickly' having 'no recollection of any effort.'[1] According to his mother he was 'exceedingly fond of study', and upon leaving school his 'whole ambition was to teach boys.'[2] Mary Brigid remembered him as 'exceedingly studious' and, even in his teens, possessing 'every attribute of the perfect teacher'[3], while Eamonn O'Neill, who attended Westland Row along with Pearse, remembered him as a 'great reader.'[4]

He was influenced by the political radicalism of his father, James, who held strong non-conformist sympathies. James's small library reflected liberal and independent-minded views and included essays of radical thinkers and colonial history.[5] The adolescent Pearse was an avid reader and undoubtedly took an interest in his father's books. Pearse's grandfather had been politically liberal and his mother, Margaret, was a Unitarian.[6]

Radicalism and free-thinking, therefore, were characteristic of Pearse's paternal lineage, while his mother's ancestry was characterised by a spirit of separatist nationalism.

Much of what we know about Pearse's youth comes from an unfinished autobiographical sketch and the memories of his family, in Mary Brigid's *The Home Life of Pádraig Pearse*, published in 1934. To a contemporary reader, these recollections bear the stamp of an adoring family and are little more than hagiography, written at a time when the public was willing to accept such memories at face value. For the historian they are useful, but must be approached with the usual critical stance necessary when reading biography. This is even more important when the authors are family and the subject a national hero, executed for his part in his country's fight for freedom. The cautions of historical methodologies aside, we cannot expect a critical, detached account of Pearse from his sister and mother. We certainly cannot expect it in the Ireland of 1934, when the fallen leaders of the 1916 Easter Rising were held in almost religious awe and former insurgents filled the front and back benches of Dáil Eireann. Mary Brigid's book, and its contributors, pre-date the post-modern uncertainties of our times and it is unfair to look to it for anything beyond what it supplies; an affectionate, uncritical account of some aspects of Pearse's life. Yet, the book contains accounts by those who knew Pearse well and cannot, therefore, be ignored by those wishing to write about its subject.

Indeed, the home life of Pearse throws much light on his adult personality. His sculptor father evidently associated with artists, some of whom made nude drawings of the young Pearse. On these occasions he would lie 'without [his] clothes in the warmth of the fire', composing stories for himself: 'Some of the longest stories I ever made up … where made up while a man was making a picture of me stretched on my face with my chin resting on my hands.'[7] This was not uncharacteristic of the late Victorian and Edwardian view of pre-pubescent children as being unsullied and symbolic of an unworldly purity.[8] The artistic, but not bohemian, influence of Pearse's father was countered by his mother, whose great-grandfather had fought in the 1798 Rebellion and whose brother was hanged for treason. His great-aunt Margaret would tell him stories of Robert Emmet and Wolfe Tome and 'had herself known the Fenians'.[9] Undoubtedly, this old woman had a profound influence upon the young Pearse and he prized her tales of the Fianna and patriots above all others. But Pearse's convert father was a nationalist in the tradition of Parnell, fair-minded and reasonable; what Edwards called 'the best kind of decent Englishman'.[10] He was a stolid Edwardian, devoting his energies to a successful monumental carving business, with modest investments in shares and an interest in liberal thought. In this last aspect he was the opposite of his wife, and it was her influence that dominated Pearse's youth. James died when Patrick was twenty-one, and throughout his extensive writings there is barely a mention of him, although the theme of motherhood appears repeatedly.

Pearse believed that the combination of the 'widely remote traditions' of his parents made him the 'strange thing I am'. Only on one other occasion does he make reference to the complexity of his personality.[11] Indeed, what is most striking when one begins to write about Pearse is how different he was from the very earnest figure of the popular imagination. His family, for example, repeatedly refer to his sense of humour and largeness of personality. Although the historian treats these recollections with caution, others too remembered him as cheerful and genial, albeit occasionally withdrawn and introspective. As a child he was possessed with a vivid imagination and would fill his days playing at being a Shakespearian hero, military general or priest. Willie and Brigid enjoyed his antics and Edwards' claim that 'to a child as romantic as Patrick, family life must have been suffocatingly dull ...' is simply not supported by family recollections and certainly never hinted at by Pearse.[12] Mary Bulfin attended St Ita's and recalled that one afternoon Pearse regaled the girls with stories about his own schooldays, and while he himself did not laugh aloud he had 'a queer little secret smile that made one feel he was having a great chuckle away down inside in himself.'[13]

His mother and sister Brigid remember him bustling about the house, late for appointments, his reluctance to get out of bed in the morning, his brief flirtation with vegetarianism and his passion for opera. According to Brigid, in later years he attended 'every opera that came to Dublin, Wagner's heavy works being his particular favourites.'[14] He was energetic, playful and somewhat pompous, but outside of the family could be shy and serious. Eamonn O'Neill, who was at school with Pearse, described him as 'extremely reserved at school', and although Patrick's cousin Alfred McGloughlin described him as unathletic, he joined both the school boxing and football teams. He was also prominent in the school debating society – an aspect of school life he encouraged at St Enda's. Pearse worked hard at school and quickly gained a reputation as a fine orator and, according to O'Neill, his peers 'liked and respected him'.[15] He was, in short, a diligent, earnest and perhaps over-serious schoolboy. He appears to have been self-conscious but, at the age of sixteen, to have quickly developed a confident grasp of public speaking, when he and others formed the New Ireland Literary Society – a forum for discussing aspects of Irish literature. Unlike others who write of their schooldays, Pearse fails to mention friends and one is left with the impression that his maintained a certain distance from his peers and revealed his true self at home, rather than socially. Certainly, his brother Willie was his closest confidant and friend throughout his life.

As a young man, Pearse was a cultural nationalist. Irish historian Mary Hayden remembers that, when she first knew him, he had little interest in politics, and despite the attempts of later generations to associate him with a particular and narrow type of Catholicism, she remarks that he 'seldom spoke' of religion. Indeed, regarding schooling, Pearse was frequently critical of the Catholic hierarchy, religious-run schools, and the Christian Brothers in particular. In an Ireland where Religious Orders had a monopoly over secondary schooling, Pearse's school was managed and operated by lay persons.

Upon leaving secondary school, Pearse acted as a monitor – a type of junior assistant teacher – at Westland Row Christian Brothers' School. Perhaps it was this experience as a monitor that helped form his earliest thoughts on the individualistic and competitive secondary school system. Westland Row was made up of middle-and working-class boys. Pearse's father's occupation as a monumental sculptor meant that he was 'trade', but being self-employed and an artisan he belonged to the lower middle-class. The Christian Brothers were renowned for no-nonsense, examination-driven teaching and their schools often provided a direct route into white-collar employment; the Civil Service in particular. Since the mid-nineteenth century their schools have been held in high esteem and while Pearse set out to create a distinctly middle-class school in Rathfarnham, Brothers schools throughout Ireland catered for those less fortunate than the St Enda's boys. Nonetheless, for the young, sensitive bibliophile, the cramming and competition must have been anathema and, given his later criticism of the Brothers' methods, must have earned his silent disapproval. The regime in Westland Row, as in other secondary schools, was one of grinding preparation for the Intermediate Examinations. The final examination was a high-stake affair; schools published their successes in the daily newspapers and vied with one another in the hope of attracting enrolments. Prior to the Intermediate Education Act 1878, schools did not benefit from direct funding (*see* Chapter Two). In order to sidestep the unpalatable prospect of funding denominational schools in Ireland, the Act allowed schools to secure funding through the awarding of cash prizes for examination success. As a result, the Intermediate Examination – the ancestor of the present high-stake Leaving Certificate – became an annual ordeal for schools and a spectator sport for the public. When first held, in the summer of 1879 – the year of Pearse's birth – *The Irish Times* described the contest as an 'intellectual tilt and tournament', with 5,000 pupils entering 'the lists'.[16] It was this element of competition, the hot-housing of individuals that many schools, particularly the Christian Brothers', excelled at. But the schools cannot be blamed. They were the victims of a terminal examination system in which the public had 'an almost superstitious reverence' and which parents understood as the best chance of securing a fighting chance for their children in the labour market.[17] This was the system that Pearse baulked at, but at which, as a pupil, he was highly successful.

While in no way exceptional, he operated well within the system and gained the required marks to allow him to enter the Royal University of Ireland two years later.[18] He studied English, French and Celtic (Irish) and was considered an excellent student.[19] Eamonn O'Neill who also attended Westland Row remembered him as 'a grave, sweet, silent boy', who never joined in 'the ordinary games at playtime' but 'often climbed up on the high window-ledge of the schoolroom and sat there reading.'[20] Edwards makes the point that, at Westland Row, he would not have developed any ability to read critically; the requirements of the intermediate rendering any such luxury superfluous. But one suspects that Pearse's romantic imagination also prevented much analysis. During his mid and late teens he read, almost exclusively, Irish myths and legends – printed versions of what his great-aunt Margaret had told him in childhood. On winning a book-prize at the Senior Grade Intermediate

in 1896 he chose Thomas Flannery's *For the Tongue of the Gael*, a book of
essays on contemporaneous Irish writing – a choice that would appear
to undermine the view that he was disinterested in critical aspects of
Irish literature. However, his later writings indicate that he was unaware
of the analytical work being done by scholars, such as Kuno Meyer, for
example. Edwards is correct when she notes that as Pearse grew older,
he read the tales with a 'childish wonder' that would have 'shaken the
sophisticated and subtle Douglas Hyde'.[21]

   The grinding contestation Pearse endured at school was shared by
thousands of boys and girls, but few founded a school that offered a
strident alternative. As we shall see later, Pearse set out to establish a
school that would challenge the entire Intermediate System. This was
Pearse's way; he was a man of action. Not content as a teenager with
the lack of highbrow literary discussion in Dublin he was a founder
member of the New Ireland Literary Society. Edwards calls the title and
the circular announcing its establishment 'pretentious' – a forgivable trait
in earnest young literary men.[22] The sixteen-year-old Pearse, president
of the society, demonstrated an ignorance of European and contemporary Irish literature that was not uncharacteristic of most boys of his age.
Drilled in the intermediate texts he had little capacity for discernment,
and his addresses were not unlike those that appeared as essays in school
annuals of the period: enthusiastic rather than insightful. But this is not
to underestimate his commitment to starting something new. Regardless
of its juvenile nature, the society was, at least, an attempt to address
what Pearse considered the absence of literary and debating societies in
Dublin. This spirit manifested itself again in a wholly different and less
conventional matter two years later, when, aged eighteen, he publicly
noted the 'poor support' which the Irish clergy had extended to the
Irish language revival.

   The schoolboy Pearse was, then, hardworking, earnest, reserved,
successful in examinations and an avid, if unadventurous, reader. His
success at school is demonstrated in the Brothers asking him to act as a
monitor at Westland Row upon leaving school. Although, given Pearse's
dislike of their method and later trenchant criticisms of the Intermediate
Examination, one wonders at their doing so. He must, as a teenager,
have given the impression that were he to become a teacher, he would
fit the mould perfectly. At home, Pearse was outgoing, fun-loving and
busy. It would be tempting to conclude that this indicated a type of split

personality but what it in fact reflects is that Pearse was, in all respects, a not untypical, socially shy teenage boy; a fact he attested to himself in later life. After his father's death he became responsible for the family and there is no doubt that the affection of his family had prepared him for this transition. But Pearse's schooling tells us nothing about him other than the rather uninteresting fact that he was, in all respects, a rather ordinary schoolboy.

However, Pearse was an extraordinary adult and the object of this book is to tell the story of his adult life in teaching rather than to provide a general biography. He was, first and foremost, a teacher and a school principal. Pearse did not join the Irish Republican Brotherhood (IRB) until 1914, but since 1908 he had operated St Enda's School. It is not surprising, but it is a scholarly injustice, that a full-scale study of his educational work has not previously appeared. However, historians have written about aspects of this work and before we consider Pearse and St Enda's in detail, we will look at these valuable contributions and what they add to our knowledge of Patrick Pearse.

READING ABOUT PEARSE

Traditionally, Pearse's educational work has been regarded as forward-looking and enlightened, given the period in which he worked as a teacher. However, the view that he was 'at his peak as a theoretical educationalist' cannot be simply taken for granted.[23] Again, given his trenchant criticism of schooling in Ireland under British rule, his work must be examined within the context of education at the period, which, it turns out, was far less restrictive than Pearse claimed. Pearse was also less than generous in recognising innovations in the school curriculum that closely resembled those he weekly advocated in the pages of *An Claimeadh Soluis* – the journal of the Gaelic League.

Again, Pearse's criticisms cannot be properly understood without reference to primary and intermediate schooling in the late nineteenth and early twentieth centuries and the contemporary reports of school inspectors, along with official and commissioned reports, provide a wonderfully detailed context against which his criticisms can be understood and examined. Pearse's work on the teaching of Irish is much neglected but gave rise to the development of sensible teaching approaches, which reveal a firm grasp of sound methodology. His emphasis upon the language as a spoken medium in many ways fore-shadows modern understandings of language acquisition and this book details his work on behalf of the language in schools and as a compulsory subject for matriculation to the National University of Ireland.

Our main focus, however, is Pearse's work at St Enda's and St Ita's, although little is known about the latter. Gertrude Bloomer, who acted as headmistress at the school, did not keep thorough records and the school's short existence means that first-hand accounts are rare. However, a strong relationship existed between the staff and pupils of both schools, helping to disperse the myth of Pearse's shyness in the company of women and shed light upon his understanding of the nature and purpose of schooling.[24] Yet this understanding, while often progres-sive, was motivated by political rather than pedagogical concerns, and within it nestle ambiguities. For example, St Enda's was similar to the model of English boarding schools typified by Rugby in England, or Clongowes Wood and Castleknock College in Ireland. Indeed, Pearse consciously imitated these to promote St Enda's and simply inverted, or substituted, the ethos to create a 'gaelic' school. This is fairly typical of school founders, but the dissenting nature of Pearse's work is not immediately apparent until examined within the broader field of educa-tional history. In other words, Pearse set out to undo the system of the time and replace it with a new model of schooling – quite a radical project. His intention was to create a school that would be stridently defiant of the type operating at the time and to offer an alternative, modelled upon an eclectic mix of Irish Ireland/Gaelic League aspira-tions; the notion of fosterage; elements of the public school ethos; and influenced by the heroic models of Cúchulainn and Robert Emmet. In short, a very personal, if not idiosyncratic, project but absolutely typical of school founders whose undertakings are informed by strongly held beliefs. Pearse's work was complex; while harking back to the past it was also modern and radical and it is not surprising that it finds echoes in the work of founders, such as Rabindranath Tagore (1861–1941) and Bertrand Russell (1872–1970), and in the work of radical theorists, such as Paulo Freire (1921–1997) and Henry Giroux (b. 1943).[25]

In viewing Pearse's educational work as a precursor to the more intensely felt enthusiasm of political activism, rather than a meaningful, separate and inherently important undertaking, historians have done him a great disservice. A copious body of educational writing, coupled with Pearse's role as headmaster and schoolteacher for eight years, deserves exclusive attention. He considered himself a teacher before all else, describing its rewards as 'richer than ever rewarded to any voyagers among treasure-islands in tropic seas.'[26] Eavan Boland's observation that Pearse's educational achievements had, by 1966, become the casualty of the 'well-bred distaste', with which the efforts of his generation were viewed fifty years after the insurrection, remains uncomfortably true.[27] Before the 1966 anniversary of the Easter Rising commentators were almost always enthusiastic about Pearse. He had become an iconic and untouchable figure, representing Catholic nationalist Ireland. In that year, Eamonn De Valera accepted the keys of St Enda's School from Margaret Pearse on behalf of the Irish state. Yet it is difficult to imagine a time when Pearse did not provoke controversy. Damned by some as reactionary and elitist, he is praised by others as being in possession of a deeply democratic and egalitarian instinct. For modern sensibilities he is a profoundly ambiguous figure, the intensity of his sombre personality, celibacy and commitment to the notion of sacrifice are strikingly at odds with the timbre of contemporary life. Pearse haunts modern Ireland's image of itself – his portrait hangs in the office of the An Taoiseach – yet, as a society, we are not sure if we subscribe to the values his generation represent. In particular, we are troubled by the thought that, somehow, the later purveyors of republican violence could, seemingly, justify their actions by reference to him. That he provided the intellectual template for later republican atrocities has proven the single most pressing concern in studies of Pearse and has resulted in an almost total disregard for his educational work.

The way in which Pearse was popularly perceived underwent a significant change in the years following the fiftieth anniversary of the Easter Rising. To some extent this has been the result of the so–called revisionist school of historical enquiry, which not only challenged traditional narratives in Irish history but also led to simplified and iconoclastic representations of Pearse. Hence, for those of us who first encountered him after the 1970s, he was parochial, reactionary, motivated by a desire to die young, and the principle apologist for the atrocities occurring on an almost daily basis in Northern Ireland – obviously a very significant sea-change had taken place in how Pearse was understood.

This change began in earnest in 1972, with the publication of Father Francis Shaw's essay 'The Canon of Irish History – A Challenge'.

The article expressed misgivings concerning Pearse's use of Catholic vocabulary and imagery to espouse militant nationalism.[28] Shaw argued that Pearse and other insurgents had misappropriated the vocabulary of sacrifice and applied it to the realm of political action. In effect, it could be argued (although Shaw does not make the connection) that Pearse had identified a relationship between the vocabulary of theology and the political resistance and liberation in a manner that was becoming increasingly popular among Latin American theologians in the 1970s. Shaw raised important questions about Pearse's legacy and his essay was important because it forced a reappraisal of Pearse at a time when sectarian tensions festered in Northern Ireland, while challenging the benign figure of Pearse that had been become an accepted part of Ireland's culture. Shaw's essay therefore prompted historians to look more sceptically at Pearse and his age.

Pearse lived at a time of considerable social and political change. Many of Pearse's generation committed themselves to radical political and cultural activism. The period witnessed the initial growth of Irish trade unionism, the founding of the National University of Ireland, the language revival and the development of an increasingly politi-cised articulate and radical middle-class, many of whom took part in the Easter Rising. Pearse was ambitious and committed. His complex personality has led commentators to analyse his relationships closely. An essay by Joe Nugent in 1996 attempted to explain the apparent complexity in terms of an Oedipean complex, in which Pearse's life was informed by an attempt to prize apart his mother (Irishness) and his father (Englishness).[29] Nugent suggests that this conflict later manifested itself in his involvement in the Rising, representing the attack upon the father figure as epitomised by England. This interesting proposition undervalues the influence of the Gaelic Revival, interest in the Irish language, Pearse's political beliefs and the wider cultural milieu in which he operated. Indeed, it has become commonplace for commentators to ignore or be unaware of Pearse's own profound insight into this marriage of nationalities, leading him to ponder whether it was this mixture that made him the 'strange thing' he became in adult life[30]

It is worth noting that those who worked closely with Pearse did not consider him a complicated personality. Usually, their recollec-tions are very positive and most praise his vision and commitment. Desmond Ryan, who attended St Enda's as a boy and later taught there, described the school as 'the soundest and most determined attempt to reform Irish education.' [31] Certainly, the accounts of Pearse's educational work written between 1916 and the 1970s tend to lack critical distance, and one is left with the impression that it is the man, rather than the work, that is being praised. And it is for this reason that his work at St Enda's has so often been overlooked and taken for granted. It has been assumed that St Enda's was noble and in some way provided a model for schooling in post-independent Ireland. As late as 1973, for example, commentators were writing blithely of St Enda's as a 'startling success', despite its debts and dramatically falling enrolments from 1914 onward. [32]

While significant works on Pearse have appeared, none claim to present a critique of his educational work. [33] Usually St Enda's is not presented as significant. The claim, by Ruth Dudley Edwards, for example, that St Enda's was simply another of Pearse's enthusiasms is unjustified given his personal and financial commitment to the project. The supposed problematic issue of Pearse's political influence upon his pupils is touched upon by Edwards who describes him as sitting, 'Every night on the bed of one or another of the boarders, chatting to him and getting to know him as an individual whose mind he might influence.' [34] However, there is no record of such a custom or instance. Indeed, Pearse was usually a sombre character, lively when among his pupils but otherwise reserved. He was aware of this and on at least one occasion makes reference to it. [35] The contention that he failed 'through his arrogance' to maintain St Enda's is contradicted by Ryan, whom Edwards describes as Pearse's 'best biographer'. [36] Yet Edwards's biography provided the first incisive and critical portrait of Pearse, and remains the essential reading for those interested in the subject.

But Edwards is not alone in underestimating Pearse's commitment to his schools. In *Patrick Pearse and the Politics of Redemption* (1994), Seán Farrell Moran argues that in opening St Enda's Pearse was indulging in escapism – Moran's valuable study almost completely ignores Pearse's educational work. This is regrettable because Pearse's financial investment in St Enda's brought him to the edge of personal bankruptcy and swallowed up his share of his late father's business. [37] It was not, in other words, a work of escapism.

Séamas O'Buachalla's *Letters of P.H. Pearse* (1980) [38] is an important collection and provides information of Pearse's correspondents,

although the author concedes the incomplete nature of the collection – some thirty letters are absent.[39] These have not been previously
employed by scholars and had not become available when O'Buachalla
published *Letters*.[40] Finally, O'Buachalla's *An Piarsach Sa Bheilg
(P.H. Pearse in Belgium/P.H. Pearse in Belgie)* (1998) provides a trilin-
gual collection of the articles written by Pearse that appeared in
An Claidheamh Soluis, under the title 'Belgium and its Schools',
between 1905 and 1907. The editor provides an introduction to the
articles, placing them in the context of Pearse's developing interest in
bilingualism.[41] O'Buachalla's collections remain significant points of
departure for those interested in Pearse and schooling, and he correctly
places Pearse within the tradition of child-centeredness.

Elaine Sisson's *Pearse's Patriots, St Enda's and the Cult of Boyhood* (2004)
provides an analysis of the relationship between life at St Enda's and
conceptualisations of masculinity in early twentieth-century Ireland,
arguing that from the 'standpoint of cultural history', St Enda's provided
a 'training ground for the teasing out of a new definition of Irish masculinity'. This view is examined within the context of ideas concerning
the 'perceived relationship between manhood and patriotism', which
was 'under constant revision in the early years of the twentieth
century'.[42] Sisson's innovative study once again focuses upon evolving
definitions of masculinity rather than Pearse as an educator. Drawing
upon visual expressions of boyhood at St Enda's, she argues that the
theatrical costumes worn by pupils in the school dramas were visual
articulations of Pearse's desire to create a reinvigorated Ireland based
upon an archaic gaelic model. This interesting avenue is undermined
by the author's claim that there is an 'almost total absence of detailed
accounts of what it was like to be a St Enda's boy'.[43] Yet a very considerable amount of such material exists and is employed extensively in
later chapters of this book. Other observations are equally unhelpful.
It is suggested, for example, that Desmond Ryan recalled how 'The boys
joked that the pervasive presence of the Hound of Ulster [Cúchulainn]
made him an "important if invisible member" of staff.'[44] The boys did
not 'joke' about this; rather, it was treated with gravitas. Ryan wrote,
'Mr Pearse begins … to tell us of the Cúchulainn saga which he subsequently continues every day … until the "dark, sad boy" has become an
important if invisible member of the staff.'[45] The brief reference to the
students from St Ita's, who were involved in dramatic productions at

St Enda's, as 'the six women' who had 'been borrowed from St Ita's for the day' greatly diminishes the importance of the regular and close links between the schools (*see* Chapter Five).[46]

Sisson's reflection that 'the subject of Pearse remains so contentious that to admit to writing on [him] presupposes that the idea is either to debunk the myths of martyrdom or to reinforce him as an icon of the past' is certainly true and captures the challenge facing those wishing to unravel the subject of Pearse.[47] The author correctly identifies Pearse as among the first to draw the attention to the vulnerability of the *Gaeltacht* way of life, and writes eloquently on the issue of his sexuality.[48] Her view that the fledgling Irish state reduced Pearse's 'ideas on pedagogy to a narrowly focused religious and nationalist orthodoxy' is certainly true.[49] Perhaps Sisson's most striking contribution is her analysis of the type of person-ality or disposition Pearse wished to cultivate in the boys of St Enda's – a combination of the virtues of pagan heroes, such as Cúchulainn and the early Irish saints. This was done through a combination of visual references in the school, such as paintings and the use of dress, especially for theatrical productions. Undoubtedly the symbolism of dress and the visual culture developed at any institution reflect, and perhaps foster, particular disposi-tions, but wider socio-political factors are also at work. The emphasis upon visual representations of the boys as early Irish saints or heroes belongs within the wider context of cultural revivalism which resulted in a reawak-ened sense of national identity and also in trifling eccentricities, such as the wearing of kilts.[50] Again, given Pearse's proclamation that St Enda's was founded to challenge the entire educational system, it is unsurprising that he was sensitive to the quality of its visual representation, both in terms of the reputation of the school and in attracting publicity.

While these works have contributed in greater and lesser degrees to our understanding of Pearse, no single volume offers a compre-hensive survey of his educational work and practice. The value of his contribution to the history of Irish education remains undecided and the intellectual rigour underpinning his work at St Enda's remains uncertain and unexamined. Yet these issues continue to provoke animated public debate.[51] The continued effort to promote the Irish language and raise awareness of national identity through heritage and culture, articulated by recent policy documents and initiatives, point to the continued potency of values that Pearse sought to place at the heart of education in Ireland.[52]

READING PEARSE: POLEMICS AND POLITICS

Writing about Pearse involves reading his journalistic, literary and political output; however, the tone of Pearse's writing was incessantly persuasive. The ever-present need to initiate and perpetuate publicity as editor of *An Claidheamh Soluis*, meant that his editorials were usually pugnacious. He quickly developed an editor's instinct for controversy and succeeded in transforming often unpromising material into provocative journalism. Pearse's aim was to persuade, and his writings in *An Claidheamh Soluis* must be read in that context.

His ability to write and deliver provocative journalism was not lost on the veteran Fenian Tom Clarke, who suggested that Pearse deliver the graveside oration at the funeral of O'Donovan Rossa in August 1915.[53] His tracts frequently resonate with religious sentiment. He wrote of 'Struggle, self-sacrifice, self-discipline, for by these only does the soul rise to perfection'[54], of teaching as a 'priest-like' task[55] and employed the analogy of 'the disciple and the master' to describe the pupil-teacher relationship.[56] Declan Kiberd has noted that it will never be fully clear whether the resort to religious rhetoric 'is sincere or tactical'[57], although it is possible that, in Pearse, the two were closely linked. While personally moved by notions of sacrifice and struggle, Pearse drew upon the vocabulary and imagery of Catholic piety, recognising in it a deep historic and cultural quality that would immediately resonate with his readers. He and his audience were immersed in the language of Catholicism; historically laden with notions of persecution, sacrifice, resurrection and triumph, and its shared imagery, vocabulary and ritual were a potent element of Irish identity – being Catholic meant not being English. Therefore, when Pearse writes about schooling in Ireland as a 'murder machine' it has a duel meaning; on the one hand referring to pedagogical poverty and on the other to its use as an agent of colonialism.

Pearse's writings about education are usually informed by concerns that extend beyond teaching and learning, and he cannot, therefore, be examined in the same manner as educational commentators such as Dewey, Montessori or Gardner, for example.[58] He does not write, foremost, as an educational thinker but as a commentator, standing just outside the traditional discourse of that discipline. This perhaps explains his seeming lack of familiarity with nineteenth and early twentieth-century educational writing, but also with what appears to be only a passing familiarity with thinkers such as Pestalozzi or Froebel, whose work his so closely resembles. The likeness he bears to other thinkers is accidental and he seems unaware, for example, that he is immersed in the late nineteenth-century culture of child-centeredness. But this is not unusual; school founders often appear from the outside (Maria Montessori's initial interest in children, for example, was medical rather than pedagogical). These thinkers often act as agents of change and are motivated by ideas of social transformation, rather than learning, and often place practice before theory, enabling school to become the laboratory for untested ideas.

Notes:

[1] See Patrick Pearse, 'My Childhood and Youth,' in Mary Brigid Pearse, *The Home Life of Pádraig Pearse*, p. 27. Pearse was awarded an exhibition in 1894 at Intermediate Certificate, Junior Grade. He obtained honours grades in Latin, English, French, Celtic, arithmetic, algebra, natural philosophy and chemistry. See MS 21096 (2) Intermediate Education Board for Ireland Certificate, Junior Grade, 1894, Pearse Papers, NLI.

[2] Margaret Pearse, 'A Mother's Golden Memories', in Mary Brigid Pearse, *The Home Life of Pádraig Pearse*, p. 34.

[3] Brigid Pearse, 'My Brothers' Love of Books – His First Attempts at Authorship' in Mary Brigid Pearse, *The Home Life of Pádraig Pearse,* p. 62 & p. 64.

[4] Eamonn O'Neill, 'Some Notes on the School and Post–School Life of Pádraig Pearse' in Mary Brigid Pearse, *The Home Life of Pádraig Pearse,* p. 103.

[5] The following are examples: Geo. Catlin, *North American Indians* (1841); Albert G. Mackey, A *Lexicon of Freemasonry* (1883); George W.E. Russell, *Collections and Recollections* (1903); Thomas Archer, *Gladstone and his Contemporaries: Fifty Years of Progress* (n.d.); Edmund Ollier, *Illustrated History of the Russo Turkish* War (n.d.) Library Collection, Pearse Museum.

[6] See Ruth Dudley Edwards, *Patrick Pearse, the Triumph of Failure*, pp. 1–10.

[7] Patrick Pearse, 'Myself – My Father – My Mother and Her People', in Mary Brigid Pearse, *The Home Life of Pádraig Pearse*, p. 7.

[8] See, Catherine Robson, *Men in Wonderland: The Lost Girlhood of the Victorian Gentleman, passim.*

[9]   Patrick Pearse, 'First Lessons and Schooldays' (*sic*) in Mary Brigid Pearse, *The Home Life of Pádraig Pearse*, p. 7.

[10]   Ruth Dudley Edwards, *Patrick Pearse, the Triumph of Failure*, p. 10.

[11]   See Chapter Five, 'Pupils' Views of Pearse'.

[12]   Ruth Dudley Edwards, *Patrick Pearse, the Triumph of Failure*, p. 7.

[13]   Mary Bulfin, 'Pádraig Pearse Among His Pupils', in Mary Brigid Pearse, *The Home Life of Pádraig Pearse*, p. 118.

[14]   *Ibid.*, 'A Social Evening and Other Diversions'.

[15]   Eamonn O'Neill, 'Some Notes on the School and Post-School Life of Pádraig Pearse'.

[16]   *The Irish Times*, 5 July 1879.

[17]   D.V. Kelleher, *James Dominic Burke*, p. 100.

[18]   Pearse was sixteen upon leaving school and therefore too young to enter university. He sat the Matriculation examination for Royal University of Ireland in 1898.

[19]   MS 21050, Letter of Commendation concerning Mr Patrick H. Pearse, from Revd J. Darlington, MA, FRUI, Dean of Studies, University College, Dublin, 25 September 1905. Pearse Papers, NLI.

[20]   Eamonn O'Neill cited in Ruth Dudley Edwards, *Patrick Pearse, the Triumph of Failure*, p. 14.

[21]   Ruth Dudley Edwards, *Patrick Pearse, the Triumph of Failure*. p. 15.

[22]   *Ibid.*, p. 16.

[23]   *Ibid.*, p. 205.

[24]   See book review of *Unstoppable Brilliance* by M. Fitzgerald and Antionette Walker in *Sunday Independent*, 9 April 2006. It has been popularly assumed that Pearse 'turned his face' against marriage but a letter from Mary Hayden reveals that he had discussed the matter generally with her and may have intended to marry later in life. Hayden writes that she hopes finally to find him 'settled as a paterfamilias with children not adopted'. MS 21054, Mary Hayden to Patrick Pearse, Pearse Papers, NLI, (n.d.).

[25] See, B. Walsh, *The Pedagogy of Protest, passim*.

[26] *The Murder Machine*, 'Back to the Sagas'.

[27] Eavan Boland, 'Aspects of Pearse', *The Dublin Magazine*, Vol. 5, Spring 1966 (n.p.). The Dublin Insurrection of April (Easter) 1916.

[28] See Francis Shaw, 'The Canon of Irish History – A Challenge', *Studies*, LXI (1972).

[29] 'Patrick Pearse and Homosexual Panic', *The McNair Scholars' Journal*, Vol. 4.

[30] P.H. Pearse, 'My Childhood and Youth', in Mary Brigid Pearse, *The Home Life of Pádraig Pearse*, p. 11

[31] Desmond Ryan, 'The Man Called Pearse', *St Enda's and its Founder, the Complete Works of P.H. Pearse*, p. 209. Pearse's 'Story of a Success' and Ryan's 'The Man Called Pearse' were published in Ryan's work *St Enda's and its Founder*, a volume of *The Complete Works of P.H. Pearse*, edited by Ryan.

[32] Raymond J. Porter, *P.H. Pearse*, Preface. Pearse's educational writings are accorded four pages in a text of 140 pages.

[33] *Patrick Pearse, the Triumph of Failure* was awarded the National University of Ireland Prize for Historical Research, 1978.

[34] Ruth Dudley Edwards, *Patrick Pearse, the Triumph of Failure*, p. 130.

[35] See Chapter Five.

[36] Ruth Dudley Edwards, *Patrick Pearse, the Triumph of Failure*, p. 114. Ryan recalled that during the occupation of the GPO during Easter Rising Pearse asked him 'if it were the right thing to do', adding that this 'was the last question I ever expected to hear from him.' While this does not necessarily reveal Pearse as an arrogant personality it perhaps points to his being unaccustomed to questioning his own actions. See Desmond Ryan, 'The Man Called Pearse', *St Enda's and its Founder, the Complete Works of Patrick Pearse*, p. 188.

[37] See Chapter Five.

[38] Séamas O'Buachalla (ed.), *The Letters of P.H. Pearse*.

[39] *Ibid.*, xxii. Letters to the following parents/correspondents, written in the 1910–11 school year, do not appear in O'Buachalla. The name of the relevant son/pupil appears in brackets. Three letters were written to Mrs Delaney and two to Mrs Andrews. Mr Fogarty (Fredrick); Mrs Murphy (Richard); Mrs Colahan (William); Mrs Peterson (Conrad); Mr Mac Dermot (John and Stephen); Mrs Gallina (Richard); Father McHugh (O'Reilly – unidentified); Father Molloy (Frank – unidentified); Mr Carleton (Tadgh); Mr Boyle (Edward); Mr Holden (unidentified); Mrs Reddin (Kenneth); Mrs Delaney (Edward); Mrs Rooney (Joseph); Mrs McGrath (Eoin); Mrs Gaynor (Alfred); Mr O'Seadh (?) (Fergus); Mrs Andrews (C.S. Andrews); Mrs Donnellan (Patrick); Mr Jennings (Horace and Antony); Mr Delaney (Patrick); Mrs Cleary (Kevin); Mr Carney (Desmond); Mr Delaney (Edward); Mrs Rowan (Joseph and James); Mrs Powell (Gilbert); Mrs O'Connor (Daniel) and Fanny (at St Ita's school). MS 21086, Pearse Papers, NLI.

[40] The Pearse Museum, Rathfarnham is located at The Hermitage, formerly St Enda's School. The museum houses a collection of school ephemera. Pearse had gone to American in 1914 to raise funds for St Enda's. Eugene Cronin returned with him to board at the school in May 1914 and spent the summer with an uncle in Bandon, Co. Cork. The collection of letters from Eugene to relatives in America and those of Pearse to his father Michael Cronin, originally stored at the Pearse Museum in Rathfarnham, were being re-located to the Kilmainham Goal Archive (KGA) at the time of writing.

[41] For the Introduction in English see pp. 105–116. The articles that comprise this volume were reproduced in the author's earlier *The Educational Writings of P.H. Pearse* (1980).

[42] Elaine Sisson, *Pearse's Patriots, St Enda's and the Cult of Boyhood*, p. 9.

[43] *Ibid.*, p. 239.

[44] *Ibid.*, p. 80.

[45] Desmond Ryan, 'A Retrospect', *St Enda's and its Founder, the Complete Works of P.H. Pearse*, p. 90.

[46] Elaine Sisson, *Pearse's Patriots St Enda's and the Cult of Boyhood*, p. 94.

[47] *Ibid.*, p. 2.

[48] *Ibid.*, p. 2, p. 61. & p. 152.

[49] *Ibid.*, p. 160.

[50] *Ibid.*, p. 151.

[51] See for example *The Sunday Times* 'Culture' 8 April 2001; *Irish Independent* 'Review', 14 April 2001; *Sunday Business Post*, 15 April 2001; *The Irish Times*: '*Ceist Staire*', *Tuarascáil*, 2 October 2002; 'An Irishman's Diary', 17 April 2004; 'Letters to the Editor', 27 April 2004 & 'Book Reviews', 3 July 2004.

[52] *Programme for Action in Education 1984–1987* stated that the 'development of our linguistic and cultural heritage should be at the core of our educational system.' The *Green Paper on Education, Education for a Changing World* (1992) stated that the aims of the primary curriculum are 'to enable students to: Communicate with clarity and confidence through speech, reading and writing in their first language. Acquire a mastery of a second language (English in *Gaeltacht* areas, *Gaeilge* in *Galltacht* areas)'. *Charting our Education Future, White Paper on Education*, 1995, noted that 'The Higher Education Authority will have a statutory responsibility for the preservation, promotion and use of the Irish language in the higher education sector …' See also Para. 31, 'Teaching through Irish', *Education Act* (1998).

[53] O'Donovan Rossa, a veteran Fenian was resident in the United States. Upon his death his remains were brought to Ireland for burial. Clarke 'noticed young Padraig Pearse whose oratory was already inspired and inspiring. At Clarke's suggestion Pearse was asked to deliver the oration at Glasnevin Cemetery … Clarke determined that this new voice should announce the tidings of the country's deliverance.' Donagh MacDonagh, *P.H. Pearse*, p. 2. (n.d. n.p.) MS 33694/G, NLI. Thomas Clarke (1857–1916) veteran nationalist, publisher of Irish Freedom, member of IRB, participant in Easter Rising, executed May 1916. On Pearse as a political writer see J.J. Lee, 'In Search of Patrick Pearse', in *Revising the Rising*.

[54] See Patrick Pearse, 'The Story of a Success', *St Enda's and its Founder*, Desmond Ryan (ed.), *The Complete Works of P.H. Pearse*.

[55] *The Murder Machine*, 'Back to the Sagas'.

[56] *Ibid.*, 'Master and Disciples.' Declan Kiberd has noted that such use of religious language was not new: 'if there is any substantive difference between the English revolutionaries of 1640 and the Irish insurgents of 1916, it is merely this: the English relied mainly on the Old Testament … and the Irish on the New.' Declan Kiberd, *Inventing Ireland: The Literature of Modern Ireland*, p. 211. See also Evan Boland, 'Aspects of Pearse', *The Dublin Magazine*, Spring 1966 and Séamas Deane, 'Pearse: Writing and Chivalry', in *Celtic Revivals*.

[57] Declan Kiberd, *Inventing Ireland: The Literature of Modern Ireland*, p. 211

[58] John Dewey (1859–1952), Maria Montessori (1870–1952), John Gardner (b. 1943).

Two

The Evolution of
Schooling in Ireland

THE HISTORICAL BACKGROUND

For centuries schooling played a crucial part in the process of cultural and religious assimilation in Ireland, and Pearse's attempts to undermine the system of the early twentieth century had historic antecedents that reached back at least to the hedge-schools of the eighteenth century.[1] The defiant nature and political resonance of his work is more readily understood when studied against the often inglorious narrative of education in Ireland under English rule.

Educational provision in Ireland, from the Tudor period until the advent of the 1831 National Education (Ireland) Act, under which the National School System came into being, was characterised by State involvement, either directly or indirectly through the support of proselytising bodies. In a speech given at Dublin's Mansion House in December 1911, Pearse remarked that the English never committed a 'useless crime'[2] and the notion of the education system as a crime enforced upon the children of Ireland remained central to his thinking. He believed that the aim of successive British administrations was the creation of an unquestioning and submissive population in Ireland, and that they began this process in the classroom was testament to their rigour. Central to the success of this project was the spread of the English language and throughout his life Pearse asserted that attempts to make the Irish language redundant were an open attack on an integral characteristic of a people. Henry Tudor (1509–1547) issued an edict in 1537 in an attempt to protect the linguistic identity of the Anglo–Irish Pale, prompted by the prevalence of Irish language and customs amongst its settlers.[3] The Act stated that 'The King's true subjects inhabiting this land of Ireland … shall use and speake commonly the English tongue and language', and endorsed a measure designed to encourage the founding of parish schools.[4]

Further efforts to establish schools were undertaken during the reign of Elizabeth I (1558–1603). Known as diocesan schools – imitations of the English grammar schools – their development was slow and arduous. The Act demanded that the archbishops of Armagh, Dublin, and the bishops of Meath and Kildare nominate schoolmasters within their respective dioceses and that the Lord Deputy appoint schoolmasters for all other dioceses. Each parish was to raise sufficient monies to build a schoolhouse and raise one third of the salary of the schoolmaster. The imposition of such expenditure upon the parishes was as offensive to Catholic sensibilities as it was poor political thinking. Having ordained the founding of the diocesan schools, the administration had to find a way of making them become a reality and at the same time prevent Irish Catholics from entering colleges and seminaries in France and Spain.[5] Relations between these two countries and post-Reformation England had suffered considerable strain over the previous five decades and Parliament feared the influence the colleges would have upon Irish students. The few diocesan schools built during Elizabeth's reign were concentrated within the Pale area and therefore, like the parish schools, presented little threat to the prevalence of Irish.[6] It should be noted, however, that even at this early stage the notion of schooling as a mechanism for assimilation and social control was understood and acted upon.

The accession of James I (1603–1625) saw the emphasis shift to the new plantation in Ulster, and, echoing the Elizabethan model, newly established free schools would be placed in the hands of the local bishops who would support them by income from rented land. As post-Reformation persecution became more virulent, Catholics of means increasingly sent their sons to foundations abroad, and it is in this period that the first official prohibitions were created to prevent Catholic families from sending children overseas.[7] It was hoped that the developing network of schools would facilitate the spread of English, the absence of which among the Irish was impeding the work of proselytism. In May 1620, King James wrote to the Lord Deputy, instructing him to place a number of Irish speakers in Trinity College so that, having been instructed in the Protestant faith, they might act as interpreters for ministers among the Irish peasantry.[8] The scheme bore little fruit, however, due to the intransigence of the native Irish and the unwillingness of ministers to commit themselves to working among isolated and resistant communities. As a result, the association of Trinity with the use of Irish for the purposes of proselytism had implications lasting into the early twentieth century, when Pearse and fellow revivalists confronted the college over its ambivalence toward the language.[9]

The antagonism that characterised relationships between Irish Catholics and the monarchy was further exacerbated during the reign of Charles I (1625–1649). Within five years of his accession, Charles forbade Catholic attendance at Trinity College in 1630, suppressed all Catholic colleges and schools. This more comprehensive control, coupled with dispossession of land, resulted in the rebellion of 1641. The confederates placed their many grievances concerning prohibitions on Catholic education before the King, when a cessation in hostilities was called in 1644. The resultant Glamorgan Treaty permitted Catholics to found schools but was rendered redundant when Oliver Cromwell came to power five years later.[10]

The Commonwealth Parliament placed all schools under the authority of a central Board of Control for Schools and devised a programme whereby the rent of confiscated lands would provide funds for schoolmasters, whose task it was to help convert the Irish peasantry to Protestantism. The new parliament was unstinting in its suppression of a people who had so recently been allied to its enemy, and the period witnessed a narrowing of the definition of education, which, until now, had been understood solely as a means of proselytism and assimilation. The Cromwellian vision, however, included the notion of serfdom. Children of poor Catholic families would be trained in agriculture and industry in schools under Protestant control. A new law provided that those over the age of ten could be legally removed from their parents and thus incarcerated. In March 1657, Cromwell argued that his plan was justified, as peasant children were 'burthensome but also unnecessary members of the Commonwealth' and if they could be apprenticed to 'religious and honest people in England or Ireland … they might … come out of their apprenticeships, to get their livings by their own industry.'[11] The new schools established under the Cromwellian regime, however, were frustrated by the prevalence of the Irish language, which represented an obstacle to every administration in Ireland. Ultimately, proselytism depended upon the spread of English as the main language spoken, and, increasingly, Irish was associated not only with Catholicism, which was viewed as inherently subversive, but as representative of that persistent otherness which hampered the political assimilation of the Irish.

The accession of Charles II (1660–1685) heralded a slight but ultimately superficial relaxation in hostility. Some lands confiscated by Cromwell were returned, although the new monarch understood that any large-scale reparation would only serve to alienate Protestant opinion at home and in Ireland. The removal of restrictions on Catholic clergy, however, was criticised as destabilising the Protestant interest in Ireland. In 1677, for example, a number of Protestant schoolmasters had a Jesuit school in Dublin closed.[12] Growing concern about the scope of concessions to Irish Catholics resulted in the proclamation of 1673, which banished Catholic bishops and priests and ordered the closure of religious communities and schools. In 1679, Titus Oates revealed the improbable Popish Plot, doubted even by the King. It caused a wave of persecution in England and Ireland, allowing the administration to introduce further restrictions.[13] The Proclamation of 1673 was re-issued in October 1678 but the execution of Archbishop Plunkett in 1681 had a sobering effect, and the four years between his death and that of the King were marked by a steady improvement in the fortunes of Catholic Ireland.[14] The hierarchy's relationship with the Dublin Parliament improved and generally Catholics enjoyed the grudging tolerance of their Protestant neighbours. By the time of Charles' death, the position of Catholic education had improved significantly.

Charles II was succeeded by James II (1685–1688), the first Catholic monarch since 1558. James' Catholicism made his position as monarch untenable and his handling of religious affairs in Ireland was frequently ham-fisted. He insisted, for example, on retaining the right to nominate clerics for positions within the Church, a prerogative that belonged solely to the Catholic hierarchy. His short reign was a precarious balancing act between the suspicions of Parliament and his Catholic belief. His endeavours were mainly concerned with restructuring the army and appointing Catholics to the judiciary, and he carried out only one significant piece of educational legislation. In 1688 he ordered that members of the Society of Jesus (Jesuits) must be appointed to any vacancies that may in the future occur in government-controlled schools.[15] His hold upon power was always slight and he fled to France upon the arrival of his son-in-law, William Henry de Nassau (of Orange), to England in November 1688.

In 1695, William initiated the Act to Restrain Foreign Education. Under its terms no Catholic child could be sent abroad to be educated in any Catholic institution or 'be resident or trained up in any private popish family.'[16] The admission inherent in the Act was that the establishment of State schools in Ireland merely resulted in Catholics of means sending their children to seminaries and colleges abroad. William died in 1702 and the following year, Queen Anne issued an ordinance stipulating that the closest relative of a child suspected of being sent abroad must bring the child before a justice of the peace within two months.[17] If the relative was unable to do so, or could not prove that the child was not abroad, then 'such child shall incur all the penalties in the Act to Restrain Foreign Education.'[18] The measure appears to be simply a continuation of the 1695 Act to Restrain Foreign Education, but in fact is more pernicious as it criminalises the child. Such severe punishment highlights the increasingly unstable position of the Catholic interest and represented a systematic continuation of the Cromwellian policy of suppression, now more fitfully informed by fears of Catholic France and Spain. What one commentator has called the 'long penal night of repression and persecution' had begun.[19] The brief respite during the reign of James II was no more than a temporary interval in a process that was initiated by Henry Tudor. Documents from the administration of Queen Anne are explicit concerning the outcome of the penal code. Sir John Percival, Earl of Egmont, declared in a letter of 1703 that 'Popish schoolmasters have been suppressed', and expressed his hope that 'the Irish youth may soon have English habit, and in one or two generations be true sticklers for the Protestant Church and Interest.'[20]

At the beginning of the eighteenth century, a group of Protestant gentry suggested the establishment of charity schools for 'The instruction of Irish children gratis in the English Tongue, and the Catechism and Religion of the Church of Ireland.'[21] By 1719 there were approximately 130 such institutions catering for about 3,000 children. The master had to be a member of the Established Church and of professed sympathy to the King. A charity school manual of 1721 stated that, through the schools, the whole nation might become Protestant and English.[22]

The scholarly ambitions of the charity schools were modest, concentrating almost wholly upon numeracy and literacy. The persistence of the hedge-schools, representing at this time a type of folk resistance to mainstream offerings, meant that they made little progress. In 1730, Hugh Boulter, Protestant Primate of Ireland, petitioned the Archbishop of Canterbury for the establishment of the Society for the Promotion of Christian Knowledge to operate in Ireland.[23] The findings of a 1731 inquiry into the state of Popery in Ireland had established that there were 549 schools operating throughout the country employing Catholic masters; the parish and diocesan schools had not proliferated, despite receiving government funding.[24] The language, hopes and methods of the Charter of Establishment are strikingly similar to the Tudor edict of 1537. Again, the Irish were to be instructed in the 'English tongue and the Fundamental Principles of True Religion.'[25] It reflected popular belief that 'the erecting and establishing of English Protestant Schools' was an effective means for 'converting and civilising … the children of Irish Natives [sic]', who were alluded to as 'deluded persons'.[26]

Before becoming incorporated in 1733, the society depended upon private donations. From 1738 to 1831 it also received government monies, and Parliament continued to finance the society after independent observers had condemned the schools connected with it as deplorable. Between 1782 and 1788 John Howard (1726–1790)[27] visited schools belonging to the society and his findings led to the enquiry of 1788, which found that children lived in cramped and squalid conditions, were under-fed, poorly clothed, overworked on land adjoining school houses and, in spite of the society's *raison d'être*, were almost all illiterate.[28]

Successive administrations funded the work of the society from the public purse. However, there were occasional dissenting voices. Chief Secretary Thomas Orde (1740–1807) introduced proposals for the re-structuring of educational provision in Ireland to the House of Commons in April 1787, remarking that Parliament was 'obliged to correct the unfortunate consequences of a want of education (in Ireland) with a rude and severe hand.'[29] He wished to see 'our fellow subjects of all religious persuasions' participate in the benefits of education; his proposals also included an improvement in the salary and working conditions of schoolteachers, and the building of schools for the 'free instruction of the poor'.[30] While supportive of the efforts of the Established Church, Orde was prepared to claim openly that, educationally, its endeavours in Ireland had fallen short. He wanted to see the Catholic peasantry profit from a more worthwhile educative experience than had historically been theirs, believing 'they have been suffered to remain as a rich metal in the mine, which no fashioning hand of an artist has hitherto attempted to polish into beauty.'[31]

In the history of Irish education, Orde's proposals were significant but hardly radical. He did not want to replace the parish schools but to reinvigorate them. In his speech to the House on 12 April 1787 he noted that 'There was something of policy as well as of charity in the institution of the parish school.' Their promulgation of 'knowledge and use of the English language' represented a strategy that was 'most excellent' and 'worthy of being perpetuated'. Orde also hoped that the 'first families' in Ireland would continue to send their children to public schools and universities in England, 'thereby (drawing) the two countries still closer … in assimilating their manners and their habits.'[32] He was the first to recognise the need for a nation-wide system of funded education for all and was prepared to call the proselytising bodies to account for the administration of schools that were in receipt of public monies. Yet it was not until 1806 that a Statutory Commission of Inquiry was created to investigate education in Ireland. It recommended that a body be created specifically to oversee schooling, supervise existing and new schools and create teacher-training institutions. It stressed that no plan for the education of the poor in Ireland could hope to be successful if it did not accept the principle of religious freedom, and recommended that in future, religious and secular instruction should be given separately. These proposals foreshadowed the 1831 Stanley letter, which outlined the founding principles of the National School System.

Political resistance to such sweeping concessions, particularly in the area of religious instruction, meant that the work of the Commission of Inquiry came to nothing and it was decided to create a Board that would deal with endowed schools only. However, by the mid-1820s the question of education for the Catholic poor had become so critical that Parliament established a commission to study the issue. The Irish Education Inquiry (1824–1827) produced nine reports on the matter, but had little immediate impact on schooling in Ireland; although it did reflect a growing realisation that change was necessary.[33] The Commission was unstinting in its criticism of the many proselytising societies and recommended that funding be withdrawn from the Incorporated Society and the Association for Discountenancing Vice.[34] It also recommended that while clergymen of the Established Church give Protestant children religious instruction, a layman, who had received approval from the local Protestant bishop, should instruct Catholics.

The momentum of reform, coupled with the need to find a solution to the Irish education problem, resulted in the appointment, in March 1828, of Thomas Spring-Rice, MP for Limerick, as head of a committee to review the findings of the principle inquiries into education in Ireland. In May 1828 the committee recommended the creation of a non-sectarian system of education under the control of a body whose sole purpose was the administration of education.[35] This pointed to a new conceptualisation of the role of the State in educational provision, a task that had traditionally been the preserve of Church bodies. Had the recommendations been implemented, the work of various proselytising bodies would have been seriously undermined. The Established and Presbyterian Churches, however, launched ferocious campaigns against the proposals, seeing them as a serious threat to the Protestant interest in Ireland. Despite constant lobbying, Spring-Rice could not persuade the government to implement his recommendations, although such a forward-looking document could not be ignored indefinitely.

The Wellington administration (1828–1830) was not conspicuous for its Catholic sympathies, and when it collapsed a more benevolent Whig cabinet took office. In October 1831, Edward Stanley, a member of the new cabinet, used the occasion of a parliamentary vote on monies for education to introduce his ideas on educational reform in Ireland. Basing his suggestions on the findings of the four reports between 1812 and 1828, he recommended the establishment of an Education Board composed of representatives of the main denominations, to have responsibility for the distribution of £30,000 annually for running costs.[36] Once the House had agreed upon Stanley's scheme, he presented a detailed written proposal to the Duke of Leinster, who was invited to become president of the new Board of Education.[37] The original letter is lost but it is known from surviving versions that Stanley made changes to his initial proposals. The onus upon teachers to see that the children attended their appropriate Sunday worship was dropped because of the opposition of Revd James Carlile, one of the two Presbyterian members of the Board. There were also objections to the proposal that Catholic children use a Roman Catholic approved version of the New Testament for religious instruction. It is unfortunate that Stanley was prepared to give way at such an early stage. While refusal may have resulted in temporary stalemate, acquiescence so early may have contributed to the culture of constant bargaining that dogged the early life of the new Board.

Stanley's proposals represented a turning point in the history of education in Ireland but were, in fact, less innovative than usually supposed, particularly when considered in the wider political context. The National System was established during a time of great political and social change in Britain and coincided with the Parliamentary Reform Bill of 1831. Though a modest piece of legislation, it reflected Parliament's realisation that the clamour for representation demanded a response.[38]

Throughout Britain, increasing numbers of disaffected groups were championing a range of causes, from a shorter working day to representation for industrial regions. The King was deeply troubled by the emergence of organised unions, especially in the north of the country.[39] Rural unrest characterised the period 1829–30; damage to property and rioting had resulted in the government taking severe measures to prevent further disturbances, and in December 1830 nine labourers had been sentenced to death for their part in instigating unrest, while in Ireland there were food riots in Limerick and Leitrim. Prime Minister Grey wanted to press on with reform but believed he needed a firmer mandate. Consequently, he persuaded the King to dissolve Parliament and, in a general election in May, returned to office with an increased majority. Ten days later, seventeen people were killed in clashes over the payment of tithes in Westmeath. The Stanley letter, therefore, was conceived in a time of considerable unrest and arguably represented little more that what was required in justice. Certainly, further provocation of the Catholic community would have been foolish. Indeed Catholic reaction was initially very encouraging. Stanley's plan recognised that they had the right to receive religious instruction from a priest during a time set aside in the school week and the hierarchy welcomed what they saw as an opportunity for Catholic children to receive schooling free from the risk of proselytism.

Catholics had become suspicious and resentful of the manner in which schools were established and operated, and no meaningful progress was possible until the suspicion of proselytism was removed. The commissioners of education for 1824–5 had recommended 'two teachers in every school, one Protestant and the other Roman Catholic, to superintend separately the religious education of the children' but it was soon found that this scheme was 'impracticable'.[40] Stanley reminded Leinster that the 1828 Committee had recommended the establishment of a system which allowed for combined literary and separate religious instruction and concluded by stating that, if a new system was to work 'the most scrupulous care should be taken not to interfere with the peculiar tenets of any description of Christian pupils.'[41] If religious freedom was to be upheld then it was necessary that the new board be comprised of men of 'high personal character' who held 'exalted station(s) in the church' drawn from the Anglican, Presbyterian and Roman Catholic communities.[42] Where an application proceeded 'exclusively from Protestants or exclusively from Roman Catholics', it would be incumbent upon the board to 'make inquiry as to the circumstances which led to the absence of any names of the persuasion which does not appear.'[43] Schools were to remain open for combined instruction for four or five days a week, and the Board was to have control over the selection of textbooks. Teachers could use what religious text they wished, provided they secured the approval of Board members of the same faith. It was not envisaged that the Board would select teachers but approve them once nominated by school managers or patrons, and teachers must first receive training in a model school to be established in Dublin.

The proposals were not innovative, as they reflected and drew upon the previous three decades of educational thinking in Ireland. No review of the system was undertaken until 1868, when intense agitation by the Catholic hierarchy over its 'mixed' (i.e mixed-denomination) nature resulted in the establishment of the Royal Commission of Inquiry into Primary Education (Ireland).[44] The inquiry lasted two years and the Report of the Royal Commission of Inquiry into Primary Education (Ireland) was published in 1870.[45]

The Royal Commission drew largely upon the annual school inspection reports, which were produced by the Commissioners of National Education and provided detailed accounts of schools throughout the country. The inspectors commonly gathered information pertaining to attendance, enrolment, subjects taught, condition of premises and so forth, but their remaining observations might range from the stench of schoolrooms to the increasing problem of the peasantry's penchant for strong tea. While occasionally idiosyncratic, the reports provide a wonderfully rich and detailed picture of the educational landscape of mid-nineteenth-century Ireland.

The inspectors usually noted what books were being used as part of the curriculum, and typically commented on those that were controversial. Generally, these contained extracts from Scripture to be used by pupils of both denominations. The schools could only use textbooks that had been approved by the Commissioners who, as Stanley had decreed, exercised 'entire control over all books ... used in the schools.'[46] Between 1830 and 1870 the Commission published an increasing number of secular schoolbooks. These were high quality, affordable and held in high regard by all sections of the community. Their low price left booksellers complaining that they could not compete and that the expanding school market was becoming closed to them. Indeed, the Report of the Powis Commission concluded that 'the use of the Board's books, though in theory forced upon no school, is in practise compulsory in all National Schools.'[47] In effect, the Board had a monopoly and some suspected that such tight control might be politically motivated. The Assistant Commissioner for the Cork District, for example, reported in 1870 that the 'un-Irish character' of books produced for schools 'provoked much resentment'.[48] Inspector Patrick Keenan noted the same sentiment and concluded that he was 'perfectly satisfied that, as in England, where different books are used in different schools, it should be perfectly practicable to do the same in Ireland.'[49]

The inspectors' reports between 1830 and 1870 provide a great deal of information, but the manner in which it was recorded makes it difficult to be certain about the overall standard of learning. A number of factors contribute to the difficulty – there was no uniformity regarding either the type (e.g. geography, arithmetic) or number of subjects reported, and levels of proficiency were often left unrecorded.[50] In the report of 1858, only three inspectors offered statistical evidence concerning proficiency in their districts.[51] In general, the standard was poor and only one inspector returned a verdict of 'satisfactory'.[52] An 1863 circular from the Commission requesting that future reports be more concise resulted in considerably less information being recorded, and very little information about proficiency was recorded between 1862 and 1870.[53] The small number of schools visited may have been responsible for this and one inspector remarked that he could give no details on test results because 'The examination of a few schools in a district can furnish no reliable data to form a correct opinion of the condition of the schools generally.'[54] This appears to question the inspection procedure generally, although the Powis Commission did not recommend any changes.

Proficiency was, however, far from acceptable. Between 1862 and 1870 only three inspectors reported an improvement in standards.[55] Statistical returns supported the general picture and the Powis Commission revealed the same lack of progress, recording that it was 'very much less than it ought to be largely due to poor funding, overcrowding and lack of attendance'.[56]

The Powis Report made more than 100 recommendations. Significantly, it proposed that the National Board should cease publishing schoolbooks but retain its sanction on what texts could be used in schools, teachers should be provided with a contract of employment (including procedures for dismissal), payment by results should be introduced, provision should be made to finance teacher accommodation, schools operating exclusively under denominational management and teacher training colleges operated by religious bodies should be incorporated into the National System, and provision should be made for training programmes for all teachers.[57] A number of these recommendations were implemented over the next decade. Catholic institutions, excluded because of their denominational character, were gradually accommodated within the system, and Convent schools were finally allowed to join in 1884.[58] These schools had grown rapidly during the nineteenth century and in 1850 there were some 102 convents in Ireland, most of which had schools attached.[59] The Report of F.H. Dale (1904) recorded 292 aided convent schools, boasting an average daily attendance of 69.7 per cent. These schools are barely noted in the reports of 1830–1870[60], although the Powis Commission recorded the almost unanimous praise for their work.[61] In general, the Report presents a picture of well-run schools, where the standard of teaching was high.

Mention of proselytism is strikingly absent from the reports, although few non-Catholic pupils attended convent schools.[62] There were 207 such schools operating in 1868 with approximately 30 per cent of these operating outside the system. They were predominantly Catholic and therefore presented the government with the anomaly of granting aid to approximately 138 schools that were in fact denominational. Yet it appears, however, that the convent schools generally did not transgress the rule of the Board regarding religious/secular instruction, nor did they exclude children of other denominations.[63]

A payment by results system was introduced in 1872. This mechanism linked award money with examination grades and while evidently a 'crude and simplistic mechanism' it was praised in 1885 for improving teacher performance.[64] However, it was generally held to be pedagogically unsound, forcing teachers to attach more importance to 'quantity than to quality'.[65] Inspector's submissions in 1897 were ambivalent about the scheme. It had positively affected pupil and teacher performance and provided at least some means of measurement[66] but was generally held to produce uninspired teaching, cramming, the exclusion of non-compulsory subjects and to contribute little to intellectual development.[67] While the mechanism was abolished only a few years later it had the effect of conditioning a generation of teachers and pupils who perceived learning as a competitive act based on rote memorising. Teachers did not need to become interested in innovative methodologies, regardless of their attractiveness, and the relationship between results and extra remuneration became deeply entrenched within the teaching community and a generation of children left school believing that learning and memorising were almost identical activities. In this way, a self-perpetuating lethargy dominated Irish classrooms for three decades, co-existing with, but unaffected by, the child-centred innovations that were spreading throughout England and Europe in the latter part of the nineteenth century.

Toward the end of the nineteenth century, the growing importance of the sciences, the identification of schooling with economic development and the preponderance of an apparently overly academic curriculum resulted in the establishment of the Commission on Manual and Practical Instruction in Primary Schools (Belmore Commission) in 1897. The Report described the national curriculum as 'one sided', leaving 'some of the most useful faculties of the mind absolutely untrained'.[68]

It recommended the implementation of a number of new disciplines and the replacement of examination fees with inspection, as had happened in England.[69] A year later, the recommendations of the Report of 1898 presented a vision for national education that was influenced by the tenants of child-centeredness. It pointed out that possibilities for developing kindergarten had been overlooked because of the overemphasis upon the 'three R's', remarking that 'in many cases this object is the one still aimed at.'[70] The Report did not, however, recommend the establishment of kindergarten schools, rather that the Commissioners hoped that teaching would become 'permeated' with its 'spirit'.[71] It recommended the introduction of drawing 'with the least possible delay'[72] and elementary science, with the emphasis placed upon practical learning.[73] In girls' schools, cookery, laundry and domestic science 'should be taught as far as may be found practicable', needlework should continue to form 'an important element' of the syllabus and that singing be taught wherever possible.[74] The Commissioners concluded that these changes were necessary because the system did little to stimulate intellectual growth and that the experience of other countries demonstrated their benefits.

The recommendations of the Belmore Commission formed the basis of the Revised Programme for National Schools in 1900.[75] The scope of the programme was wide, child-centred and largely utilitarian. It promoted a more child-friendly vision of schooling and while its recommendations, like those of the Powis Commission, may have been difficult to implement, they permeated educational discourse and encouraged new ways of thinking about schooling.

In 1902, Local Education Authorities were established in England, having the power to levy rates for schools and in this way raised 50 per cent of education costs.[76] Chief Secretary George Wyndham pointed out that local contributions in Ireland had always been low due to crippling poverty and recommended that an English inspector prepare a report comparing educational provision in the two countries.[77] However, the 1904 Report of F.H. Dale argued that a 'lack of any local interest' and not poverty was the reason for poor contributions. Dale also found that the condition of school premises had changed very little since 1870; that the buildings were frequently unsuitable, dirty and cold; teachers were often paid less than their English counterparts and instruction suffered in small schoolhouses that were 'unsuitably staffed' and poorly attended.[78]

In the same year that Dale's report was submitted, the Gaelic League
secured the sanctioning of the Bilingual Programme in *Gaeltacht*
regions.[79] This represented an important victory for Pearse, who had
campaigned on the issue since becoming editor of *An Claidheamh Soluis*.
He was unable to secure the support of the League for the Irish Councils
Bill (1907), which proposed the amalgamation of all local Boards into
one Irish Council. This would include the National and Intermediate
Boards, as well as the Departments of Agriculture and Technical instruction. He wrote that if the Bill was passed, 'the schools will be ours.'
The Catholic hierarchy, Gaelic League and the Irish Party under John
Redmond opposed the Bill and it was withdrawn. Dale's report had
demonstrated that schooling in Ireland was underfunded, understaffed
and under attended, in much the same way it had been in 1870 when
the Powis Commission published its findings. While it had embraced a
more child-centred approach to instruction and the curriculum, cultural
nationalists such as Pearse could claim, with some legitimacy, that the
emphasis upon Ireland's place within the Empire which permeated
schoolbooks, coupled with the curricular neglect of the Irish language
and continued under-funding, made the system appear unaccountable,
unrepresentative and symptomatic of a political inheritance that was not
representative of the increasingly strident voice of nationalist Ireland.

BRITAIN AND IRELAND IN THE NINETEENTH-CENTURY

The period in which Pearse opened St Enda's was one of great change
in educational thinking and practice. Nineteenth-century England
was characterised by the rise of religious scepticism, the decline of the
country aristocracy, the spread of organised labour movements and
the increasing competitiveness and strength of American and German
manufacturing. The human cost of the Industrial and Agricultural
Revolutions was laid bare in the slums of cities such as Manchester,
Liverpool and London. Squalor led many to question the economic
basis upon which late nineteenth-century society operated, and contributed to the quickening development of trade unionism. The work of
writers such as Charles Darwin (1809–1882) encouraged the growing
tendency of middle-class intellectuals and freethinkers to abandon the
institutional Church, while figures such as T.H. Huxley (1825–1895)

queried the religious orthodoxies of the previous century.[80] Socialist groups questioned the assumption of a preordained class system thereby emboldening an increasingly sceptical working class.[81] The period witnessed the rise of decadent art and the influence of aestheticism, championed by figures such as Aubrey Beardsley (1872–1898) and Oscar Wilde (1854–1900).[82] The traditional position of the country landowner in the social hierarchy was undermined by the importation of cheap American wheat in the late 1870s. Estates throughout England were abandoned by farm labourers migrating to the cities in search of work, adding further to overcrowding and unemployment.

The dehumanising effects of urban squalor prompted groups such as the Arts and Crafts Movement to promote alternative visions of living and to attempt radical reappraisals of the socio-economic conditions of late Victorian Britain. Toward the end of the century, William Booth (1829–1912) famously captured the troubled nature of Britain by asking whether there was not a 'darkest England' to mirror 'darkest Africa'.[83] The possibilities of socialism appealed to the disaffected and also to middle-class intellectuals and reformers.[84] Working-class discontent became pervasive. The Independent Labour Party was founded in 1893 and by 1906 had won a number of major concessions, including the Workers Compensation Act (1897), the Factory Act (1901) and the Trades Disputes Act (1906).

The process of agitation and change was repeated in Ireland, although legislation was slower to materialise. As early as 1890 Michael Davitt (1846–1906) had published the first issue of *Labour World* and the following year founded the Labour Federation in Cork. The Belfast Labour Party was founded in 1892. Arthur Griffith's (1871–1922) National Council campaigned for the eradication of slum dwellings in Dublin and James Larkin (1874–1947), two of whose sons attended St Enda's School, acted as organiser for the National Union of Dock Workers in Belfast in 1907.[85] Larkin led the Belfast dockworkers' strike in May 1908 and in August founded a branch of the Dock Workers Union in Dublin.

In 1909, Hanna Sheehy-Skeffington (1877–1946) and Margaret Cousins (1878–1954) founded the Irish Women's Franchise League, and in December of that year, the Housing of the Working Classes (Ireland) Act authorised the Dublin Cooperation to build and finance the construction of new housing in inner city Dublin.[86] 1911 witnessed the publication of the *Irish Worker*, official organ of the Irish Trade and General Workers

Union, and the founding of the Irish Women's Suffrage Federation and the Irish Women's Workers Union. In September, Sir Edward Carson (1854–1935) campaigned against the introduction of Home Rule and in March 1912 Pearse addressed a demonstration in its favour. In June of that year the Irish Labour Party was founded and 1913 witnessed the creation of the Ulster Volunteer Force and the Dublin lockout.

PEARSE AND THE NEW EDUCATIONAL MOVEMENTS

Changes in socio-economic thinking were mirrored in ideas about schooling. Central to the rise in interest in education, particularly in England, was the notion that it could act as an antidote to industrial decline and international competition. Simple skills, traditionally learned by apprenticeship, were in decline and advocates of technical instruction urged that school curricula keep pace with industrial change. In 1881 the Royal Commission on Technical Instruction was appointed to study the provision of manual instruction abroad.[87] It identified technical instruction as a key component in the education of the labouring classes and its recommendations resulted in manual training becoming included in the Code of Instruction in Great Britain in 1890. Predictably, the cost of equipping schools meant that progress was slow.

Of those who advocated the inclusion of practical subjects perhaps none were more successful than supporters of the natural sciences. The relationship between scientific discovery and industrial progress became increasingly apparent in the mid-nineteenth century, particularly in Britain and Germany where technical innovation resulted in spectacular improvements in industrial production. Basic scientific instruction had been sanctioned for elementary schools in Britain in 1876 but teachers were unenthusiastic having received little in the way of training. The school code of 1890, however, made Elementary Science a permanent feature of the school timetable while in 1895 the teaching of basic science became compulsory and an obligatory course in teacher training colleges from 1904. The perceived correlation between scientific and commercial progress in the public mind added to the status of the subject and its advocates were anxious to highlight the benefits.[88] Those involved in the teaching of science developed new methodologies and particular emphasis was placed upon the notion of 'discovery', or experimental learning. This added further to the status of the subject and allowed its advocates to press for increased resources.[89] The promotion of science as a school discipline, coupled with the obligation upon elementary school teachers to undertake instructional training, was crucial to its progress.

While the Industrial Revolution had brought massive economic benefits, late nineteenth-century Britain retained a broad agricultural base. In 1884 the Technical Instruction Committee recommended that the principles of agriculture be made compulsory for pupils in the higher grades in rural schools, although lack of funding and insufficient training resulted in a hesitant response.[90] In 1899 the school code encouraged teachers to tailor lessons to local needs and encouraged village teachers to foster in their pupils an 'intelligent knowledge of the surroundings of ordinary rural life'.[91] Two years later the Code of Regulations for Public Elementary Schools included nature study as a subject, which, it insisted, should be taught 'with special reference to the surroundings of the scholars, and to the natural features, industries, and plant life of the locality.'[92] In 1908 the Board published guidelines and specimen courses on horticulture for schools, and two years later, Pearse re-located St Enda's to The Hermitage in Rathfarnham, noting that in its previous location the 'city was too near, the hills too far' – he also employed a gardener who also gave horticultural instruction.[93]

Traditional academic subjects, such as history and geography, did not remain removed from the early twentieth-century emphasis upon the practical. Teachers of history in particular were encouraged to design lessons that utilised the immediate locality. In 1904, Pearse insisted that this formed an essential component of history lessons.[94] The discipline was not taught with any regularity in Britain at the beginning of the twentieth century and was not made obligatory in elementary schools until 1904. Apart from the introduction of new subjects, such as manual and technical instruction, the period also witnessed a growing emphasis upon practicality and relevance in teaching. Hence mathematics, for example, might include tasks such as balancing household bills, and again, teachers were encouraged to employ instructional objects in the classroom. If possible, a child should not simply read about an experiment or a swallow's nest, but take part in the experiment or see the nest. The exponents of this view of teaching emphasised the relationship between doing and knowing; that the former was a fundamental prerequisite of the latter.

Advocates of a more practical curriculum introduced the notion of relevance and insisted that a correlation existed between what was learned in school and economic progress; a somewhat dubious approach. In this they identified schooling as serving the common good. But these were not usually educationalists and so were forced to seek pedagogical justifications to support their views. Like T.H. Huxley, their understanding of education was not primarily informed by any insight into or concern for learning *per se*, but by the need to make educational content meet the demands of the market place.[95] While many aspects of the movement toward a more utilitarian curriculum were reflected in Pearse's project at St Enda's, he rejected absolutely the notion that schooling should be informed by commercial or economic considerations.

The movement toward practical learning did not represent a rejection of the child-centeredness of Johann Pestalozzi or Friedrich Froebel, but its proponents were prepared to jettison much of the thinking that informed good practice toward the end of the 1900s. Pestalozzi's conviction that schooling was merely the facilitation of human nature in its growth to moral maturity reflected Rousseau's belief in the elemental goodness of Man: 'Every philosophical investigator of human nature,' wrote Pestalozzi, 'is ultimately compelled to admit that the sole aim of education is the harmonious development of the faculties and dispositions which, under God's grace, make up personality.'[96] In *How Gertrude Teaches Her Children* (1801) Pestalozzi defined instruction as 'nothing more than (helping) human nature to develop in its own way.'[97] Pearse's insistence upon the right of individuals to 'grow on their natural lines ... to their own perfection ... to develop ... in God's way' and that schooling had to do with 'fostering the growth of things', may have had its origins in Pestalozzi's now ubiquitous metaphor of the teacher as gardener[98], which was an all pervasive metaphor at the period. 'True education', Pestalozzi wrote, is like the work of the gardener under whose care a thousand trees blossom: 'He contributes nothing to their actual growth; the principle of growth lies in the trees themselves ... he only waters the dry earth ... he only drains away the standing water ... so with the educator.'[99]

In 1916, Pearse insisted that 'the conditions we should strive to bring about in our education system are (those) favourable to the growth of living organisms – the liberty and the light and the gladness of a ploughed field under spring sunshine.'[100] Pestalozzi's insistence that the solution to the 'problem' of education for all children, regardless of circumstances or ability, lay in 'developing the fundamental human powers' was much later re-articulated in Pearse's dictum that education lay in fostering the 'right growth of personality'.[101] Pearse does not cite Pestalozzi, but the metaphors he employs and his general notion of schooling as a process of growth indicate that he cannot have been ignorant of his work.[102]

Educational discourse in nineteenth and twentieth-century Europe was also much influenced by work of the German educationalist Friedrich Froebel, who admired Pestalozzi's emphasis upon the relationship between learning and the natural growth of the child. His first school, established in 1816, grew quickly but he was 'a mere babe in the wilderness of economic reality' and it closed in 1829.[103] Froebel operated a number of schools between then and 1837, when he opened an elementary school at Keilhau. It was here that he became convinced of the importance of activity in learning and in 1840 established two further kindergarten at Rudolstadt and Blankenburg for the 'psychological training' of young children by means of 'play and occupations'.[104] Froebel's insistence upon the value of the natural environment in schooling is reflected in Pearse's work at The Hermitage, where he created vegetable and flower gardens.

Like Pestalozzi, Froebel was interested in the process of learning. Observation led him to create learning equipment ('gifts') that later formed the basis for the instructional materials developed by Maria Montessori (1870–1952). His work was informed by a desire to discover ways of creating learning environments that were appropriate to the child's stage of intellectual development, what Montessori later referred to as 'sensitive periods'. Kindergarten spread throughout Germany and Europe. In England, the 1905 Suggestions for Schools officially recognised the merit of Froebel principles: 'The leading principle which determines the methods of education suitable to early childhood is the recognition of the spontaneous activities of the children ... the process of education up to five or six years of age consists in [ensuring that] as little constraint as possible is put upon free movement whether of body or mind.'[105]

Like Froebel, Pearse strove to create an environment in which learning could flourish unhindered by an overemphasis upon methods or examinations. He wanted his pupils to have access to the natural environment and like Pestalozzi and Froebel his school boasted a working garden, horticultural instruction, nature walks and studies and an emphasis upon outdoor life as holistically beneficial. In this, as in much besides, Pearse clearly belongs within the child-centred tradition.

The turn of the century witnessed a new openness to teaching methods, coupled with a more sympathetic understanding of childhood. In Ireland, this was reflected in the Revised Programme of Instruction for Primary Schools (1900).[106] The importance of the nursery school movement, pioneered in England by Margaret and Rachel McMillan in the first decade of the twentieth century, was officially recognised in the Fisher Education Act (1918).[107] Generally, the growing awareness of the centrality of the child in the learning process encouraged a more progressive attitude toward schooling. The period in which Pearse was working at St Enda's was increasingly characterised in Britain by under-standings of schooling that were markedly similar to those he advocated between 1903 and 1916. The Montessori Society, for example, aimed to 'unfold the latent energy of the child'.[108] E.G.A. Holmes' dictum that the function of education was 'to foster growth'[109] was strikingly similar to Pearse's insistence that schooling should facilitate 'natural growth'.[110] In 1901 Harold Gorst wrote that education was concerned with the development of the 'faculties with which Nature had endowed' the child.[111] In 1902 R.E. Hughes described the function of schooling as the 'unfolding of the disposition of the pupil.'[112]

A decade later, Pearse complained that the teacher in Ireland had not been at liberty to 'seek to discover the individual bents of his pupils, the hidden talent that is in every normal soul.'[113] In 1912 he repeated an unnamed colleague's summary of the position at St Enda's: 'If a boy shows an aptitude for doing anything better than most people, he should be encouraged to do that, and to do it as well as possible.'[114] At the 1915 British Conference of New Ideals in Education delegates spoke of 'a new spirit, full of hope' that was 'stirring in education', the essence of which were 'reverence for the pupil's individuality and a belief that individuality grows best in an atmosphere of freedom.'[115] In 1912, Pearse asserted that schools were places where 'young souls' demanded 'the largest measure of individual freedom consistent with the common good, freedom to move and grow on their natural lines, freedom to live their own lives ... freedom to bring themselves to ... their own perfection.'[116] While Pearse does not refer to contemporaneous writings on the subject, making only a single reference to Montessori, the vocabulary he employs generally

demonstrates his immersion in child-centred understandings. Again, his
pantheistic leanings were strong and his belief in the power of the natural
world to inspire and instruct, to offer solace and respite, was characteristic of the Victorian nature movements that spawned walking clubs and
amateur naturalist groups in the nineteenth century.

His understanding of the role of the teacher, however, was utterly at
odds with the doctrines promoted by advocates of child-centredness.
Montessori, for example, insisted that the teacher do little more than
facilitate the child's activity, while others counselled that the teacher must
'as far as possible efface himself'.[117] Pearse, on the other hand, believed
that the teacher was central to the learning process and entrusted with a
'priest-like office'[118] although he echoed Holmes' view that teachers
must avoid any attempt to 'mould' pupils to their 'will'.[119] He was quite
resolute on this issue, writing that: 'What the teacher should bring to
his pupils is not a set of readymade opinions … but an inspiration and
an example … his main qualification should be, not such an overmas-
tering will as shall impose itself … upon all weaker wills … but rather
so infectious an enthusiasm as shall kindle new enthusiasm.'[120] Again,
his use of the analogy of 'disciple and master', for example, was at odds
with exponents of child-centeredness who insisted that the teacher was
'the servant and not the master'.[121] Indeed, Pearse's only reference to
Montessori concerned the 'insufficient importance' she attached to the
role of the teacher.[122]

The most significant aspects of Pearse's work at St Enda's, therefore,
were informed by a combination of the move toward a more utilitarian conceptualisation of education which had developed, in parallel
with the quite dissimilar development of child-centred understandings
of the educative process, in the late nineteenth and early twentieth
century. In effect, Pearse's work drew upon seemingly opposing
traditions – while influenced by the child-centred movement he
evidently did not believe that this meant excluding practical or applied
subjects. He reflected the wider belief in the early years of the 1900s
that, ultimately, all subjects could be taught in such a way as to make
them more attractive to children. His thought is located where the
child-centred and utilitarian traditions meet. Pearse was conscious of
the practical needs of his pupils and society generally, but he did not
believe that imaginative teaching and effective learning were mutually
exclusive. The syllabus at St Enda's reflected his desire to cater for less

academically able pupils and provide a comprehensive and relevant education. The Prospectus of St Enda's (1909) pointed, for example, to the place of Physical Science in the life of the school and expressed the belief that the new 'biological laboratory' would 'give facilities for the prosecution of more advanced nature study', adding that 'the new physico-chemical laboratory completes the equipment of the school for the proper teaching of Experimental Science.' Pearse also advised prospective parents that 'arrangements were being made' for pupils who wished to pursue 'higher scientific studies' to attend a course at the Royal College of Science.[123] This was characteristic of Pearse, who strove constantly to introduce his pupils to a wider appreciation of any discipline, despite very limited resources.

The emphasis placed upon the study of the natural world and horticulture in the early decades of the twentieth century was reflected in Pearse's provision for nature studies at the very restricted site at Rathmines. He described nature study as an 'essential part of the work at St Enda's ... not mere dry-as-dust teaching of the rudiments of zoology, botany, and geology' but 'an attempt to inspire a real interest in and love for beautiful living things.'[124] Nature study began in the school garden and was reinforced by outings to 'suitable spots' in the vicinity.[125] Even at the Rathmines site, 'practical gardening and elementary agriculture' were taught and any boy could take a plot of ground which he could 'plan out and cultivate according to his own taste'.[126]

The similarity between the vocabulary Pearse employed when speaking about nature, and that used by contemporaneous advocates of nature studies is particularly striking. R.E. Hughes, author of *Schools at Home and Abroad* (1905) wrote, for example, that 'our little ones' must be lead 'out into the fields ... up hill and down dale, by rushing rivulet ... our hill sides shall be classrooms ... we will train them to know and to love every flower that blooms and every wind that blows.' Still more reminiscent of Pearse was E.G. Holmes' romantic view that stones were charged with 'mystic forces' and flowers 'laden with meaning'.[127] Reflecting on The Hermitage, Pearse wrote that the stream 'makes three leaps within our grounds ... I hear the roar of the nearest cascade, a quarter of a mile off at night from my bedroom. It reminds me of the life out there in the woods, in the grass, in the river ... the shyer creatures of the mountains, and hidden places abide with us ... as if they felt at home here.'[128]

Pearse was drawn to the The Hermitage because it would allow the boys 'intercourse with the wild things of the woods and the wastes', they would 'learn much' by observing their 'fellow-citizens of the grass and woods and water'.[129] This reference to 'fellow-citizens' is strikingly modern and at the same time hints at the influence of Romanticism in Pearse's temperament, the attraction of wilderness, empathy for wildlife and the romance of ruined buildings all feature in his writing.[130] Yet his view was not wholly sentimental. Ultimately the natural environment demonstrated the fundamental truth of existence: 'There is red murder in the greenwood … it is murder and death that make possible the terrible thing we call physical life … life lives on death.'[131]

The developments in schooling occasioned by the work of the practical educationalists and child-centred movement also influenced classroom practice in Ireland. Teachers groups, such as the Irish National Teachers Organisation (INTO) and, what later became the Association of Secondary Teachers in Ireland (ASTI), demonstrated a sincere commitment to developments in methodology. The INTO were particularly proactive. Their Programme for National Schools (1922) was informed by key elements of child-centred thinking. It denounced the 'cramming of dates and details' and suggested that teaching in arithmetic, for example, have 'a local basis' that connected 'the school work of the pupils with their environment.'[132]

The Irish Agricultural Aid Organisation was founded in 1894 to promote trade and in 1900 the Department of Agricultural and Technical Instruction was established. The creation of a specific department reflects the importance placed upon the acquisition of agricultural and technological skills and their essential place in Ireland's future economic progress.[133] The 1897 Commission on Practical and Manual Instruction (Belmore Commission), which had preceded the establishment of the Department, was established in response to fears that technical education in National Schools was falling behind that of England and Scotland. Its investigation was wide-ranging and drew upon systems in Belgium, Holland, France, Germany and Switzerland.[134] The Commissioners found that woodwork and metalwork were highly regarded by pupils in England and Wales while teachers reported that these disciplines complimented the more academic subjects by 'quickening the intelligence' and demonstrating the 'value of exactness'.[135] The findings of the Belmore Commission significantly altered the way teachers thought about primary schooling in Ireland through the introduction of new subjects such as elementary science and physical drill, the promotion of kinder-garten methods and the attempt to make schools into welcoming and stimulating environments. Its recommendations were accepted by the National Board and incorporated into the 1900 Revised Programme for National Schools.[136] Scarcity of resources, lack of teacher training, insuf-ficient funding and the conservatism of existing practice all contributed to a tardy response, although some progress was made.[137] The programme introduced elementary science into Irish National Schools and training programmes were organised for teachers in major cities.[138] By 1909, six months after Pearse had opened St Enda's, the Elementary Science course included nature study, hygiene, experimental science and domestic science for girls and mixed gender schools. In 1909 the Department of Agriculture and Technical Instruction hosted a summer course in rural science and school gardening, followed by a wider programme of teacher training, and in 1911 the National Board introduced rural science and gardening as an optional subject for National Schools.[139]

The curriculum of St Enda's closely reflected these changes, although Pearse strove to give the programme an Irish inflexion. The introduction of physical drill to the post-Belmore curriculum reflected the legacy of the Social Reform movement, which campaigned, in diverse ways, on its behalf throughout the nineteenth century.[140] Again, life at St Enda's reflected this development and while hurling and football were the core sporting activities, physical education played an important role: 'All the boys are taught Drill and the various exercises of the Gymnasium ... the boys are taught to prize bodily vigour, grace, and cleanliness, and the advantages of an active outdoor life are constantly insisted on.'[141]

Pearse was undoubtedly influenced by Rousseau, Pestalozzi and Froebel. Certainly, he was influenced by the dynamism of the child-centred movement and was equally committed to developments in science teaching, animal husbandry and botany, all of which were catered for at St Enda's. The school also offered vocational subjects, such as shorthand and bookkeeping.[142] The emphasis he placed upon experimental science, physical education, horticulture and agriculture reflect his preparedness to embrace practical and applied disciplines. Simultaneously he positioned himself within a tradition that sought to emphasise the less utilitarian aspects of education: the importance of the natural environment, the notion of teaching as an act of nurturing growth, the emphasis upon the centrality of the child and the notion of learning by experience, all indicate that much of Pearse's thinking can be traced to the child-centred movement. The images, metaphors and analogies he employed – 'fostering', 'growth', 'natural powers', 'individual freedom' and 'grow on natural lines' – position Pearse firmly within that tradition. However, the very political nature of his work added a dimension that was not usual in the work of child-centred advocates, although common in that of the radical educators. Again, Pearse's developing understanding of schooling was very much influenced by the nature of provision under the British administration. Therefore, when he speaks of freedom for the child, this can be understood in ways that remove it outside the arena of traditional child-centred understandings, even though rooted in that tradition. Pearse incorporated elements of the movements discussed above into an understanding of schooling that was located in a specific historic moment. But for him, any meaningful engagement with the issue of education in Ireland must embrace not only the advances of the child-centred movement but also, what he considered, the limitations of the prevailing system or 'murder machine', which, he believed was founded upon a centuries-old disposition of distrust.

Notes:

[1] See P.J. Dowling, *The Hedge Schools of Ireland* & Antonia McManus, *The Irish Hedge School and its Books, 1695-1831*.

[2] See Louis Le Roux, *P.H. Pearse*, p. 103. The source for this remark was Emile Montégut's essay on John Mitchel (1815–75), founder of the *United Irishman*, patriot.

[3] Indeed the necessity of making the Irish an English-speaking people had occupied the Crown since the twelfth century. The Statutes of Kilkenny (1366) attempted to prevent English settlers in Ireland from 'forsaking the English language, fashion, mode of riding, laws and usages'. Richard II asked the Pope to instruct the Irish hierarchy to encourage the population to learn English, *see* Norman Akenson, *Irish Education: A History of Educational Institutions*, pp. 15–16. All bracketed dates following the names of Regents represent years enthroned.

[4] An Act for the English Order, Habite, and Language (28 Henry VIII. c. 15) Irish Statutes (1786) I. 119–22 in *c.* Maxwell, *Irish History from Contemporary Sources (1509-1606)*, p. 113.

[5]   By the first decade of the nineteenth century diocesan schools accounted for only 432 students. In 1831 there were twelve schools catering for 419 students. See D. Akenson, *The Irish Education Experiment*, p. 27.

[6]   D.B. Quinn suggests that as 'the techniques and resources of sixteenth-century governments were severely limited … it is not surprising that before 1603 no decisive successes in the Anglicizing program had been won.' See David Beers Quinn, *The Elizabethans and the Irish*, pp. 10–11.

[7]   See text of Richard Conway S.J. '1611, at Salamanca in Corcoran', *Education Systems in Ireland form the Close of the Middle Ages*, p. 21.

[8]   King James to the Lord Deputy, Oliver St John, May 1620, cited in Corcoran, *Education Systems in Ireland from the Close of the Middle Ages*, p. 23.

[9]   See Chapter Three.

[10]   The promise of concessions to the Confederates in return for an army. See R.F. Foster, *Modern Ireland, 1600-1972*, pp. 97–8.

[11]   Cromwell to the Council at Dublin, 28 March 1657, cited in Corcoran, *Education Systems in Ireland from the Close of the Middle Ages*, p. 29.

[12]   See L. Stephen Rice SJ to Rome, 15 July 1677, cited in Corcoran, *State Policy in Irish Education*, p. 82.

[13]   Between 1662 and 1678 there had been a number of restrictions, mainly economic, placed upon Ireland. The Popish Plot accusation allowed the administration to re-enact the type of anti-Catholic legislation characteristic of the preceding Cromwellian regime.

[14]   Oliver Plunkett (1629–81), professor of theology at College of Propaganda in Rome; Bishop of Armagh 1670; accused of conspiring in Popish Plot, executed 1681; canonised 1975.

[15]   This was typical of James' strategy. Mindful of the importance of Protestant sensibilities at home and in Ireland, his approach was generally cautious. Hayden and Moonan capture its spirit by remarking that the 'Lord Lieutenant was directed to quietly slip Catholics into vacant offices when opportunities presented themselves.' See Mary Hayden and George A. Moonan, *A Short History of the Irish People Part II*, p. 307.

16 Irish Statutes, 7 William III. c. 4. Cited in Corcoran, *State Policy in Irish Education*, p. 91.

17 Penal Code, 1703. ii Anne, c. 6. Cited in Corcoran, *Education Systems in Ireland*, p. 30.

18 *Ibid.*

19 See Benignus Milliett OMF, 'Survival and Reorganization 1650–95' in Patrick J. Corish (ed.), *A History of Irish Catholicism*, Vol. 3, p. 62.

20 Letter of Sir John Percival, Earl of Egmont, Dublin to London, 16 October 1703 cited in Corcoran, *Education Systems in Ireland*, p. 31.

21 Sir C.S. King, *Archbishop King's Autobiography and Correspondence* (1906), cited in Corcoran, *State Policy in Education*, p. 96.

22 *Charity School Manual* (extract) 1721, cited in Corcoran, *Education Systems in Ireland*, p. 32.

23 This society supported various organisations that operated schools with an end to winning adherents to the Established Church. The society had made considerable progress in Scotland in the early decades of the eighteenth century. This encouraged Boulter to request the charter from Parliament. See Charles Withers, 'Education and Anglicisation: The policy of the SSPCK toward the education of the Highlander, 1709–1825', *Scottish Studies*, No. 26, 1982. Two previous submissions to Parliament had been refused. See D. Akenson, *The Irish Education Experiment*, pp. 29–30.

24 See Corcoran, *State Policy in Education*, p. 103.

25 Charter for English Protestant Schools in Ireland Dublin 1733, cited in Corcoran, *State Policy in Education*, p. 109.

26 *Ibid.*

27 John Howard, humanitarian, social reformer and author of 'State of the Prisons in England and Wales … and an Account of Some Foreign Prisons' (1777).

28 See D. Akenson, *The Irish Education Experiment*, p 35.

29 'Mr Orde's Plan of an Improved System of Education in Ireland: submitted to the House of Commons, April 12, 1787', *Union Pamphlets 8, Caldwell & Orde's Speeches, 1785, 1787, Absentees 1783, 1798, the Crisis.*

[30] *Ibid.*, p. 31 & p. 124.

[31] *Parliamentary Register*, vii. 487, cited in D. Akenson, *The Irish Educational Experiment*, p. 64.

[32] 'Mr Orde's Plan of an Improved System of Education in Ireland, submitted to the House of Commons, April 12, 1787', *Union Pamphlets 8, Caldwell & Orde's Speeches, 1785, 1787, Absentees 1783, 1798, the Crisis.*

[33] *The First Report of the Irish Education Inquiry 1825* outlined the previous prohibitions regarding Catholic education in Ireland, commented upon the effectiveness of the schools of various bodies and made the recommendations outlined above. *The Second Report ... 1826* provided statistical analysis regarding school attendance; *The Third Report ... 1826* was concerned with the Foundling Hospital; *The Fourth Report ... 1827* with the Belfast Academical Institution; *The Fifth Report ... 1827* with the Diocesan Schools; *The Sixth Report ... 1827* with the Hibernian Society for the Care of Soldiers' Children; *The Seventh Report ... 1827* with the Royal Cork Institution; *The Eighth Report ... 1827* with the Roman Catholic College of Maynooth; *The Ninth Report ... 1827* was a summary of the Commissioners progress to date.

[34] *The First Report of the Irish Education Inquiry 1825* was highly critical of the Charter Schools. While it praised the Kildare Place Society for its work with the Irish poor it concluded that it had become an agent of proselytism (p. 59). The authors recorded that they were 'obliged to suggest the expediency of gradually withdrawing the public aid from that Society.' (p. 99) They also found that the Catholic view of the London Hibernian Society, as 'actuated by a Spirit of Hostility to their Church' was not without foundation (p. 81).

[35] See D. Akenson, *The Irish Education Experiment*, p. 102.

[36] The amount seems generous. Indeed there had been no educational expenditure in England and Scotland since 1800. Yet, while all interested parties seemed to desire an end to the funding of proselytising societies, they continued to enjoy financial aid from government. Corcoran claims that as late as 1840 the Kildare Place Society and the charter schools received £60, 000 whereas the National Board was granted only £50, 000. See Corcoran, 'Financing the Kildare Place Schools', *The Irish Monthly*, June 1932, p. 812.

[37] For the debate on the withdrawal of funding from the Kildare Place Society and the establishment of a National System see *Hansard, Parliamentary Debates*, 5th Ser.,Vol. 6, cols. 1124–1305. In introducing the National System Stanley was concerned to convince the House that the Kildare Place Society was commonly 'suspected of being a proselytising Society' and that it was generally held that teacher appointments were made on denominational grounds (Stanley's introductory remarks, col. 1251).

[38] The Reform Bill added about half a million voters to the register.

[39] In March 1831 William IV told Prime Minister Grey that soon it might be 'vain to hope to be able to resist … or to check disturbances of every kind, amounting possibly to open rebellion' which would be instigated by those who had recently 'formed unions for the furtherance of illegal purposes'. *Correspondence of William IV and Earl Grey*, Vol. I, pp. 179–180. See Asa Briggs, *The Age of Improvement*, p. 248.

[40] The Stanley Letter, see D. Akenson, p. 395.

[41] *Ibid.*, p. 396.

[42] *Ibid.* When the board were finally decided upon it comprised seven members, three were Anglicans, two were Presbyterians and two were Catholic. It was therefore, unrepresentative of the religious composition of nineteenth-century Ireland, which in 1834 was as follows: Anglican 11 per cent; Presbyterian 8 per cent; Roman Catholic 81 per cent. Source: D. Akenson, *Small Differences, Irish Catholics and Irish Protestants 1815-1922*, Appendix A, p. 154.

[43] The Stanley Letter, D. Akenson, p. 397.

[44] Mixed-denominationalism was a founding principle of the National School System. In 1868 Cardinal Cullen referred to the mixed system as a 'most formidable attempt upon the religion of this country' and an attempt to root out Catholicity 'by force or by fraud'. See *Irish Ecclesiastical Record*, Vol. V, 1869.

[45] Commonly referred to as the Powis Report as such reports are popularly known by the name of the Committee Chairman, here Lord Powis.

[46] Stanley Letter 'Version A', D. Akenson, *The Irish Education Experiment*, App. p. 398–9.

[47] *Royal Commission of Inquiry into Primary Education* (Ireland) *1870*, Vol. I, Part I, p. 348.

[48] *Royal Commission of Inquiry into Primary Education* (Ireland) *1870*, Vol. I, Part II. Part III–Primary Schools, Chapter IX 'School Books', p. 351. See also the remarks of Canon O'Toole who complained that the nationwide use of one set of books was 'the most effective way' of limiting intellectual development (p. 350) and Major O'Reilly MP who remarked that the monopoly on books was seen by some as politically motivated: 'designed on the part of the English Government to blot out all records of Ireland, to eliminate every patriotic sentiment from the breasts of Irishmen' (p. 350).

[49] *Royal Commission of Inquiry into Primary Education* (Ireland) *1870*, Vol. I, Part II. Part III–Primary Schools, Chapter IX 'School Books', p. 353.

[50] For example see, *Thirty-Sixth Report by the Commissioners of National Education 1869*, [C120] (H.C., 1870), App. c. General Reports: Report by M. Fitzgerald, Head Inspector, p. 170.

[51] See *Twenty-Fifth Report by the Commissioners of National Education 1858*, [2593] (H.C., 1860), Vol. II. App. B. General Reports: Report by James Patten, Head Inspector, V. Proficiency of Pupils, p. 107, Report by Timothy Sheahan, Summary III. Results of Examination of Pupils, p. 135, Report by W.H. Newell, V. Proficiency of Pupils, p. 172.

[52] *Ibid.* Report by W.A. Hunter, p. 219.

[53] For example see: *Twenty-Ninth Report by the Commissioners of National Education 1862*, [3235] (H.C., 1863), Vol. I. App. c. Report by Timothy Sheahan. *Thirty-First Report by the Commissioners of National Education 1864*, [3496] (H.C., 1865), Vol. I. App. c. Reports by James Patterson and John E. Sheridan. *Thirty-Second Report by the Commissioners of National Education 1865*, [3713] (H.C., 1866), Vol. I. App. c. Reports by John E. Sheridan, James Patterson and Timothy Sheahan. *Thirty-Fourth Report by the Commissioners of National Education 1867*, [4026] (H.C., 1867–8), Vol. I. App. C Reports by M. Fitzgerald and T. Sheahan. *Thirty-Fifth Report by the Commissioners of National Education 1868*, [4193] (H.C., 1868–9), Vol. I. App. C M. Fitzgerald and Timothy Sheahan. *Thirty-Sixth Report by the Commissioners of National Education 1869*, [C. 120] (H.C., 1870), Vol. I. App. C M. Fitzgerald, where the inspector does not refer to the schools at any stage, concentrating instead on teacher remuneration.

[54] *Thirty-First Report by the Commissions of National Education 1864*, [3496]
(H.C., 1865), Vol. I. App. c. General Reports: Report by Timothy Sheahan,
Head Inspector, p. 143.

[55] See *Twenty-Ninth Report by the Commissioners of National Education
1862*, [3235] (H.C., 1863), Vol. I. App. c. General Reports: Report by
John E. Sheridan. *Thirty-Second Report by the Commissioners of National
Education 1865*, [3713] (H.C., 1866), Vol. I. App. c. General Reports:
Report by J.F. Fleming. *Thirty-Fourth Report by the Commissioners of
National Education 1867*, [4026] (H.C., 1867–8), Vol. I. App. c. General
Reports: Report by James Patterson.

[56] *Royal Commission of Inquiry on Primary Education* (Ireland) *1870* Vol. 1.
Part X. Conclusions and Recommendations in the General Report 1, p. 522.

[57] *Ibid.*, Reports of Assistant Commissioners, Synopsis of Reports of
Assistant Commissioners Part X. Conclusions and Recommendations in
the General Report.

[58] The Catholic hierarchy in particular won a number of concessions
during the 1880s. In 1880 the Board sanctioned the use of schoolrooms
as places of worship. In 1882 monastic schools were allowed to join the
National System and the following year denominational training colleges
were sanctioned. Also during this decade the Board allowed religious
emblems to remain on classroom walls throughout the day.

[59] See Caitriona Clear, *Nuns in Nineteenth-Century Ireland*, p. 38.

[60] See *Thirty-First Report by the Commissioners of National Education, 1864*,
[832] (H.C., 1847), App. C, General Reports: Report by James Patterson,
p. 150. See also *Thirty-Fourth Report by the Commissioners of National
Education 1867*, [4026] (H.C. 1867–68), App. c. General Reports: Report
by Timothy Sheahan, p. 149.

[61] *Report by the Commission of Inquiry into Primary Education* (Ireland) *1870*,
see for example: Vol. II. Reports of Assistant Commissioners, Synopsis
of Reports of Assistant Commissioners, Mr Coward, p. 6; Thomas
Harvey, p. 31 and Patrick Cumin, p. 23; p. Le Page Renouf, p. 21. See also
Vol. III. Evidence taken before the Commissioners from 12 March to
30 October 1868, Evidence of Edward Sheridan, question 4802, p. 208;
Patrick Keenan question 1578, p. 68 and Frederick O' Carroll, question
4283–84, p. 189. F.H. Dale (1904) reported that the 'order and tone of the

Convent Schools are excellent and the instruction, as a whole, is distinctly superior to that given in the ordinary National Schools …' See *Report by Mr. F.H. Dale, His Majesty's Inspector of schools, Board of Education on Primary Education in Ireland, 1904,* [Cd 1981] (H.C., 1904).

[62] In his evidence before the Powis Commission Patrick Keenan stated that, nationally, 'the number of Protestant children who (in 1867) attended convent schools was exactly seventy–three.' See *Royal Commission of Inquiry into Primary Education* (Ireland) *1870,* Vol. III. Evidence taken before the Board from 12 March to 30 October 1888, Evidence of Patrick Keenan, question 1563, p. 67.

[63] *Royal Commission of Inquiry into Primary Education* (Ireland) *1870,* Vol. II. Reports of Assistant Commissioners, Report by Thomas Harvey, p. 497. See also Vol. III. Evidence taken before the Commissioners from 12 March to 30 October 1868, evidence of Edward Sheridan, question 4802, p. 208.

[64] See D. Akenson, *The Irish Educational Experiment,* pp. 320–321.

[65] *Proofs of General and Special Reports of Inspectors (and others) Prepared for Publication in the App. of the Commissioners' Annual Report for the Year 1895,* [8142] H.C. 1896, Mr A.J. Codrington, District Inspector, Roscommon, p. 170.

[66] *Ibid.* James A. Coyne, District Inspector, Tralee, p. 141.

[67] *Ibid.* Mr Power, Head Inspector, Dublin, p. 15; Mr S.E. Strange, Head Inspector, Belfast, p. 31; Mr Codrington, District Inspector, Roscommon, pp. 170–1.

[68] *Commission on Manual and Practical Instruction in Primary Schools under the Board of National Education, 1897,* [C. 8383] (H.C., 1897), Part I, p. 4.

[69] *Ibid.* Part I. i–ix, Part III, p. 54.

[70] *Commission on Manual and Practical Instruction in Primary Schools under the Board of National Education, Final Report by the Commissioners 1897,* [C. 8923] (H.C., 1898), Part I. Section I, pp. 9–10.

[71] *Ibid.*

[72] *Ibid.* Part I section III, Drawing, p. 3. See also Part II, Section III, Drawing, p. 32.

[73] *Ibid*. Part II, Section IV, Elementary Science (2), p. 38.

[74] *Commission on Manual and Practical Instruction in Primary Schools under the Board of National Education in Ireland, First Report by the Commissioners 1898*, [8383] (H.C., 1897), Part I, Section VI, Cooking, Laundry and Domestic Science, p. 3.

[75] See Revised Programme of Instruction in National Schools, published in App. to the *Annual Report by the Commissioners of National Education, 1902*, [Cd 1890] (H.C., 1903).

[76] *Ibid*. III. 9, efforts by Chief Secretary Wyndham to reform Irish education, 1902, p. 154–5. George Wyndham was Chief Secretary between 1900 and 1905.

[77] George Wyndham (1863–1913), Chief Secretary for Ireland, 1900 also great-grandson of Lord Edward Fitzgerald.

[78] *Report by Mr. R.H. Dale, His Majesty's Inspector of Schools, Board of Education on Primary Education in Ireland, 1904*, [1891] (H.C., 1904). Summary.

[79] See Thomas A. O'Donoghue, *Bilingual Education in Pre-Independent Irish-Speaking Ireland*.

[73] 'Education Under Home Rule?', *An Claidheamh Soluis*, 4 January 1913.

[80] Thomas Huxley, biologist, agnostic and leading exponent of Darwinism in England. His *Essays Upon Some Controversial Questions* was published in 1892. See Cyril Buddy (ed.), *T.H. Huxley on Education*.

[81] Darwin's *The Origin of the Species* was published in 1859.

[82] Aubrey Beardsley, English artist and libertine. Oscar Wilde, playwright and novelist.

[83] William Booth, *In Darkest England and the Way Out* (C. Knight, London, 6th ed., 1970). Booth was the founder of the Salvation Army, a religious congregation dedicated to the relief of poverty.

[84] See Brian Simon, *Education and the Labour Movement 1870-1918*, Chapter One.

[85] Arthur Griffith, supporter of the Gaelic League and constitutional nationalist until Easter 1916, president of Sinn Féin, member of group that negotiated Treaty of 1921, elected president of Dáil Eireann in January 1922. James Larkin, trade unionist and nationalist.

[86] Hanna Sheehy–Skeffington, co-founder of the Women's Franchise League, member of Irish Socialist Party, participant in the Easter Rising, rejected the Treaty of 1921, member of first executive of Fianna Fáil, funded Women's Social and Progressive League, 1938.

[87] The Royal Commission on Technical Instruction 1881 published its findings in 1884.

[88] See T.H. Huxley, *Science and Culture and Other Essays*, pp. 4–5.

[89] On methodology see H.E. Armstrong, *The Teaching of Scientific Method and other Papers on Education*.

[90] *Second Report of the Royal Commissioners on Technical Instruction (1884)* Vol. I, p. 534–37.

[91] Board of Education, 'The Curriculum of the Rural School' (Circular 435) April 1900, cited in R.J.W. Selleck, *The New Education 1870-1914*, p. 129.

[92] Code of Regulations for Public Elementary Schools, 1905, cited in R.J.W. Selleck, *The New Education, 1870-1914*, p. 129.

[93] 'By Way of Comment', *An Macaomh*, Vol. II, No. 5, Christmas 1910.

[94] See 'The Philosophy of Education', *An Claidheamh Soluis*, 12 November 1904, p. 6.

[95] See T.H. Huxley *Science and Culture and Other Essays*, *passim*.

[96] J. Pestalozzi, 'Views and Experiences', in J.A. Green (ed.) *Pestalozzi's Educational Writings*.

[97] J. Pestalozzi, 'How Gertrude Teaches Her Children', in J.A. Green (ed.) *Pestalozzi's Educational Writings*, p. 87.

[98] *The Murder Machine*, 'The Murder Machine' & 'Of Freedom in Education.'

[99] J. Pestalozzi, 'Address To My House', in J.A. Green (ed.) *Pestalozzi's Educational Writings*, pp. 194–5.

[100] *The Murder Machine*, 'The Murder Machine.'

[101] *Ibid.*

[102] There are no volumes of Pestalozzi's work at the library in the Pearse Museum or in the Pearse Collection, Kilmainham Archives.

[103] J. White, *The Educational Ideas of Froebel*, p. 11.

[104] *Ibid.*, p. 13.

[105] *Suggestions for the Consideration of Teachers and Others Concerned in the Work of Public Elementary Schools*, Board of Education, p. 22.

[106] On the informing principles of the Revised Programme and an overview of its success after a decade of operation see W.J.M. Starkie (1860–1920) Chairman of the Board of Intermediate Education and Resident Commissioner of National Education for Ireland, *The History of Irish Primary and Secondary Education During the Last Decade* (1911). Starkie concurred with the late Sir Joshua Fitch's commendation of the system as the 'broadest and most elastic ever produced in any European country,' p. 22.

[107] On the work of the McMillan sisters see S.J. Curtis, *Education in Britain Since 1900*, pp. 60–1 & pp. 69–70.

[108] *Report of the Conference of New Ideals in Education*, Stratford-on-Avon, Introduction iii, cited in R.J.W. Selleck, *The New Education 1870-1914*, p. 212.

[109] E.G.A. Holmes, *What Is and What Might Be*, p. 3.

[110] *The Murder Machine*, 'Of Freedom in Education.' This remark formed part of a speech Pearse gave in the Mansion House, Dublin in December 1912. Holmes' *What Is and What Might Be* was published in the same year.

[111] H. Gorst, *The Curse of Education*, p. 127.

[112] R.E. Hughes, *The Making of Citizens*, p.18, cited in R.J.W. Selleck, *the New Education 1870-1914*, p. 212.

[113] *The Murder Machine*, 'Of Freedom in Education.'

[114] *Ibid.*

[115] *Report of the Conference of New Ideals in Education*, Stratford-on-Avon, 1915, Introduction, p. iii, cited in R.J.W. Selleck, *The New Education 1870-1914*, p. 211.

[116] *The Murder Machine*, 'Of Freedom in Education.' These comments had originally formed part of an address given at the Mansion House, Dublin in December 1912.

[117] E.G.A. Holmes, *What Is and What Might Be*, J.A. Green (ed.), p. 164.

[118] *The Murder Machine*, 'Back To The Sagas.'

[119] E.G.A. Holmes, *What Is and What Might Be*, p. 50.

[120] *The Murder Machine*, 'Master and Disciples.' In this Pearse echoed Froebel who lamented the treatment of the child as if he were a 'piece of wax, a lump of clay which man can mould into what he pleases.' Friedrich Froebel, *The Education of Man*, p. 8, trans. W.N. Hailman.

[121] N. MacNunn, *A Path to Freedom in the Schools*, p. 113. Nevertheless there were similarities between Pearse and the child-centred movement on this issue. Pestalozzi, for example, had written of the teacher as the child's 'trusted friend' while Pearse believed that the teacher should be a 'tolerant and genial friend'. See Adolphe E. Meyer, *Grandmasters of Educational Thought*, p. 228 & *The Irish Review*, June 1914.

[122] See *The Murder Machine*, 'Master and Disciples.'

[123] *Prospectus of Scoil Éanna (1909)* Pearse Papers, NLI: 'Nature-Study and Physical Science.' In the 1914–15 school year twelve First Year boys studied Preparatory and Junior Grade Experimental Science; three Second Year boys studied Junior Grade and seven Third Year boys took a special course in chemistry in middle and senior grades. See 'Department of Agriculture and Technical Instruction for Ireland, Time Table of Classes in Experimental Science, Drawing, Manual Instruction, and Domestic Economy in Day Secondary Schools. Session, 1 August 1945 to 31 July 1915', Pearse Papers, NLI.

[124] *Prospectus of Scoil Éanna* (1909).

[125] *Ibid.*

[126] *Ibid.*

[127] E.G.A. Holmes, *The Montessori System of Education* (Board of Education, London, 1912), p. 26.

[128] 'By Way of Comment', *An Macaomh*, Vol. II. No. 3, Christmas 1910.

[129] *Ibid.*

[130] See H.G. Schenk, *The Mind of the European Romantics*, p. 44.

[131] 'By Way of Comment', *An Macaomh*, Vol. II. No. 3, Christmas 1910.

[132] See *National Programme of Primary Instruction*, p. 5. Although, as we have seen, this was hardly a new insight.

[133] Discussion concerning the relationship between the economic welfare of the state and systems of education tend to be characteristic of industrialised communities. The desire to introduce into the curriculum those disciplines and skills that will result in economic progress, as noted above, was first articulated in the mid-nineteenth century. The relationship between schooling and the economy has remained as a significant aspect of educational and socio-economic discourse in Ireland, as witnessed, for example, by reports and policy documents such as: *Investment in Education* (1965); *Draft Green Paper: Education for a Changing World* (1993) and *Charting Our Educational Future* (1995). The interrelationship between economic thinking and educational policy, as articulated in the latter two documents, was outlined in J. Coolahan (ed.), *Report of the National Education Convention*, (1993).

[134] See T.J. Durcan, *History of Irish Education from 1800*, p. 91.

[135] *Ibid.*

[136] See 'The Revised Programme', Appendix, *Reports of the Commissioners of National Education (1900 to 1921)*.

[137] In 1911 W.J.M. Starkie noted that, when introduced, insufficient support from Treasury and Government had impeded the implementation of the Revised Programme. See W.J.M. Starkie, *The History of Irish Primary and Secondary Education During the Last Decade* (1911), p. 4.

[138] See T.J. Durcan, *History of Irish Education From 1800*, p. 121.

[139] *Ibid.*, p. 122.

[140] See R.J.W. Selleck, *The New Education 1870-1914*, Chapter Five.

[141] *Prospectus of Scoil Éanna*, (1909).

[142] Before the changes brought about by the Revised Programme of 1900, bookkeeping took the place of agricultural studies in urban schools. Agricultural studies were compulsory in all rural schools for boys in the fourth and higher standards where a male teacher presided. See T.J. Durcan, *A History of Irish Education form 1800*, p. 96.

Three

The Tongue of the Gael

The rejuvenation of the Irish language and the creation of a bilingual Ireland were fundamental aspects of Pearse's educational thought and work. As editor of *An Claidheamh Soluis* he constantly sought to promote the language, and at St Enda's he attempted to create a bilingual environment where Irish would be 'taken for granted.'[1] He played a key role in securing the Bilingual Programme for Schools in 1904 and the matriculation in Irish as requirement for the National University of Ireland and his educational thinking is most compelling when writing about how the Irish language might be taught. This chapter details how Pearse fought to secure Irish within official education policy generally, encouraged schools, teachers and training colleges to embrace it and looks in detail at his work in the area of bilingualism.

Like Pearse's thinking on schooling generally, his views on the place of the language are more fully understood when addressed within the context of the history of the language at the period. Long before the stirrings of the Gaelic Revival the language had symbolised the contest between two cultures, and by the early twentieth century had attained a symbolic significance for Pearse and the revival movement.

THE IRISH LANGUAGE IN THE NINETEENTH-CENTURY

The survival of the Irish language in the twentieth century is due in no small part to Pearse's insistence, as editor of *An Claidheamh Soluis*, that it be provided for at national, secondary and university levels. Permeating the debate, however, was the long history of Irish under British rule. At the beginning of the twentieth century, the Irish language was perilously close to extinction in all but a few pockets along the west and southern seaboards.

Table 1. Percentage of people able to speak Irish 1851 & 1861

	Leinster	Munster	Ulster	Connaught
Year: 1851	3.5	43.9	6.8	50.8
Year: 1861	2.5	36.3	6	44.9

Source: The Census of Ireland for the Year 1851, [582] Part IV, Report on Ages and Education, Dublin 1855. *The Census of Ireland for the Year 1861*, [3026] Table XXIX.

Table 1 illustrates that, nationally, the number of people who could speak Irish only, or Irish and English, fell from 23.3 per cent in 1851 to 19.1 per cent in 1861. The distribution of people who could speak only Irish in 1861 was: Leinster 0.2 per cent, Munster 4.1 per cent, Ulster 1.2 per cent and Connaught 8.5 per cent.[2] The national percentage of persons who spoke Irish only, therefore, was 2.8 per cent. The proscriptions of the seventeenth and eighteenth centuries were partly responsible for this, but the famine of 1843–7 decimated the population of the western and southern seaboard, traditional strongholds of the language.[3]

Irish was in decline before 1845 and there is evidence that in some parts of the country the switch to English was happening among the younger generation. Stories about 'tally sticks' are given substance by findings that point to the decrease in native speakers less than ten years of age from 100 per cent in 1811–12 to 3 per cent in 1861–71 in Kilmallock, Co. Limerick.[4] In Callan, Co. Kilkenny, 64 per cent of the population spoke Irish in 1821, a figure that had fallen to 31 per cent by 1831.[5] The magnitude and speed of the decline is striking – the Census of 1851 records that the percentage of native speakers in County Kilkenny was just 0.2 per cent. By 1891 the national percentage of children under ten years who were native speakers had fallen to approximately 3.5 per cent.[6] There were other factors militating against the language in the nineteenth century: the perceived benefits of acquiring English; the initial failure of the National School System to include Irish and the ongoing effect of post-famine emigration. Often, the hedge-school lessons were conducted in English, and before 1856 there is no significant mention of the language in the Commissioners' reports.[7] In 1812 Henry Grattan wrote the following to the Secretary of the Board of Education: 'The diversity of language, and not the diversity of religion, constitutes a diversity of people. I should be very sorry that the Irish language should be forgotten; but glad that the English language should be generally understood ...'[8]

When the National System was established in 1831 it made no provision for the teaching of Irish, causing the Catholic Archbishop Mc Hale to describe its schools as 'graves of the national language'.[9] Nor was the National Board inclined to allow its use.[10] Indeed, in 1834 the Commission refused an application for a teacher of Irish to be appointed to a National School on the grounds that the request did not come within the framework of the Board's plan of education in Ireland. In 1844, a school manager was refused permission to teach Irish during ordinary school hours. The refusal of the Board to allow for teaching through Irish resulted in the anomaly of children in *Gaeltacht* regions attending schools where lessons were given in English. Taught in an incomprehensible language, they were, in effect, denied access to education on a par with the English speaking communities, and the apparent worthlessness of Irish was therefore reinforced.

It was not intended that the system should cater for children other than through English and when Inspector Patrick Keenan visited a number of islands off the west and southern-seaboards in 1855 he reported that the islanders wanted to learn English.[11] 'This passion,' he noted, was due to their seeing 'that prosperity has its peculiar tongue as well as its fine coat.'[12] He submitted that the National System had failed the islanders because they had not yet acquired English; hence the number of Irish speakers was increasing, even though, on some islands, parents punished children who were discovered speaking Irish.[13] The islanders' wish to learn English led Keenan to suggest that a bilingual system be instituted instead of one in which pupils were 'forced to learn the vocabulary and the grammar of a strange language before they are taught the alphabet of their own.'[14] A bilingual system would mean that the islanders would be taught Irish 'grammatically and soundly' and then English 'through the medium of their native language'.[15]

Patrick Keenan's observations, repeated again in 1857 and 1858, were ignored.[16] In 1879 Irish was introduced into primary schools as an extra subject, for which results-fees could be earned.[17] The concession was of little value as it applied only to children from fifth class upward, a stage few progressed beyond and was informed solely by the understanding of Irish as an aid to acquiring English.

It has been correctly noted that the very small number of schools teaching Irish before 1900 hardly amounted to a language revival.[18] However, the increasingly influential Gaelic League was instrumental in securing recognition for the language in the Revised Programme of Instruction for Primary Schools (1900). The programme permitted the teaching of Irish as an optional subject during ordinary school hours with the proviso that this did not impede instruction in other subjects.[19] Irish was included in the intermediate school curriculum in 1878 and although impeded by an unequal allocation of marks in comparison to other languages, it became an increasingly popular choice in the first two decades of the twentieth century.

This popularity was reflected in the numbers opting to study it in National Schools. While small, when measured against national enrolment, it continued to rise, and by 1904, 95,487 pupils were studying Irish in 1983 schools.[20] This increase took place while the number of monoglot Irish speakers continued to decline from 38,192 in 1891 to 20,953 in 1901. The Report of the Commissioners for 1905–6 recognised the 'educational necessity for instruction in Irish in Irish-speaking and bilingual districts', and acquiesced in the League's demand for bilingual teaching in those areas.[21] The increasing popularity of Irish, however, resulted in a rise in fees expenditure from £995 in 1901 to £12,069 in 1904.[22] The Treasury was unwilling to sustain the increased expenditure for extra subjects and in 1905 it was announced that from January 1906 the payments would cease. In 1904 fees for these subjects, other than Irish, amounted to a mere £2,297; a figure that could be sustained without difficulty.[23] In all probability it was the cost of the growing demand for Irish, rather than the cost of extra subjects as a group, that caused the Treasury to waver. In 1906 the parliamentary grant for education in Ireland was £1,138,422. The cost of Irish as an extra subject (£12,069) therefore represented 0.01 per cent of the educational budget – less than half the salary cost of the Dublin Office of the Commissioners of National Education.[24]

The Commissioners 'recognised' the need for instruction in Irish in 'Irish-speaking and bilingual districts' but only for 'children who are wholly or largely Irish-speaking'. They were unprepared to consent to the removal of fees 'except on the condition that the savings thereby effected should ... be applied to purposes of national education.'[25] The official disposition toward the language, despite the accepted 'strong sentiment in its favour and the interest ... taken by the teachers and the pupils' was evidently indifferent, if not hostile.[26] Yet Irish was quickly becoming the most popular extra subject in National Schools, enjoyed strong public support and was obviously necessary in *Gaeltacht* areas. The contrast between provision for Irish and official support for English was historically resonant and Pearse accused the Commissioners of entering 'an unholy compact with the arch-enemy of Ireland' (the Treasury), thereby abandoning any claim they might have had to represent the interests of education in Ireland.[27] In August 1905, he warned readers of *An Claidheamh Soluis* that the 'fight' was now with 'the British Treasury and the British Government'.[28] When the Treasury announced the withdrawal of fees for Irish in 1905, there were 1863 schools teaching Irish to approximately 100,000 children. Despite the announcement, the number of schools opting to teach Irish rose to 2,072 the following year, but Pearse insisted that Irish could not flourish due to competition from compulsory and fee-paying subjects.[29]

In March 1907, Augustine Birrell (1850–1933), president of the Board of Education and recently appointed Chief Secretary for Ireland, announced that a new but lower fee would be introduced. Pearse, however, pledged the League to a campaign to ensure that the 'full grant was restored'.[30] According to the Commissioners, the new scale of fees for both bilingual and ordinary schools reflected the 'growing popularity of the study of the language' and, in order to further encourage this, the Commission proposed the appointment of six 'organisers' of Irish instruction who would travel throughout the country training teachers.[31] In 1907, the number of schools teaching

Irish rose to 2,861, an increase of 168 on the previous year. By 1908, Irish was being taught in 3,047 schools.[32] Pearse welcomed these initiatives, and while the full fee was not restored he conceded that 'reasonable facilities and encouragement' were 'now afforded for the introduction of Irish teaching into our schools.'[33]

Regardless of the new scale of fees and the provision and support of undertakings, such as evening classes and summer courses, the number of schools which taught Irish dropped in 1910 to 2,800. The number of pupils learning Irish in 1911–12 had fallen by 44,000 since 1907, one year after the fees were lowered.[34] In his summary report for the session, D. Mangan, secretary to the Commissioners of National Education, complained that progress was generally poor and insisted that greater proficiency would result if the teaching of Irish were 'earnestly and systematically carried out.' He dismissed the teaching of Irish as an optional subject, remarking that 'there is not much of it and most of it is of an inferior kind'.[35] Yet at this time 34 per cent of pupils were studying Irish as an option. According to his report, 'few' of the Gaelic League evening schools taught Irish.[36] Teaching methodology in the National Schools, was condemned as 'dull, routine and commonplace … calculated to give children a distaste rather than a love for Irish.' However, he conceded that teachers were doing 'a good deal for the language.'[37]

But for Pearse, the most pressing obstacles to the revival of Irish in National Schools were not smaller results-fees or ineffectual teaching; ownership of policy and control of its implementation were the crucial factors, and in *An Claidheamh Soluis* he repeatedly insisted that the Board was an interloper in Irish affairs and the agent of a foreign power. Commenting on the departure of Arthur Balfour's administration in December 1905 he wrote: 'Our objection to them as controllers of the educational systems of Ireland was simply this, that they were British. Being British, they had no right to interfere with our schools. Morally, they were no more entitled to dictate what should be taught to children in Connemara than they were to dictate what should be taught to children in Yokohama.'[38]

If the Board could not be removed then it must be moulded to suit the requirements of the League. For the Board, Pearse's demands represented one more of many and while the first decade of the twentieth century witnessed a renewed interest in Irish, English remained the dominant language.[39] A co-complier of the Vice Regal Committee of Inquiry into Primary Education (Ireland) 1918 submitted that he had, 'grave doubts in assenting to the encouragement of the system by which special grants are given in bilingual schools and for the teaching of Irish as an extra subject ... Either Irish is the national language or it is not. If it is not, there is no need to teach it. If it is, its teaching should need no encouragement.'[40]

By 1911 Pearse had resigned as editor of *An Claidheamh Soluis* and was beginning his third year as headmaster at St Enda's. Despite being instrumental in securing bilingual schooling in Irish-speaking districts and the place of Irish as a compulsory requirement for matriculation to the National University of Ireland, he was no longer a dominant voice in the language movement. His time was divided between the demands of St Enda's and St Ita's and his increasing commitment to the Irish Republican Brotherhood, which he had joined in February 1914.

In 1918–19, the number of schools that earned fees for Irish was 1,261, a fall on the previous year. In 1920 the number was 1,525, an increase of 264. The Report of the Commissioners of National Education (1919–20) outlined six causes for the rise, including the continued State support for bilingual schools and the freedom accorded to schools to teach Irish as an extra subject for remuneration.[41] However, as late as 1920, teachers could only begin to teach Irish from the Third Standard. The position of Irish as an ordinary subject taught during regular school hours for the lower rate remained unchanged.[42] By 1920, twenty-three colleges for training teachers in Irish had been recognised by the National Board.[43] *The Eighty-Sixth Report of the Commissioners of National Education in Ireland 1919–20* estimated that, since their inception in 1906, approximately 3,000 teachers had been registered as competent to teach Irish in National Schools. The position that Irish had come to occupy, as Ireland assumed independence, is reflected in the place assigned to it in the Irish National Teachers Organisation's National Programme Conference (1922), which was accepted by the fledgling Dáil Eireann as 'embodying the new government's view in regard to National School education policy.'[44] This decision ushered in a new and, arguably, equally contentious era in the history of Irish in schools.

IRISH IN INTERMEDIATE SCHOOLING 1878-1922

The position of the Irish language was not considered when the Intermediate Education (Ireland) Act of 1878 was initially drafted. Only when the Bill was debated in Parliament did Irish members query provision for the language. The inclusion of Irish was due, in large, to the work of the Society for the Preservation of the Irish Language, founded in 1876. But Irish did not carry the same marks as other languages. The Preparatory Grade examination was worth 500 marks while the remaining grades received 600. However, French and German were worth 700 in all grades and English, Latin and Greek merited 1,200 marks.

The Gaelic Union believed that the lower marks reflected antipathy to the language.[45] Hence in 1880 it announced that it would award financial prizes to the pupils who secured the highest marks in Irish that year. Consequently the number of candidates rose from nineteen in 1879 to 117 in 1880. The prize money was made available again in 1881 and 116 students took Irish. In 1882, when no money was offered, the number of candidates dropped to seventy-two. Gradually, however, the numbers securing a 'pass' in Irish rose from 272 in 1889 to 503 in 1897.

In 1898, Douglas Hyde, in his capacity as Intermediate School Inspector of Celtic, was able to point to a renewed interest in Irish at intermediate level and an improvement in the 'calibre' of student generally. The German scholar Kuno Meyer (1858–1915), also acting as an Intermediate Inspector, reported in 1902 that if the best students 'were but given a chance of continuing their Irish studies at a University, an inestimable benefit would be conveyed on the cause of Irish studies both in their native land and abroad.'[46]

In 1904–5, the number of students taking Irish rose from 2,527 to 3,218. Ranking the languages in order of number of candidates demonstrates its strong position: French (9,156), Latin (4,029), Irish (3,218), German (1,101), Greek (1,081) and Italian (34).[47] Of twenty-seven subjects in the honours category, Irish was the sixth most popular. In the final examinations in 1905 the percentage of students who passed Irish with honours was 17 per cent, third behind Italian (26.4 per cent) and German (28.6 per cent). The total percentage of students who passed Irish in 1905 was 81.1 per cent, the same as German. Only Italian had a higher pass rate (88.3 per cent).[48] The results demonstrate that there was a keen appetite for Irish at intermediate level.[49] In 1906 the numbers taking Irish at intermediate level rose to 4,087; only French had a larger enrolment.[50] While the total percentage of students passing intermediate Irish had decreased from 80.1 per cent in 1905 to 78 per cent, the percentage passing with honours increased from 65.4 per cent to 80.7 per cent in the same period.

These achievements occurred in spite of curricular amendments made between 1903 and 1905 that ignored Irish. For example, in 1903 the experimental science course included the direction that all students taking this course must also take French or German – Irish was not an option. Again, in 1903, the mathematical course included only obligatory English. In 1904 pupils taking this course were directed to also take Latin, French or German, again Irish was not permitted as an option. In 1904, money prizes were awarded only for Greek and German, not Irish, despite its popularity.[51]

More students were examined in 1907 than in 1906, although the percentage passing with honours dropped from 80.7 per cent to 68.7 per cent. The percentage passing with honours fell again in 1908 and 1909.[52] In 1908, when Pearse opened St Enda's, the total number of candidates examined in intermediate Irish was 4,843, the percentage that passed with honours was 70.1 per cent, the second highest average percentage pass with honours in any subject for that year apart from Italian, which, as always, was taken by only a handful of students. The total pass rate for Irish for the year was 74.7 per cent.

The period between 1903 and 1909 coincided with the debate about compulsory Irish for matriculation to the National University of Ireland (NUI) and Pearse's term as editor at *An Claidheamh Soluis*, and presents a mixed picture. In 1908 it was announced that, from 1914, Irish would be an obligatory subject for matriculation to the NUI. The imminent requirement did not have any immediate effect upon pupil performance. In 1913, the number of candidates examined in Irish was 5,842; a drop of 1,451 on the figure for 1912 (7,293).[53] While the number rose again in 1915 to 6,356, it was at its lowest since 1909 (6,076). The percentage of students passing with honours also dropped from 80.8 per cent in 1909 to 65.3 per cent in 1915.[54] In spite of the fluctuations in the pass rate, the overall number of pupils enrolling for Irish at intermediate level rose almost annually from its introduction into the schools. Between 1908, when Pearse opened St Enda's, and the end of the War of Independence in 1921, the number studying Irish in intermediate schools rose from 5,885 to 8,332. In 1920, Irish was the fastest growing language in intermediate schools, with 58 per cent of candidates presenting for the examination in that year. However, the popularity of the language was not to last and its position, and the means by which it should be taught, was at the forefront of debates regarding education in independent Ireland. Indeed, the ambivalence of the teaching profession in particular had caused Pearse to identify it as an obstacle to, rather than a vehicle of the language revival.

THE TRAINING COLLEGES AND IRISH

Pearse believed it was the duty of teachers to teach Irish regardless of remuneration or whether or not the subject was classified as an 'extra' or 'ordinary'.[55] He demanded that it be taught and that the government fund any extra training the teachers might require.[56] In 1903 he even suggested that, in areas where the teaching of Irish was 'inefficient and uninteresting', the community should employ external teachers.[57] According to Pearse, teachers were best placed to facilitate the 'Irishising' of the schools. They were 'the most important factor in moulding the character of a school' and as such should be 'warmly Irish in sympathy'.[58] The teacher should 'regard himself as a worker for Ireland.'[59] He was critical of the National School teachers for failing to employ Irish at their annual Congress in 1907.[60] Even teachers who supported the language revival were not making sufficient progress due to their reliance upon 'antiquated' teaching methods.[61]

Indeed, it was by reflecting upon language teaching that Pearse's views on teaching generally began to develop. Encouraging teachers to use Irish in everyday conversation with pupils was certainly an enlightened approach.[62] He also condemned the hasty correction of translated passages while pupils hurriedly marked exercises 'right' or 'wrong', a 'method' too prevalent 'in many Christian Brother's Schools, Diocesan and other Colleges'.[63] The aim of the teacher should not be to get through the lesson quickly but 'to teach; a point which, though fairly obvious, is sometimes strangely overlooked'.[64]

His criticisms were echoed by Una Ní Fhaircheallaigh, Advising Examiner in Irish with the Intermediate Board, who noted in 1907 that enthusiasm for the language was spreading but 'in a large number of schools the teacher still adheres to antiquated methods of teaching.'[65] She was candid about the obstacles: 'If Irish is to be taught as a living language … it is absolutely necessary that the teachers be trained, and that examinations be oral as well as written.'[66] Pearse also encouraged teachers to adopt new methods and to attend the training colleges organised by the Gaelic League.[67] But, if teachers were to teach the language effectively, the training colleges would have to show them how.

When Pearse became editor of *An Claidheamh Soluis* in 1903 there were seven official training colleges in Ireland.[68] These were incapable of meeting the demand for qualified teachers and by 1900 only about half of National School teachers were trained. The colleges also found themselves under pressure to provide for Irish as, by 1903, it was the fastest growing non-compulsory subject in National Schools.[69]

The colleges were endeavouring to provide teachers for an under-funded system that was facing increasing demand while also trying to respond to the more child-centred curriculum of the Revised Programme for Schools (1900).[70] Understandably, they tended to ignore Irish as it was not obligatory in schools.[71] The entrance examination, known as the King's Scholarship Examination, contained the following compulsory subjects: geography, arithmetic, algebra, geometry, book-keeping, practise of teaching, history, drawing, needlework, domestic economy and hygiene, vocal music and english.[72]

In 1904, the Commissioners announced that Irish would be included in the final examinations of the training colleges as an optional subject. While Pearse welcomed this, he pointed out that because Irish was only offered as an option — examination marks not counting toward a candidates final grade — the measure did little to assist the language revival. That the colleges were reluctant to commit resources to a non-compulsory subject is reflected in the small number of teachers trained in Irish in 1905 when the six training colleges (excluding the Church of Ireland College, Dublin) trained ninety-one teachers or 18 per cent of graduates. The Report of the Commissioners of National Education (1905–6) pointed out that 'within the past ten years' over 1,000 teachers had obtained certificates of competency to teach Irish.[73] However, there was a significant gap between the number of teachers of Irish and the number of schools teaching it. While only 105 schools taught Irish in 1899 this number had risen to 1,983 by 1904. In 1905 fees were paid for Irish as an extra subject in 1,185

National Schools, mathematics had the second largest number of claims for payment but this represented only 361 schools. In the previous year £2,000 was paid in fees for Irish while mathematics earned £1,896.[74] According to Pearse the colleges were making no effort to supply the 'large and growing' demand for teachers of Irish.[75]

Pearse complained that it was not included in the schedule along with ordinary lectures. But the colleges had to meet the demands of a substantial curriculum.[76] In 1904 the following subjects formed the Programme of Instruction for National Schools: reading, writing and spelling, grammar, composition, arithmetic, kindergarten, manual instruction, drawing, object lessons, elementary science, cookery, needle-work, singing, physical drill, Irish, French, Latin, arithmetic and algebra, geometry and mensuration and instrumental music.[77]

The pressure was not alleviated by time. In 1908, Marlborough Street Training College opened with the largest number of male applicants since 1902 and a full complement of female students. The General Report on the Training Colleges for 1908–9 complained of the 'undue labour' imposed on the Professor of Method and called for a second appointment 'to cope with the heavy work'.[78] Again, in the 1910–11 session, the Commissioners warned that 'pressure from the over-crowded curriculum' was 'the greatest danger that has to be guarded against'.[79] Despite the introduction of an entrance fee in 1911 the total number of applicants to the colleges was still in excess of the number of places available.[80] The authorities at Mary Immaculate Training College Limerick, for example, complained that 'the strain towards the end of the session' had become 'excessive'.[81]

Nonetheless, since 1905, Pearse had been attempting to persuade the colleges to include Irish in the schedule of ordinary lectures and to make it a required subject for admittance to training.[82] By this, he meant that those candidates who had Irish should 'be allowed credit for that ... in competition with others'.[83] The syllabi of the colleges, however, tended to reflect the curriculum as prescribed by the Board.[84] If Pearse wanted them to commit resources to Irish then he would have to convince the Board to change the status of the language in schools. He believed that the demand existed, pointing out that in 1903 over 10,000 children in 2,018 National Schools had been taught Irish.[85] Indeed, the increase in the number of schools teaching Irish had been impressive, as illustrated in Table 2.

Table 2. The number of National Schools in which Irish was taught 1899–1904

Year	1899	1900	1901	1902	1903	1904
No. of Schools	104	88	1,198	1,586	2,018	1,983

Source: *The Seventy-Eight Report of the Commissioners of National Education in Ireland, School Year, 1911–1912*, [Cd. 6042] H.C. 1912, pp. 86–7.

Yet Pearse believed that a campaign to make Irish compulsory in the colleges would be counter-productive and accepted that, while not compulsory in schools, the colleges had no more than a moral duty to make provision for the language in training.[86]

In March 1907, Birrell called the attention of the House of Commons to the small number of teachers qualified to teach Irish. He reminded the House that, though the government provided thirty prizes annually to the Training Colleges to assist them in attracting candidates willing to study Irish, the number eager to do so remained small.[87] Indeed, a report by the Leinster Branch of the League for the same year showed that of the 16,000 schoolchildren in the province, only 5,000 (31 per cent) were being taught Irish. Consequently, a new rule requiring appointees to schools in Irish-speaking areas to have a knowledge of the language was, in effect, unworkable. Yet, cognisant of popular sentiment, Birrell concluded that it was inevitable that, in time, the managers of Training Colleges would be obliged to provide for Irish.

In 1908 the Commissioners announced that from 1911 the colleges would require applicants to pass an examination in a second language at the entrance examination.[88] Pearse responded by stating simply that teachers should be prepared for 'the advent of Bilingualism' and that the school managers should be persuaded to avail to the full of the 'large facilities for Irish teaching afforded by present regulations of the Board'.[89] Of the 1,192 teachers who qualified in 1908–9 only seventy (0.06 per cent) were competent to teach Irish; a drop of 0.03 per cent since 1905.[90]

The situation in the colleges did not improve. In 1910 only thirty-two (0.05 per cent) of the 641 teachers who qualified did so with a certificate to teach Irish.[91] At this time Irish was taught in 2,500 of the 8,000 National Schools (31 per cent) representing a decrease from

3,000 (37.5 per cent) in 1909.[92] The colleges remained unwilling to
include Irish other than as a subject to be studied voluntarily outside
lecture hours. As late as 1911 the Commissioners of National Education
recorded that, 'owing to the heavy call on the King's Scholars' time and
study for other matters, little can be done in the way of obtaining a
satisfactory grasp of a second language – especially of one so difficult as
Irish – in the spare hours of a College session, unless the students enter
with a good foundation already laid … Progress in the study of the
language can therefore be made only in the classroom'.[93]

Yet Irish was excluded from classrooms below the Third Standard,
received no fee as an extra and only a reduced one as an option. Very few
teachers were competent in the language and, faced with students who
knew little Irish and entering a profession where it was not necessary,
the colleges were unwilling to make any significant concessions. Securing
Irish as compulsory for matriculation to the National University of
Ireland became imperative if the language was to survive in intermediate
schools. Trinity College was considered hostile to Catholicism and indifferent to the Irish language; the latter being given considerable weight
by a report of the Royal Commission on Trinity College, Dublin, and
the University of Dublin. Generally, revivalist enthusiasts shared Eoin
McNeill's summary of the position of Trinity as 'sullenly aloof … from
the whole intellectual movement of modern Ireland.'[94] The position
of Trinity, coupled with the increasingly perceived unsuitability of the
Royal University of Ireland and pressure, in particular from the Irish
Catholic hierarchy, resulted in the introduction of the Irish Universities
Bill (1908), leading to the establishment of the National University of
Ireland (NUI) with constituent colleges at Cork, Dublin and Galway.
While the Bill was, fundamentally, a response to calls for university
education for Catholics, Pearse was unconcerned with matters spiritual,
remarking that 'the setting up of a College or University as Catholic
as Trinity is Protestant might conceivably leave the provision for Irish
higher education as unsatisfactory as it is today.'[95] For him, the 'fundamental objection to Trinity' was its hostility to nationalist aspirations
and the Irish language in particular. It is not unfair to claim that Pearse's
overriding interest in the proposed NUI was in how it might facilitate
the Irish language revival and he embarked on a campaign in the pages
of *An Claidheamh Soluis* insisting that a new university could not claim
to be 'national' if it did not require Irish as a prerequisite for entrance.

His logic: if Irish became necessary for matriculation then every intermediate school in Ireland would be forced to teach it and teach it well.

IRISH AND THE NATIONAL UNIVERSITY OF IRELAND

'We take it for granted,' Pearse wrote in February 1908, that 'from
the outset Irish would be a compulsory subject at the Matriculation
Examination.'[96] While a university should 'train the intellects of its
students' and 'lead them to a high degree of culture', the new university
must, nonetheless, meet Irish needs and interests, otherwise it would
replicate the failure of the school system.[97] Not all language revivalists
shared Pearse's views. In December 1908, the General Secretary of the
Gaelic League told a meeting at the Catholic University, that the League
would be satisfied 'if it was decided that Irish should be made obligatory
at the end of four years.'[98] Others held that any new university should
contribute to the economic as well as the intellectual life of the country.
F. Cruise O'Brien, writing in *The Leader* in August 1908, complained
that the Royal University had done little in this respect, accusing it
of producing yearly 'a certain number of ... uneconomic persons ...
more or less useless to the community.'[99] O'Brien saw little connection
between 'training in Ireland' and 'the whole condition of the country',
concluding that if the new university was possessed of a 'true spirit of
Nationalism' then its graduates would 'live in Ireland with a crust rather
than ... in India on two thousand a year.'[100]

Eoin MacNeill was anxious to stress that 'mere' instruction in
the language should take place in the schools, rather than university.
He pointed out that provision for the various branches of Irish Studies
in itself could not impart a national spirit to the institution, observing
that the 'self-same group of studies will be carried on in universities
outside of Ireland.'[101] Again, views on compulsion varied. A letter from a
Dr McWalter to the *Freeman's Journal* in January 1909 reflected the views
of many:'Liberty demands that if a student wishes to take Irish he must be
free to take it and get credit for it in the same way as Greek, or French or
German.'[102] In September 1909, *The Leader* called for the new university
to offer more applied and technological courses;'what the country wants
is practical men ... industrialists ... men who will make a living to other
peoples benefit.'[103] Evidently there were significant differences about

the nature and purpose of the new university and it is testament to the vigour of the League's campaign that it won widespread popular support for compulsory Irish, at a time when there were calls for more utilitarian provision in higher education. It also reflects the symbolic place of the language in Irish society in the first decade of the twentieth century.

Pearse was anxious that the language movement was adequately represented on the governing bodies of the new university. Hence his exasperation, five years previously, when the Report of the Royal Commission on University Education in Ireland had made no mention of representation for 'the people', as Pearse referred to members of the Gaelic League and its sympathisers.[104] His vision of the new university might be defined as an institution that contrasted with Trinity College in atmosphere, ethos and curriculum. 'Ireland,' he wrote, in 1904, had no use for another 'British institution as Trinity College is ... we want an Irish University.'[105] Douglas Hyde, the President of the Gaelic League, defined the League's demands as follows: 'We press now for a University that shall be Irish in the fullest and broadest sense of the word ... It must recognise that Ireland is a separate entity ... with a separate national life, language, literature and history ... the only hope of a new university doing good to Ireland will be to have it frankly and robustly national.'[106]

Pearse agreed, arguing that any proposal would secure the League's support provided it reflected the 'interests of Irish–Ireland'.[107] The form of the new university was of little consequence to Pearse, whose interest lay solely in ensuring that Irish became compulsory for matriculation.

When the Irish University Bill came before the House of Commons in March 1908, Pearse praised it as 'an honest Englishman's honest attempt'.[108] His main reservation was the proposed composition of the governing body of University College, Dublin. Five of the thirty-five members of the body were to be elected by graduates. Undergraduate students were to have no representation, whereas they would in Belfast. The composition of the governing bodies of the individual colleges also concerned him, as the Bill did not allow for adequate control by the 'hands of Young Ireland.'[109]

The proposed Senate was not unsympathetic to the language revival and included several members of the movement, but it was not to have any authority in drawing up the statutes of the new university or have any involvement in the appointment of the first body of professors. [110]

The Bill proposed that a Statutory Commission, composed of seven members, be appointed to perform these tasks; three appointed by the Crown and four by the Senate. Pearse objected on the grounds that, as the Crown appointed the Senate, the government retained too much authority, an arrangement that would not guarantee the place of the Irish language. Regarding the proposals for the Senate of the National University, he complained that only one woman had been included; an anomaly that offended his democratic instinct: 'Is one woman – would even two women or for that matter six women – be sufficient representation of the interests of what is, after all, the more important half of Ireland's population?'[111]

In May 1908 the Irish Universities Bill was given its second reading in the House of Commons and forwarded to Grand Committee. Pearse urged that this was the time to secure modifications. To encourage Irish studies the Bill should be amended to ensure that the NUI provided scholarships, studentships and fellowships in Irish. A course in Irish studies should be offered, a Faculty of Irish established in each college, and provision made for the education of native speakers in their own tongue. Pearse hoped to see the University become a bilingual institution in time, and therefore suggested that a date be fixed 'after which none should be eligible for professorships or other offices unless able to conduct the teaching or other business of their offices in Irish.'[112]

While the University Bill was before the Statutory Commission, the view was expressed that making Irish compulsory for matriculation to the new university was an act of coercion, a view shared by the Irish liberal Francis Sheehy-Skeffington (1878–1916).[113] Pearse's response was unconvincing. Arguing that nearly every action of our daily lives was 'more or less compulsory' and that it was 'no more tyrannical' to make Irish compulsory than 'Latin, English, Logic, Algebra'[114], he failed to make a cogent counter claim.[115] Compulsion was imperative because the new university would serve as a 'nerve centre for the whole educational system of Ireland'.[116] The urgency Pearse brought to bear on the debate was considerable. He insisted on the right of Ireland to operate its own national university and the tone of his argument was unflinchingly political: 'Intellectual freedom must precede political or national freedom; the first care of every race struggling to maintain their national existence is to educate their people on national lines, and through the medium of their own language.'[117]

If Irish were compulsory for matriculation it would encourage schools to implement the bilingual system, which as yet they had 'not touched.'[118] When they began to provide for Irish in a meaningful way, National Schools would follow. Without compulsion even those schools that were working hard to promote Irish would find it difficult to continue attracting pupils to the language. If Irish was not made compulsory then the new university should be treated as a foreign institution: 'The people,' Pearse warned, 'will no longer willingly acquiesce in a campaign of mind murder, nation murder, which is the end aim of West-British education.'[119]

A mass meeting was held at the Rotunda, Dublin, in December 1908 to call attention to the issue and respond to remarks made by Revd William Delany SJ one week earlier.[120] Delany was a member of the Gaelic League but opposed to the idea of Irish as compulsory for matriculation.[121] He was an important figure in the wider debate, and drawing on his own experience as President of University College, Dublin, observed that approximately 90 per cent of students there generally chose to present in a language other than Irish. Speaking of Pearse's lectures on elementary and advanced Irish at the College during the term of 1905–6, he reported that 'attendance was very unsatisfactory and considerable expense was incurred'.[122] A series of lectures by Eoin MacNeill the following year drew similarly low numbers. Delany also argued that a compulsory requirement would drive students into Trinity College or to Belfast.

Nonetheless the campaign for compulsory Irish for matriculation won widespread popular support. Large meetings were held throughout the country including one of more than 10,000 in Tuam, Co. Galway. Douglas Hyde reflected the mood, stating that 'as the Irish language did not die naturally but was killed by force … a little gentle pressure is necessary for its restoration', only its being made compulsory, he argued would convince 'the Gaelic Irishman' that 'after 300 or 400 years of oppression is he at last ceasing to be the underdog in Ireland.'[123] The campaign culminated in a demonstration by more than 100,000 people in Dublin in September 1909 and represented the zenith of the influence and popularity of the Gaelic League. In the same year, Pearse finally resigned as editor of *An Claidheamh Soluis* to concentrate on his work at St Enda's.[124]

The campaign for compulsory Irish bore fruit in 1910, when the Senate of the National University of Ireland announced that it would be obligatory for entrance from 1913. It was a famous victory for Pearse and the

League, and the announcement was greeted with celebrations in many
parts of the country.[125] But the *London Times* suggested that the poor of
Ireland were 'eminently shrewd' and wanted their sons to be 'barristers
or solicitors, doctors or engineers. They will ask what use Irish will be
to their children in such pursuits or in anything.'[126] The campaign had
caused tensions within the League and many members had objected to
such a strenuous fight on an issue that concerned so few people. But the
campaign for compulsion had acquired symbolic significance. It came
to represent growing nationalist aspirations and added momentum to
the cultural revival movement; another current in the swelling tide of
national fervour in pre-1916 Ireland.

Pearse's work for Irish on a national level was mirrored by his unre-
mitting articles in *An Claidheamh Soluis* and elsewhere concerning
how Irish should be taught. This is an aspect of Pearse which has been
ignored. Edwards' portrayal of him as passing from one grand enthusiasm
to another has little basis in reality. While Pearse campaigned tirelessly on
behalf of the language, *viz a viz* its place in the school curriculum and
national life, he also applied himself zealously to the practical matter
of how teachers should teach it. In doing so he produced a vast corpus
of insightful and workable methodology. It is this work that has been
neglected by historians, occluded by the more glamorous events of the
Rising, but which occupied most of Pearse's adult life.

THE TEACHING OF IRISH

The processes Pearse described for teaching Irish reflected his growing
grasp of methodology; the apparatus of how teachers help pupils learn.
He recommended that only Irish be spoken during an Irish lesson and
suggested that about four hours per week be allocated to the language.[127]
He submitted that one hour was an appropriate length for a lesson and
his article, 'The Secondary School: Thoughts and Suggestions' (1906)
outlined how that hour might be divided. The first fifteen minutes
might be dedicated to homework correction. He warned that 'even here
method is important ... too often the correction of pupils' exercises is
a performance of a very perfunctory character.'[128] The 'crude' method
whereby the teacher called out answers as the pupils marked their
exercises 'right' or 'wrong' was anathema to Pearse, who suggested

instead, that pupils themselves should read their homework aloud, their classmates offering corrections or alternatives.[129] This, Pearse recommended, should be written on the blackboard and the teacher should give any further explanation that might be necessary. He admitted that 'all this ... will make the correction of exercises a longer process than it generally is' but was unapologetic: 'The teacher's aim should be not to get through things with the greatest possible rapidity, but – well, to teach; a point which is sometimes strangely overlooked.'[130]

Once homework was corrected, the teacher should make his tour of the classroom, but 'should leave his cane behind ... to inflict corporal punishment for a mistake is surely the very acme of stupid and purposeless folly.'[131] The spectacle which Pearse had 'frequently seen' of teachers 'punishing boys for faults in their homework on the delightfully simple principle, 'one slap for each mistake' was 'nothing short of criminal'.[132] This did not mean that Pearse was opposed to the use of corporal punishment in principle but there is only one recorded instance of his employing it at St Enda's, and that in the case of a boy who had been cruel to an animal, behaviour that Pearse abhorred.[133] Once the teacher had completed his tour he could begin the lesson proper. Regrettably, Pearse nowhere provided a comprehensive lesson plan outlining how a teacher might proceed through the full one-hour lesson. He did, however, suggest a model weekly plan as follows:

Suggestion for School Timetable

Monday	Revision of Home Work. Composition
Wednesday	Revision of Home Work. Text (...) with grammar, etc.
Thursday	Revision of Home Work. Conversation.
Saturday	Revision of Home Work. Text.

Source: 'The Secondary School: Thoughts and Suggestions', *An Claidheamh Soluis*, 13 January 1906.[134]

At St Enda's, Pearse reserved time each week for *Sgéalaidheacht* (story-telling), reflecting his belief in its importance in the educative process and in particular its appeal to the imagination.[135] While advocating the Direct Method he stressed that he was unwilling to commit teachers to 'the fads of any one maker of methods books'.[136] Teachers should employ the teaching method that most suited their pupils: 'The good teacher must create his own method; and his own sympathy, insight and ingenuity will serve him better than all the maxims of all the best theorists.'[137]

Whilst Pearse insisted that Irish be taught and teachers should be free to decide upon methodology, he consistently recommended the Direct Method, or methods closely modelled upon it. The method was founded on the basis that language was taught as a living medium. Hence, a fundamental principle was that language teaching should not be book based. In teaching vocabulary, for example, he recommended that, rather than offering a simple translation of a word, its meaning should instead be demonstrated. Therefore, if a teacher wished to introduce the Irish word for 'window', rather than simply telling the children the translation was '*fuinneog*' he should say '*fuinneog*' and point to, or tap on, the classroom window at the same time. This represents the most basic mode of operating the Direct Method. Pearse explained the basis of the method: '[it] connects the words and phrases of the new language ... with the ideas for which in the new language those words and phrases stand. With this end, names of things are taught, not by giving the equivalents in the known language, but by showing the things themselves ...'[138]

Pearse had observed the method being used in Belgian classrooms and believed that, because it was practical, it appealed to teachers and pupils alike. For example, after learning the word for 'coat' in Irish, the teacher could, pointing to his own coat, ask the pupils whether or not they thought it was a nice coat and so on. The first step was always the simple naming of objects – a desk, for example – after which he could introduce actions; 'I am placing my hands on the desk' and so on.[139] The basic principle of the method was that language was taught as a living medium, using practical examples based on objects and pictures, or a combination of both. Pearse recommended that lessons occasionally consist of games, such as leapfrog or marbles, with vocabulary being introduced as appropriate. Small dramatic presentations or figures drawn on the blackboard could also be used. The extent to which Pearse was ahead of his time, in thinking about learning by doing, is demonstrated in his 1906 observation that 'pupils should not be merely listeners and spectators of but actual participants in all that goes on.'[140] Indeed, he insisted, it was 'always best to allow the class to take an active part in the giving of the lesson.'[141]

The Direct Method, as advocated by Pearse, relied less upon the use of textbooks than the originality and ingenuity of the teacher. Indeed, for

Pearse, textbooks represented merely an aid to what he called 'live' teaching.[142] Schoolbooks were a source of supplementary information which the pupil 'may take home with him for the purposes of reference' and 'a mere adjunct'.[143] And while basic grammars were required, Pearse insisted always that 'good teachers will succeed despite bad books'.[144] Indeed, the teacher was 'infinitely more important' than the textbook because by hearing the language spoken the pupils were encouraged to consider it as a living medium. The example set by the teacher was all important. Intermediate schoolteachers were particularly well placed and more likely, for example, to have a smaller group than his counterpart in the National School and less likely to be diverted by monitors or pupil-teachers. In order to teach an effective lesson in Irish to an intermediate class the teacher must have 'undivided control of his class' and be 'free to concentrate his attention on that class only'.[145] That the 'duty' of the teacher was to speak Irish was an axiom of 'Gaelic League teachers' and that they should speak the language informally around the school was a sound pedagogic principle. 'The fact is,' Pearse argued, 'that apart from the appeal of Irish to the child's national sense – the experience of using familiarly a new and unwonted language is so strange and interesting that children will, when quietly encouraged by the teacher, do so out of very glee and childish wonder.'[146] This willingness to engage pupils in conversation as a teaching tool, points to a more enlightened view than was common at the time: 'We have been in schools in which the pupils would as soon think of making a casual remark to the teacher as a prisoner in the dock of asking the judge on the bench to give him a light' and this, Pearse contended, was 'an unhealthy state of affairs'.[147]

PEARSE AND BILINGUAL EDUCATION

The Gaelic League was finding it difficult to convince teachers and school managers of the intrinsic value of the Irish language. In 1901, the percentage of the population who could speak Irish was 14.4 per cent, a drop of 8.9 per cent since 1851, while the percentage of people who spoke only Irish had fallen from 4.9 per cent to 0.5 per cent in the same period.[148] By 1904 Pearse's thinking on the plight of the language had changed. Perhaps unwilling to admit to significant indifference, he began focusing upon methodology and the bilingual method in particular, as a viable solution to the unproductive language teaching of the time. By 1901, 15.3 per cent of the population spoke only Irish, some Irish or Irish and English. Of that figure only 0.13 per cent could speak both Irish and English, in other words, were bilingual. The remaining 84.7 per cent spoke only English.[149] Therefore, less than 1 per cent of the population was bilingual. Inspired by the success of the language movement in Wales, and in particular their championing of bilingualism, Pearse began to see in the bilingual method the most promising means of revitalising the language.[150] Pearse's visit to Belgium in 1905 convinced him of the benefits of bilingualism, and from September 1906 to March 1907 he wrote almost exclusively upon the subject in *An Claidheamh Soluis*.[151] The Gaelic League had been campaigning for bilingual education in *Gaeltacht* regions since the early 1900s and in 1904 secured the introduction of the Bilingual Programme in those areas. This was in response to the anomaly of Irish-speaking children being instructed through English, an incongruity Pearse believed to be destructive of the Irish language and educationally bankrupt. In a letter to the press in 1900 he complained that, in reality, a master was permitted to explain a word or phrase in the vernacular (in this instance, Irish) if a pupil could not understand the English equivalent, yet even this power was further limited by the small number of teachers who could speak Irish.[152] What the League wanted was 'the teaching of Irish grammatically and soundly to Irish-speaking children, and the teaching of English … through the medium of Irish.'[153] However, that was not in fact a true definition of bilingual education and Pearse's evolving understanding became more refined after his visit to Belgium in 1905.

In developing a national strategy, Pearse divided the country into three regions: those where Irish was the only language spoken by children starting school, those where the majority spoke both Irish and English equally and those areas where most of the children spoke English and understood a little Irish. In all these regions some form of bilingual education should be introduced. Because of the situation in the *Gaeltacht* areas, Pearse initially concerned himself exclusively with the application of bilingualism there. But he did not insist on the use of Irish as the first medium of instruction. If a child from a *Gaeltacht* region was more familiar with English then, Pearse argued, his instruction should be in that language.[154] However, concurrent instruction in the second language should begin as soon as possible.

Hence, a bilingually educated child should be able to read a passage in Irish and explain it in English or vice versa. When teaching other subjects, such as geography or arithmetic, initial instruction should be given in the vernacular and then in the second language. The extra work required to teach a lesson, in which emphasis was as much upon language acquisition as content, demanded considerable enthusiasm and commitment from teachers and pupils. However, Pearse was, as usual, emphatic: 'The mind and soul of Ireland cannot be saved without large, very large demands on the capacity and energies of teachers.'[155]

Before the Bilingual Programme was officially sanctioned for *Gaeltacht* areas, schools were reluctant to employ the method, fearing they might be in breach of National Board regulations. Pearse insisted that there was nothing in the Board's rules to prevent bilingual teaching and his resolve to see the method widely used was in reaction to the poor standard of teaching Irish which he described as 'sham teaching'.[156] The prevalence of non-Irish-speaking inspectors placed another obstacle in the way of schools wishing to teach bilingually and, until April 1904, pupil proficiency was tested by written examination only. It is hardly surprising Pearse felt that the Board were only grudgingly facilitating the language.

In response to incessant lobbying by the Gaelic League, the Commissioners announced the introduction of the Bilingual Programme for National Schools in April 1904. It was intended for use in *Gaeltacht* and bilingual areas. In the schools that were sanctioned to use the programme, Irish would be taught concurrently with English from infant grade. In *Gaeltacht* regions, Irish would also be the medium of instruction. The methodology, as prescribed by the Board, was similar to that advocated by Pearse. The Programme stated that: 'As in the ordinary programme, each lesson may be given (1) in the "first" language with the cultivation of an intelligent observation for its principal aim, and (2) then in the second language for the purpose of further impressing the points learned, and teaching expression in the new language.'[157]

The Bilingual Programme was an important achievement for Pearse as it officially sanctioned Irish as the medium of instruction in Irish-speaking areas. Pearse was now confronted with the possibility of widespread indifference from the schools. The advent of the programme meant that he had to persuade managers and teachers that it was worth implementing. But he insisted that the Board demonstrate its commitment to it by providing

Irish-speaking inspectors to oversee the schools that adopted it.[158] He also considered that the Board were duty-bound to provide for the training of teachers in the methodology of bilingual instruction. It was the responsibility of the schools to implement the programme initially:'The whole thing is entirely in the hands of the teachers and managers of the Irish-speaking districts … Heretofore it was the Board that was on trial; now it is the country.'[159] Pearse insisted that the Board should provide travelling instructors to conduct training in bilingual methodology. Programmes operated by the training colleges during the summer holidays might support these 'term-time' courses. It was then up to the Board to ensure a steady supply of Irish-speaking teachers who were trained in bilingual methods. Only a small minority of National and intermediate teachers were fluent speakers and research carried out by the Gaelic League, in the summer of 1904, indicated that teachers felt that the Bilingual Programme would increase their workload. Pearse admitted that it would make greater demands but argued that increased effort would result in greater efficiency.[160] This would happen, he reasoned, because teachers, particularly in *Gaeltacht* areas, would be teaching in a language the children understood, hence both would be engaging in an educative experience quite unlike the 'amazingly absurd system … under which instruction is from the first hour conveyed in a language utterly unknown to the child.'[161]

Pearse offered various guidelines for schools in *Gaeltacht* areas.[162] A school that had decided to adopt the programme should employ it from infant classes upward and all infant teaching should be done through Irish for the first year. Pupils should be taught the alphabet, basic literacy, elementary mathematics and all other exercises proper to infant grade. While this was not strictly bilingual in method, Pearse pointed out that the programme stated that it was not intended that Irish and English should be taught concurrently to infants and that the teachers could decide which language was employed first.[163] He advised that teaching through English should begin only when this first year of instruction through Irish was complete. But, as he was outlining practice for *Gaeltacht* regions, he advised that the teacher should not hesitate to use the vernacular to explain 'a new English word or idea'.[164]

In *Gaeltacht* areas, therefore, all Irish writing, reading, singing and so on should be carried out exclusively through Irish, while the teaching of English would be done mainly through English, the vernacular being employed if necessary to assist comprehension. All other subjects should be taught through Irish first and then through English. Everyday school commands should be given in Irish only. Such a system would, according to Pearse, finally produce 'an educated bilingualist', a child who was primarily an Irish speaker but with a mastery of English.

THE BELGIAN MODEL OF BILINGUAL EDUCATION

Pearse's ideas were based upon bilingual teaching in Wales and Belgium. He visited Wales on a number of occasions and knew many Welsh-language enthusiasts there. In the summer of 1905 he spent five weeks visiting schools in Belgium. A letter of introduction from Dr W.J.M. Starkie, Resident Commissioner of National Education in Ireland, to his counterpart in Belgium, M. van der Dussin de Kastergat, meant that Pearse was generously facilitated during his visit. The Director General in the Ministry of the Interior, M. Charles Remy, was particularly interested in Pearse's work and provided him with information on Belgian educational policy generally.[165] Pearse visited both primary and secondary schools (public and private) and two universities. He was deeply impressed by what he saw in Belgian classrooms. Discovering a bilingual system of education that was enthusiastically embraced, State supported and educationally progressive, he became convinced of the necessity to pursue a similar programme in Ireland. The Belgian model represented an infallible solution to the Irish language problem. Between August 1905 and March 1907 his editorials in *An Claidheamh Soluis* were devoted almost exclusively to a detailed exposition of bilingual education in Belgium. He wrote two series of articles. The first, which ran from August 1905 to March 1906, was mainly concerned with the socio-political history of Belgium and the rise of the language movement there. The second, which appeared between September 1906 and March 1907, was concerned with the schools he visited and presented an explanation and analysis of the bilingual method in practise.

THE DEVELOPMENT OF BILINGUALISM IN BELGIUM

The history of Belgium reflects that of Ireland in that, from the sixteenth century, it was subject to foreign rule. However, while Ireland was subject only to the English Crown, Belgium was, at various times, subject to a succession of European powers. By the end of the eighteenth century, part of northern Belgium, inhabited mainly by Flemish Belgians, fell to Holland, while much of southern, or Walloon Belgium, came under French control. The Flemings were of German extraction and lived mainly in the north-western region while the Walloons, largely of French extraction, inhabited Flanders. The Flemings spoke Flemish while the Walloons spoke French. By 1790 those parts of Belgium which were not under the control of Holland or France were ruled by Austria. The French Revolution brought an end to Austrian control and Belgium came under French rule. The Treaty of Paris united Belgium with Holland to form the Kingdom of the Netherlands. But the Walloons were not prepared to ally themselves with the Dutch, who in turn proscribed their language and set about establishing Dutch culture and language as the template for the new Kingdom. The Walloon territories broke into revolt and, as the tide was turning in their favour, the Flemish regions of the north rose to join them and Holland was forced to withdraw, causing the collapse of the kingdom of the Netherlands. Apart from historic ties and a shared Catholicism, the Flemings too had been victims of discrimination during the short life of the kingdom. There was then common cause between the Flemings and Walloons and this united the two groups.

Pearse was interested in this episode in the history of Belgium because a fundamental cause for the Walloon uprising against the Dutch had been Holland's moves to proscribe their language. The shared Catholicism, common Protestant persecutor and an official policy of language proscription were aspects of Belgian's past, which, he believed, closely paralleled aspects of Ireland's history. However, Belgium was composed of two quite distinct groups and with the fall of the Kingdom of the Netherlands a new language question arose. The French-speaking Walloons had initiated the revolt against the Dutch. Once the Dutch had retreated and a new free Belgium established, the Walloons showed themselves unwilling to recognise the Flemish language, which they considered tainted by its relationship with the Teutonic Dutch. Hence the Flemings, who had risen to assist the Walloons against the Dutch, now found their French-speaking neighbours employ the same strategies against their language that the Dutch had used to suppress the Walloon tongue. Finding their language ignored, the Walloon's rallied to its cause and a campaign was initiated to secure its place in the new state.

Like the language revival in Ireland, a renewed interest in Flemish language and culture resulted in theatres and clubs opening throughout the region, magazines and newspapers appeared in Flemish, and language classes were organised. The movement quickly began securing concessions. By 1905, knowledge of Flemish was compulsory for any candidate seeking work in the civil service and judiciary. While the vernacular was used in local courts in Flemish and Walloon districts, the High Courts of Brussels were conducted in the language of the litigant.

Pearse recognised that the situation in Belgium was similar but not identical to that in Ireland. Flemish was widely spoken and not on the 'very brink of the grave'.[166] Again, Belgium was not a bilingual country, but one in which two languages were spoken, one by each community although, by the late nineteenth century, the creation of a bilingual state was government policy. Pearse was impressed to find that official and public documents were published in both languages. In public museums and galleries inscriptions were bilingual, the language which appeared on top depending upon whether the institution was in a Flemish or French-speaking area: 'It is Flemish and French in Flanders and French and Flemish in the land of the Walloons.'[167] Also, the role of the State in the development of bilingual schooling was very different in Belgium where the acquisition of the second language was government policy. While the second language could be other than French or Flemish, in practise it was usually one of these and the government encouraged schools to begin teaching children through their first language. Parity of treatment for Flemish had not been secured without effort but Pearse could see no reason why a similar victory could not be won in Ireland.

A Belgian government circular of 1899 declared that 'the movement in favour of the teaching of a second language in the various institutions of public instruction is neither so widespread nor so active as the Government would wish.'[168] The circular called the Bilingual Programme a 'patriotic work' through which 'closer bonds' would 'unite one to the other the members of the Belgian family.'[169] Pearse's wry remark: 'Fancy the "National" Board addressing such a Circular to its Inspectors!' is not altogether trite.[170] While bilingual education was officially sanctioned in Ireland in 1904, its introduction was couched in the language of caution, schools could employ it 'subject to (the Commissioners) approval in the case of each school in which it is proposed to introduce such a system …'[171] and again, the Commissioners must be 'satisfied that instruction in the ordinary day school subjects will not be interfered with.'[172]

The fundamental difference between Belgium and Ireland was that the former was an interdependent and sovereign state while the latter was subject to direct rule from Britain. Hence, language policy in Belgium, formulated and implemented by a national parliament, was directed at the social, economic and cultural progress of Belgium. Language policy in Ireland, on the other hand, was dictated by the perceived public desire for the language and the place of vernacular languages in British colonial thinking.

BILINGUAL TEACHING IN BELGIUM

The secondary schools in Belgium were under the direct control of the State, whereas primary schools answered to local authorities. A degree of uniformity throughout both levels was secured by a combination of inspection, publication of guidelines for teachers, consultation documents and so forth. All schools were inspected, including the ecoles privees of the religious orders. There were three types of primary school: kindergarten, ecole primaire and the ecole primaire superieure. The last institution was designed to give a post-primary schooling to able pupils whose circumstances precluded secondary schooling. Primary education was free, but not compulsory. This contributed to the high rate of illiteracy.[173] Pearse was prepared, probably with justification, to explain this by pointing to the long proscription of the Flemish language, which would have meant that Flemish-speaking children would have left school having been instructed in French, but knowing little or nothing of the language. There were two types of secondary school: the ecole moyenne and the Athenee. The former offered a commercial type course, while the programme of the Athenee was based upon the traditions of classical liberal education. Both were fee paying. While primary education was freely available to all, access to secondary schooling was restricted to those who could afford it, although the fee was usually modest.

The different types of schools meant that parents could choose one that offered a predominantly academic or vocational type of education. While second language teaching was optional, Pearse found that it was 'in practice taught almost everywhere'.[174] A school he visited in Brussels devoted just over half as much time to the second language as the mother tongue and a school in Antwerp did likewise. Second language teaching was 'no mere make-believe'; the minimum amount of time spent teaching the second language in Belgian schools (three and a half hours) represented the maximum amount of time devoted to second language teaching in Ireland.[175]

Despite Pearse's claims that bilingual schooling was widespread, the circular of 1899 had admitted that second language teaching was not so 'widespread nor so earnest' as the government desired.'[176] According to the circular, lack of progress in bilingual education was due to teachers giving 'abstract and too exclusively grammatical … lessons and exercises' and called for language teaching to be based upon the 'naturalistic' (Direct) method.[177] Pearse found in the circular an echo of his own thoughts. He had always insisted that the language revival in Ireland was impeded by uninspiring teaching methods. The Direct Method advocated by the Belgian government was based upon the principle that the second language should be taught through conversation as a spoken language with grammar being introduced later. The emphasis upon spoken language is important. While Pearse was a keen advocate of the method, he ignored the fact that Irish pupils, teachers and parents had little or no experience of Irish as a spoken medium. The Direct Method was successful in Belgium, largely because children had neighbours, classmates or parents who spoke the second language hence its acquisition was practical and relevant. And, as previously mentioned, in 1901 only 15.3 per cent of Irish spoke only Irish and less than 1 per cent was bilingual. Unsurprisingly, then, Pearse paid close attention to how bilingual schooling operated in practice in Belgian classrooms.

At the Ecole Communale, a primary school at Etterbeek, a suburb of Brussels, Pearse observed the work of a M. de Cleene, who had developed a method whereby the work in all suitable subjects for any given week shared a common theme. When Pearse visited, the theme for the week was 'the wind'. Manual subjects were concerned with manufacturing, using windmills as a starting point and the class learned

'Song of the Wind' during singing lessons. Pearse observed M. de Cleene conduct a lesson in French using a model windmill as a starting point. After questioning the pupils on the lesson she then gave another lesson in Flemish, carefully avoiding repetition of the first part of the lesson. Again, when this lesson finished the pupils were questioned, this time in Flemish. The windmill was used to extend lessons into the realms of geography, the use of the windmill in the Low Countries, history and industry in Belgium and so on, first through French, then Flemish.[178] Pearse was impressed and observed that in these schools teachers were concerned to have children 'observe and think' before teaching them to read and write.[179] If a child were encouraged to think in a language, he would inevitably start speaking it.

The lessons Pearse had observed in Belgium all displayed the same use of child-centred bilingual methodology and played an important part in forming his own philosophy of how language should be taught. Most of these were observed at Molenbeek St Jean, a school in the Flemish district of Brussels. The simplest Direct Method lesson he observed saw the teacher positioning a boy in front of the class and asking them to name the parts of the body. Again the vocabulary was elementary: nose; ear; chin and so on and he commented that it was likely that the use of one of the pupils, rather than a picture for example, was a good starting point as it appealed to the children's sense of fun.

At the same school Pearse observed the use of cardboard figures and accessories know as L'Image Animee. They were the invention of M.J. Mehauden, the school principal and a colleague, Mr M.G. Wynincx. An ensemble of such items had been produced by which scenes could be created to teach vocabulary and act as a stimulus for conversation and composition. The models were pinned to the board and the teacher began to tell a story. The teacher would then develop the lesson, asking and prompting questions. One teacher pinned a horse to the board and asked the children to count the legs, she then wrote the figures '1, 2, 3, 4' on the blackboard and then rapt on the desk four times and announced, '*Le cheval a quatre jambes.*' She then asked the class how many legs does a boy have, continuing with similar basic questions designed to teach the vocabulary of numeracy. The novelty, common sense and appropriateness of this teaching aide so impressed Pearse, that he provided readers of *An Claidheamh Soluis* with the address where they could purchase a set of the Images.[180]

Before discussing the use of the Direct Method in teaching 'colour' in Belgium, Pearse described common practice in Ireland as follows:

> The teacher holds up a book and says: 'Tá an leabhar glas. Bhfuil an leabhar glas?' 'Tá an leabhar glas!' choruses the class, and the teacher complacently passes on to another word, thinking that he has taught the meaning of 'glas.' The pupils know indeed that the book is 'glas', but as to whether 'glas' has reference to its size, shape, weight, material, price … they have not been afforded an inkling.[181]

Pearse recounted several methods he witnessed in Belgium, including the use of the coloured disks from the science laboratory, coloured ribbons suspended on the blackboard, books showing blocks of colour and the use of coloured chalk. Using one or more of these, children were introduced to the names of colours while teachers utilised practical conversation, such as the colour of one's shoes or shirt, to help the pupils employ new vocabulary.

The same method was employed in teaching 'comparisons.' In a lesson where German was being taught, the teacher introduced the terms for 'long' and 'short' by comparing a long rule with a short pencil, his middle with his little finger and so on. Each time rein-forcing the new words *'lang'* and *'kurs'*. In teaching 'position' the same use was made of everyday stimuli and new vocabulary was gradually introduced. Placing a book on the desk the teacher would state: 'The book is on the desk', then placing it below the desk, would say 'The book is beneath the desk.'[182] Once mastered, the teacher would place the book on the table asking 'where is the book?'[183] In teaching vocabulary relating to 'action' a pupil might be asked to lift a book and then asked to describe what he had just done before the class were asked to describe the child's action.'[184] In this way vocabulary was built up into phrases and sentences.

The Image Animee were also used by a number of teachers when teaching Composition. Pearse observed a lesson at Molenbeek St Jean Girls School given by a Madam Beudin. The pupils were initially given no guidelines; rather, Madam Beudin created a small scene on the blackboard and then instructed the girls to begin their composition. When finished, the pupils read their work and the class was invited to offer corrections. Pearse noted the sound pedagogic principles of observation, imagination and criticism but was most impressed by the freedom to compose original work. The lesson encouraged the children to 'think for themselves'[185] rather than memorising the work of others. Where possible, teachers used the immediate environment as a teaching aide. A teacher at the Ecole Froebel in Antwerp used a projected image of the town port and began the lesson by asking questions. The pupils were asked what they saw: 'Which river?' 'What was on the river?' 'Were they large ships?' 'What did that mean?' The teacher drew the attention of the class to the cathedral in the background, another projected image showed its interior. This was followed by questions on Rubens. The next image was of paintings by Rubens and Van Dyck. In this way the pupils discovered that it was a busy port, with transatlantic links; that it had a manufacturing industry; that it's cathedral housed paintings by a famous painter called Rubens; that it had a wonderful art gallery and that Antwerp was a very old and historically significant city. All this was achieved without the use of a textbook and by images of landmarks with which the children were very familiar.

However, the situation in Belgium was very different from that in Ireland. The Belgian government, unlike the British administration, actively encouraged and supported the spread of bilingualism. Belgian teachers taught spoken languages which the children encountered daily. Pupils and parents in Ireland were faced with the economic necessity of choosing English above Irish, a situation that did not exist in Belgium in relation to French and Flemish. What might be termed a 'colonial mindset' did not exist in independent Belgium. In Ireland the assumption of English mores was common and the Irish language played little part in Ireland's definition of itself.[186] Flemish had not been suppressed with the same vigour, or for the same length of time, as Irish had been. Pearse himself admitted that 'the tally, the ferule and the cane were spared, those "enlightened" methods were reserved for … the Anglo Saxon in Ireland.'[187] Finally, while the Belgian government encouraged bilingual schooling throughout Belgium, in Ireland it was sanctioned only in *Gaeltacht* and bilingual areas.[188]

Nonetheless Pearse worked tirelessly to spread the credo of bilingual teaching and hoped that widespread bilingual education would help reverse the decline of Irish, although he did not recommend that it be the compulsory second language in non-Irish-speaking areas, nor should English be forced as a second language upon schools in Irish-speaking areas.[189] In March 1906 he summarised the League's position as follows: 'A. Districts in which Irish is the Home Language: First Language, Irish; Second Language, English (with the option of French, German, etc., instead); B. Districts in which English is the Home Language: First Language, English; Second Language, Irish (with the option of French ...).'[190] He was always anxious to stress that bilingual schooling was not education in, but through, a language. This was the position he adopted at St Enda's where, while Irish was the first language, English was commonly spoken among the pupils.

But the schools were disinclined to adopt bilingualism. According to the League's own figures, only 110 had adopted the programme by 1908. Although Pearse spoke of bilingual education being 'common-place in Ireland',[191] it was, in reality, adopted only in schools where staff or management were sympathetic to the language revival movement. While becoming popular with schools in Connaught, the *Gaeltacht* region of Connemara seemed reluctant to embrace it. Historically, Irish was associated with poverty while English had become the language of the economic emigrant. Indeed, many teachers in Connemara did not speak Irish.[192] In 1907 there was, for example, only one bilingual school in Co. Clare, few in Co. Kerry and none in Co. Waterford.[193] After the League's Ard Fheis in 1908, Pearse wrote in *An Claidheamh Soluis* that 'the alternative for the moment is not one between an Irish-speaking and an English-speaking Ireland. It is between Bilingualism and Englishism [*sic*].'[194] He saw no hope of Irish becoming a living language so long as it was taught as a school subject. Its revival lay in its becoming the medium of instruction and conversation. He insisted that the next generation would either be bilingualists or 'a generation of English speakers with (or without) a smattering of Irish'.[195] In particular, Pearse encouraged those in *Gaeltacht* areas to adopt the Bilingual Programme and called on the League to embark on a campaign to persuade all concerned parties of its value.[196] But these areas displayed little enthusiasm and, generally, it remained the experiment of the minority. The percentage of National Schools employing the Bilingual Programme rose from 0.004 in 1906–7 to 0.03 in 1921–2.[197] The success, which Pearse often claimed for the League's campaign, had no basis in reality.

Bilingual education never became a significant feature of Irish schooling in Pearse's lifetime. The history of the Irish language since independence demonstrates that popular consensus about the desirability of Irish has not been matched by willingness to become conversant in the language. The post-independence policy of instruction through the medium was questioned by the Irish National Teachers' Organisation (INTO) in the 1930s, and even though successive governments encouraged secondary schools to promote the language, few became truly bilingual.[198]

Father John Macnamara's important 1966 study of the Irish experience of bilingualism demonstrated that attempts to create bilingual schooling had failed. Irish children grew up in an English-speaking society and consequently there were no incentives to adopt Irish. Bilingual schooling worked best, he suggested, in countries such as America, where immigrants wished to learn the first language of their adopted home.[199] However, Macnamara also found that a 'balance-effect' existed whereby children who developed skills in one language tended to have a weaker grasp of the other. He also found that, overall, the remaining subjects tended to suffer when taught through the medium of Irish and argued that 'where Irish has been for the most part well taught by the "Direct Method" over a period of forty years, results are not very encouraging.'[200] He also found that children in the *Gaeltacht* regions had suffered 'most seriously of all', performing poorly in English, Arithmetic and Irish.[201] While generally he found that children in secondary schools had a reasonably good knowledge of Irish, he concluded that the aim of restoring Irish was no nearer 'than at the turn of the century when Douglas Hyde founded the Irish League.'[202] A half a century after Pearse's death then, not only had bilingualism failed to be adopted as national educational policy but where it was employed as a method of instruction it actually damaged pupil's progress in other school subjects; a more damning refutation of Pearse's ideas is hard to imagine.

PEARSE'S LEGACY: IRISH IN SCHOOLS

The Irish language was largely unspoken in mid-nineteenth century Ireland. It was not the language of the 1798 rebellion, the campaign for

Catholic emancipation or the repeal of the Act of Union. O'Connell had addressed his great rallies in English.[203] But Pearse had worked for a bilingual, not Irish-speaking, nation. Frustrated with conventional politics in post-Parnell Ireland, many idealistic young men and women gave their energies to the League and achieved impressive results. Language enthusiasts secured the teaching of Irish at National School level as an extra and an ordinary subject, it had been included as an extra subject in intermediate education since its inception in 1878 and the Gaelic League had secured Irish as compulsory for matriculation to the National University of Ireland. The League had overseen the development of a network of evening classes throughout the country in the late nineteenth and early twentieth centuries.[204] It had established training colleges for those wishing to teach through Irish, although by 1910 only seven of these had been granted recognition by the National Board,[205] by 1915 this figure had risen to seventeen and by 1919 there were twenty-three such colleges.[206] A Bilingual Programme had been sanctioned in *Gaeltacht* and bilingual regions and a vigorous interest in both Irish language and history had been generated. Finally, by 1926, when the first census under an independent government took place, it was found that the percentage of Irish speakers had risen from 17.6 per cent in 1911 to 18.3 per cent. The rise was small but significant because it represented the first increase since 1881.[207]

In 1922 INTO recommended that all children should be taught Irish and that a number of other subjects be taught through Irish, although only one third of lay teachers in National Schools held the Bilingual or Ordinary Certificate.[208] In the same year, the Association of Secondary Teachers in Ireland (ASTI) reported that one third of its members 'had no knowledge of Irish'.[209] The rehabilitation of Irish was a keystone of the new State and a number of schemes were implemented during the 1920s to promote the language, including its introduction as an essential subject for student teachers. The 1926 census revealed that the number of Irish speakers of school age, that is up to fourteen years, had almost doubled since 1911.[210]

In the same year more than half of the teaching profession had an official qualification to teach Irish. However, the use of Irish at primary level was hindered by the teachers' lack of fluency and in 1922 the school programme was refined so that Irish was employed only where the children were able to follow the lessons 'profitably and easily'.[211]

From 1932 candidates for the Leaving Certificate Examination had to present Irish as a subject. To encourage schools to employ Irish, a system of grant-linked grading was introduced. Grade 'A' schools used Irish as the medium of instruction in all subjects apart from modern languages, Grade 'B' employed Irish for some subjects and Grade 'C' taught Irish as an ordinary subject. By 1930 only twenty-one of the 300 schools (0.7 per cent) had achieved Grade 'A' status, although by the middle of the decade Irish was taught as an obligatory subject in national, vocational and secondary schools.[212]

However, the 1940s witnessed growing criticism of mandatory Irish. Primary teachers questioned its value to pupils for whom there was no obvious educational benefit. *A Plan For Education* published by the INTO in 1947 called for oral, rather than written, competence to be prioritised, and a proposal in the early 1950s recommended the abolition of written examinations as a way of encouraging pupils to learn to speak Irish. It was suggested that 'a minimum standard for oral Irish be tested by the inspector' after which 'every method and aid' be employed 'to make the Irish hour the one bright spot in the day'.[213] The emphasis upon learning to speak the language as a living idiom had, of course, been central to Pearse's thinking.

The 1926 census revealed that the total number of Irish-only speakers had dropped by 120,000 (18 per cent) since 1891. However, while the provinces of Connaught and Munster lost approximately 100,000 native speakers, the number of monoglot speakers in Leinster rose dramatically in the same period. This represented a reversal of the traditional diminishing influence of Irish from the western to eastern seaboard and reflected the strength of the Gaelic League in Leinster, the most populated of the four provinces.[214] While there is no way of knowing what percentage of this number spoke Irish fluently, it was probably between 5 and 10 per cent.[215] By 1966 the number of native speakers had dropped to less than 70,000, representing less than 20 per cent of what it had been before 1922. This represented a 'disastrous decline', which, according to one commentator, 'could scarcely be described as evidence of a successful social revolution.'[216] The comment illustrates the contested nature of the outcome of the language revival. Commentators agree only that the position of the Irish language remains uncertain.[217] Perhaps, in retrospect, it was naïve of the Gaelic League to allow the new government to shoulder responsibility for the language after 1922. The mistake is nowhere more evident than in the almost immediate decline in the number of League branches from 819 in 1922 to 139 in 1924.[218]

The number of National Schools teaching through Irish rose from 228 in 1931 to 704 in 1939, representing almost 14 per cent of all primary schools, while another 26 per cent were teaching partly through Irish.[219] However, the necessity of compulsory Irish at school level became a contentious issue again in the 1970s. In 1974 the requirement to pass Irish to secure the Intermediate and Leaving Certificates was abolished. But State-funded schools were obliged to continue teaching Irish while the requirement to secure a pass in Irish for matriculation to NUI colleges meant that secondary schools continued to offer the language to Leaving Certificate level. While the 1970s seemingly witnessed increasing public ambiguity, a survey carried out in 1975 found that the majority of the population still perceived the language as closely linked to cultural identity and supported its maintenance and transmission.[220] However, 25 per cent of primary teachers felt that too much time was given to the language and one year later 50 per cent felt that there had been a decline in the standard of Irish since 1966.[221] In 1979 there were only 160 Irish-medium schools, a fall of 420 since 1960. In the same year only twenty-two secondary schools were using Irish as the medium of instruction, a drop of 110 since 1969.[222]

Yet recent years have witnessed a growth in gaelscoileanna (schools which teach through the medium of Irish). In 1993–94 there were twenty-four such schools, excluding Irish-medium schools in *Gaeltacht* areas. Between 1993 and 2000 another fourteen were established and they continue to expand. The debate as to whether Irish should remain compulsory at school level continues, usually centring upon its relevance.

A very significant factor in the decline of Irish was, and remains, the global popularity of English. When, in the early 1920s, British educationalists began to support the vernacular, rather than English, as a means of instruction in the colonial territories, Crown representatives pointed out that the people wanted to learn English and that any change would be regarded as an attempt to deny them the opportunity to improve their standard of living.[223] English was perceived as the language of progress and the imposition of the vernacular would be resented as an attempt to deny access to the means of self-betterment.[224] The English language was viewed as culturally, socially and economically essential – just as Patrick Keenan had observed in his visits to the islands in 1855. This was a phenomenon beyond the abilities of the Gaelic League to rectify.

It is not possible to point to one cause for the demise of the language after the 1960s. Public ambivalence, the absence of a coherent language policy at government level, adolescent perceptions of Irish as unfashionable and irrelevant, the growing popularity of European languages encouraged by travel, the development of the European Union and the limited scope for Irish usage in professional or personal life in Ireland meant that, while more people at the beginning of the twenty-first century may speak and understand more Irish than in the early 1900s, the status of the language is possibly no greater. The geographical location of the *Gaeltacht* regions as natural homes of the language is no longer certain. They represent less than 2 per cent of the national population, are scattered and are not necessarily populated by Irish-only speaking inhabitants.[225] While they represent the historic home of the language, it is possible that in the future the *Gaeltacht* will not be synonymous with a given geographical region but may be preserved and developed among disparate groups of language enthusiasts.[226] In this, the position of the language is little changed. Writing in 1997, Pádraig Ó'Riagáin remarked that 'a member of the Gaelic League in the 1890s, returning to the Ireland of the 1990s, would surely have wondered what, if anything, had changed in the intervening years.'[227]

The place of the language in Irish society has, however, changed considerably since Dr Salmon of Trinity College Dublin suggested that 'no one with any sense of humour' could refrain from 'laughing at such a show, as the affectation of speaking Irish has become.'

Irish is taught nationally in primary and secondary schools and is a compulsory requirement at Leaving Certificate for admission to the National University of Ireland.[228] Its compulsory introduction throughout the school community in the 1920s meant that it became incumbent upon the training colleges to introduce Irish to their curricula, just as Pearse had foretold. Until recently the requirement upon candidates wishing to teach in the national, secondary or vocational sectors to obtain a certificate of competency in Irish continued to lend official recognition to the language in public service appointments.

In contemporary Ireland each Catholic parish typically celebrates one Mass each Sunday in Irish. No such arrangement existed in the first decade of the twentieth century. The choice of Irish language media, such as TG4 and Radio na *Gaeltacht*a, the daily broadcasting of national news in Irish coupled with the many State uses of the language are testament to the principle of choice which was at the heart of Pearse's belief regarding the language. For Pearse, freedom to choose to speak Irish was as important as its actual acquisition, a characteristic of his essentially democratic instinct.

Notes

[1] See 'The Primary Schools', *An Claidheamh Soluis*, 26 December 1904, p. 4.

[2] *The Census of Ireland for the Year 1861*, [3026] (H.C., 1862), p. 49, Table XXIX.

[3] The population in Ireland fell by 1,947,635. See Seán O'Lúing, *Celtic Studies in Europe and Other Essays*, pp. 190–1. See also, Janet Leyland, 'Outposts of the Gael: The Decline of Gaelic in the Great Blasket and St Kilda', in Ullrich Kockel (ed.), *Landscape Heritage and Identity, Case Studies in Irish Ethnography*.

[4] See Martin Ball and James Fife (eds), *The Celtic Languages*, p. 437. A 'tally stick' was a small stick attached to a piece of stick and hung around a child's neck. Those who broke the prohibition against speaking Irish had the instances notched upon the stick and the tallied number of notches represented the number of slaps they would receive. Similar devices were common in Wales, Scotland, Kenya and provincial France. See Gwyneth Tyson Roberts, *The Language of the Blue Books, the Perfect Instrument of Empire*, p. 33. For an outline of the decline of the Irish language in the late eighteenth century see 'The Strange Death of the Irish Language, 1870–1800', in Gerard O'Brien (ed.), *Parliament, Politics and People, Essays in Eighteenth-Century Irish History*.

[5] See 'The Strange Death of the Irish Language, 1870–1800', in Gerard O'Brien (ed.), *Parliament, Politics and People, Essays in Eighteenth-Century Irish History*. By 1841 the figure had fallen to 11 per cent.

[6] Martin Ball and James Fife (eds), *The Celtic Languages*, p. 437. On Irish in Kilkenny see also p. Birch, *St Kieran's College, Kilkenny*, pp. 43–5.

[7] See Reports of the Commissioners of National Education 1836–1856. See also, D. Akenson, *The Irish Education Experiment*, p. 51 and J. Coolahan, *Irish Education: History and Structure*, p. 7.

[8] L. Rt Hon. Henry Grattan, to the Secretary of the Board of Education, 1812, cited in T. Crowley, *The Politics of Language in Ireland 1366–1922*, p. 134.

[9] *Ibid.*

[10] See D. Akenson, *The Irish Education Experiment*, p. 381.

[11] In 1855 Keenan visited Tory, Innisboffin, Gola, Owey, Arranmore, Rutland and Innisfree. This was also the experience of English visitors to the Scottish isle of St Kilda in the late nineteenth century. See Janet Leyland 'Outposts of the Gael: The Decline of Gaelic in the Great Blasket and St Kilda', in *Landscape, Heritage and Identity, Case Studies in Irish Ethnography*, p. 70.

[12] *The Twenty-Third Report of the Commissioners of National Education, 1856*, [2304] (H.C., 1857–8), IV. Appendix B, General Reports, No. 1. General Report by Patrick Joseph Keenan, Head Inspector, p. 143, Table 56. On the relationship between the English language and social mobility see also T. Crowley, *The Politics of Language in Ireland 1366-1922*, p. 134.

[13] More than fifty years later the Irish playwright J.M. Synge noted in *The Aran Islands* that 'in the older generation … I do not see any particular affection for Gaelic. Whenever they are able they speak English to their children, to render them more capable of making their way in life.' See J.M. Synge, *The Aran Islands*, p. 68. Regarding Synge and Irish see Declan Kiberd, *Synge and the Irish Language*.

[14] *The Twenty-Third Report of the Commissioners of National Education, 1856*, [2304] (H.C., 1857–8). IV. Appendix B, General Reports: Report by Patrick Keenan, Head Inspector, p. 144.

[15] *The Twenty-Third Report of Commissioners of National Education, 1856*, [2304] (H.C., 1857–8). Appendix G. Head Inspectors' Reports: Report by P.J. Keenan, p. 75.

[16] See *Twenty-Fourth Report of the Commissioners of National Education, 1857*, [2456–1] (H.C., 1859) and *Twenty Fifth-Report of the Commissioners of National Education, 1858*, [2593] (H.C., 1860), Reports of, P.J. Keenan, head inspector.

[17] The designation 'extra subject' indicates that the subject could be taught but outside normal school hours, that is not as part of the 'ordinary' school course.

[18] D. Akenson, *The Irish Education Experiment*, p. 382.

[19] Fees could not be earned when Irish was taught as an 'ordinary' school subject during regular school hours.

[20] See *Seventy-First Report of the Commissioners of National Education, 1904*, [2567] (H.C., 1905), p. 90, Table 58. In 1899 only 105 schools were teaching Irish, see Table 54.

[21] *The Seventy-Second Report of the Commissioners of National Education, 1905-6*, [3154] (H.C., 1906), p. 21, Irish.

[22] See *Seventy-First Report of the Commissioners of National Education, 1904*, [2567] (H.C. 1905), Table 56.

[23] *Ibid.* The five 'extra' subjects were: Irish, French, Latin, mathematics and instrumental music. The total expense to the Treasury of the extra subjects was £14,366.

[24] See *The Seventy-Second Report of the Commissioners of National Education, 1905-6*, [3154] (H.C., 1906). This calculation is based upon the 'Statement of Account', p. 105.

[25] *Ibid.*

[26] *Ibid.* On the relationship between Commissioners and government policy see Gwyneth Tyson Roberts, *the Language of the Blue Books, the Perfect Instrument of Empire*, Chapter Four.

[27] 'A National Board Minute', *An Claidheamh Soluis*, 26 August 1905, pp. 6–7.

[28] *Ibid.*

[29] See 'The Irish Fees', *An Claidheamh Soluis*, 23 March 1907, p. 7. Pearse is reflecting the position of the Education Committee of the Gaelic League. In May 1906 it had noted that were Irish an 'ordinary' subject, schools would have great difficulties 'making room for it within ordinary hours'. Minutes of the Education Committee of the Gaelic League, 25 May 1906, MS 9797, NLI.

[30] *Ibid.* Augustine Birrell, president of the Board of Education, 1906; Chief Secretary for Ireland, 1907; established the National University of Ireland and Queen's University, Belfast, 1908; resigned, 1916.

[31] *The Seventy-Third Report of the Commissioners of National Education, 1906-7,* [3699] (H.C., 1907), p. 11, Irish Language.

[32] See *The Seventy-Eight Report of the Commissioners of National Education, 1911-12,* [6986] H.C. 1912, pp. 86–87.

[33] 'Irish in the Schools', *An Claidheamh Soluis,* 12 October 1907, p. 7.

[34] See *The Seventy-Fourth Report of the Commissioners of National Education, 1907-8,* [4291] (H.C., 1908), p. 12, Irish and *The Seventy-Eight Report of the Commissioners of National Education, 1911-12,* p. 46, Table 54.

[35] *Appendix to the Seventy-Eight Report of the Commissioners of National Education, 1911-12,* [7061] (H.C., 1912), Section I, p. 149.

[36] *Appendix to the Seventy-Eight Report of the Commissioners of National Education, 1911-12,* [7061] (H.C., 1912), p. 150 and *The Seventy-Eight Report of the Commissioners of National Education, 1911-1912,* [6986] (H.C., 1912), p. 44, Table 52. There were eleven such institutions run by the Gaelic League at this time. Since their inception 945 students had qualified to teach Irish.

[37] See *Appendix to the Seventy-Eight Report of the Commissioners of National Education, 1911-12,* [6986] (H.C., 1912), Section I, p. 150.

[38] 'The British Liberals and the Irish Language', *An Claidheamh Soluis,* 16 December 1905, pp. 6–7. The following year Pearse wrote that the English Government was unable to meet the League's educational demands because it was 'unable to understand either us (the League) or them'. *Ibid.* 24 November 1906, p. 4.

[39] See T. Garvan, 'The Politics of Language and Literature in Pre-Independence Ireland', p. 59, in *Irish Political Studies,* Vol. 2 (1987). For a cogent defence of government policy and the Commissioners subsequent implementation see W.J.M. Starkie, *The History of Irish Primary and Secondary Education during the Last Decade* (1911).

[40] See *Vice-Regal Committee of Enquiry Into Primary Education* (Ireland) 1918, Reservation by Mr Headlam, p. 32.

[41] See *The Eighty-Sixth Report of the Commissioners of National Education 1919-20,* [Cmd. 1476] (H.C., 1920), Irish Language (1) − (6), pp. 8–10.

[42] See *The Eighty-Sixth Report of the Commissioners of National Education 1919-20,* [Cmd. 1476] (H.C., 1920), p. 9. (2).

[43] *Ibid.,* pp. 29–30.

[44] John Coolahan, *Irish Education: Its History and Structure,* p. 41.

[45] The Gaelic Union, formed in 1880, was an offshoot of the Society for the Preservation of the Irish Language.

[46] *Report of the Intermediate Education Board 1902,* [Cd. 1670] (H.C., 1903), xxiv. Kuno Meyer, scholar and founder of the School of Irish Learning, now the School of Celtic Studies in the Dublin Institute for Advanced Studies. Appointed to the Chair of Celtic at Berlin in 1911.

[47] Spanish, which only had ten candidates, three of whom failed, is excluded.

[48] Again, due to the small number of candidates, Spanish is excluded.

[49] See *Report of the Intermediate Education Board 1905,* [Cd. 2944] (H.C., 1906), Table IV.

[50] *The Report of the Intermediate Education Board 1906,* [Cd. 3544] (H.C., 1907), Table IV.

[51] See 'The Function of Nationalism in Education', *An Claidheamh Soluis,* 5 December 1903, p. 4. For a discussion on the implications of the position of subjects on the curriculum see Barry M. Coldrey, *Faith and Fatherland,* pp. 106–7.

[52] *The Report of the Intermediate Education Board 1909,* [Cd. 5173] (H.C., 1910), Table IV. The number of boys in Senior Grade who passed Intermediate Irish with Honours fell from 23.2 per cent in 1908 to 12.2 per cent in 1909. The corresponding figure for girls was 23.2 per cent to 12.8 per cent.

[53] See *The Report of the Intermediate Education Board 1912,* [Cd. 6893] (H.C., 1913), Table IV and *The Report of the Intermediate Education Board 1913,* [Cd. 7555] H.C. 1914, Table IV.

[54] *The Report of the Intermediate Education Board 1915,* [Cd. 8369] (H.C., 1916), Table I.

[55] 'Should We Demand Fees for Irish as an Ordinary', *An Claidheamh Soluis*, 23 March 1908, p. 9.

[56] 'The Irish Fees', *An Claidheamh Soluis*, 23 March 1907, p.7 and 'The Bilingual Programme: A Need', *An Claidheamh Soluis*, 2 November 1907, p. 7.

[57] 'An Educational Policy', *An Claidheamh Soluis*, 12 December 1903, p. 4.

[58] 'The Secondary School', *An Claidheamh Soluis*, 25 November 1905, pp. 6–7.

[59] *Ibid*. On the role of nationalism in St Enda's see Chapter Four.

[60] 'The Teachers', *An Claidheamh Soluis*, 13 April 1907, p. 7.

[61] 'The Work of the Schools', *An Claidheamh Soluis*, 20 April 1907, p. 7.

[62] See 'Live Teaching in the Secondary School', *An Claidheamh Soluis*, pp. 6–7.

[63] 'The Secondary School', *An Claidheamh Soluis*, 13 January 1906, pp.6–7.

[64] *Ibid*.

[65] 'In the Secondary Schools', *An Claidheamh Soluis*, 23 November 1907, pp. 6–7.

[66] The continued reluctance of the Intermediate Board to allow oral Irish examinations was considered by Pearse to be another means of shackling the progress of spoken Irish. However, the Board did not have sufficient numbers of inspectors who were fluent in the language. In 1953 Micheál O'Guiheen, recorded, that in his youth, an inspector who visited to the Great Blasket island, off the west coast of Ireland, 'hadn't a word of Irish … but to our misfortune he had plenty of English …' Micheál O'Guiheen, *A Pity Youth Does Not Last*, p. 12. Giving evidence before the Royal Commission on University Education, 1902, Douglas Hyde remarked that Lady Augusta Gregory had visited the islands and 'found on one…that the only person on the whole island who did not know Irish was the schoolmaster.' See Gaelic League Pamphlets, No. 29. *Irish in University Education, Evidence Given Before the Royal Commission on University Education, 1902*, p. 20, Dr Douglas Hyde Examined.

[67] See 'Irish in the Schools', *An Claidheamh Soluis*, 12 October 1907.

[68] Central Training Establishment, Marlborough Street, Dublin; St Patrick's College, Drumcondra, Dublin, Our Lady of Mercy College, Carysfort, Dublin, De La Salle College, Waterford, Church of

Ireland College, Dublin, St Mary's College, Belfast, Mary Immaculate
College, Limerick.

[69] In 1900, eighty-eight schools taught Irish and by 1903 this figure had
risen to 2,018. See *The Seventy-First Report of the Commissioners of National
Education, 1904*, [Cd. 2567] (H.C., 1905), p. 53, Revised Programme, Table 54.

[70] See *Report of Mr F.H. Dale, His Majesty's Inspector of Schools, Board of
Education on primary education in Ireland, 1904*, [Cd. 1981] xx, 947.

[71] However, Eoin MacNeill had taught Irish at St Patrick's Training
College, Drumcondra, Co. Dublin in 1898.

[72] 'The Training Colleges', *An Claidheamh Soluis*, 18 June 1904, pp. 6–7.

[73] *The Seventy-Second Report of the Commissioners of National Education
1905-6*, [Cd. 3154] (H.C., 1906), p. 22.

[74] *The Seventy-First Report of the Commissioners of National Education 1904*,
[Cd. 2567] (H.C., 1905), p. 53. Revised Programme, Tables 54–56.

[75] 'The Training Colleges', *An Claidheamh Soluis*, 8 April 1905, pp. 6–7.

[76] *Ibid.*

[77] *The Seventy-First Report of the Commissioners of National Education 1904*,
[Cd. 2567] (H.C., 1905), Table 58, p. 90.

[78] *Appendix to the Seventy-Fifth Report of the Commissioners of National
Education, 1908-9*, [Cd. 5062] (H.C., 1910). Section I, p. 8.

[79] *Appendix to the Seventy-Seventh Report of the Commissioners of National
Education 1910-11*, [Cd. 7061] (H.C., 1911), Section I, p. 11.

[80] *Ibid.* Section I, p. 5.

[81] *Ibid.*, p. 14.

[82] See 'The Training Colleges', *An Claidheamh Soluis,* 8 April 1905, pp. 6–7.

[83] *Ibid.*

[84] For example see *Seventy First-Report of the Commissioners of National
Education, 1904*, [Cd. [2567] (H.C., 1905), Table 58 and *Report of the Intermediate Education Board 1904*, [Cd. 2580] (H.C., 1905), Table V, lxiv.

[85] 'The Training Colleges and Irish', *An Claidheamh Soluis,* 22 April

1905, p. 6–7. See *The Seventy-First Report of the Commissioners of National Education 1904*, [Cd. 2580] (H.C., 1905). Table 54. During the period 1899–1904 more schools began teaching Irish than any other subject, the number rose from 105 to 1,983.

[86] Yet he did not accept *per se* the argument against compulsion. When the League were accused of coercion in wanting to make Irish part of the core curriculum he remarked that Irish would be compulsory in the same way as say catechism or arithmetic, yet the Board is not accused of coercion in insisting they be taught. In 1911, however, the League did call for Irish to be made compulsory in training colleges. See Pádraig O'Fearaíl, *The Story of Conradh Na Gaeilge*, p. 33 & 39.

[87] In 1906–7 a scheme had come into effect whereby King's Scholars could win prizes of £5–10 'who at the close of training pass the general examination and obtain certificates of competency to teach Irish.' See *The Seventy-Third Report of the Commissioners of National Education, 1906-7*, [Cd. 3699] (H.C., 1907), p. 10. See also Pádraig O'Fearaíl, *The Story of Conradh Na Gaeilge*, p. 33.

[88] See *Appendix to the Seventy-Fifth Report of the Commissioners of National Education, 1908-9*, [Cd. 5062] (H.C., 1908), p. 7 & *Appendix to the Seventy-Seventh Report of the Commissioners of National Education 1910-11*, [Cd. 7061] (H.C., 1911), Section I, p. 8.

[89] 'Irish in the Training Colleges', *An Claidheamh Soluis*, 28 March 1908 (emphasis in original).

[90] See *Appendix to the Seventy-Fifth Report of the Commissioners of National Education, 1908-9*, [Cd. 5062] (H.C., 1910), p. 4, 'The Training Colleges', Table A.

[91] See Padraig O'Fearaíl, *The Story of Conradh Na Gaeilge*, p. 39.

[92] *Ibid.*, p. 42. By 1913 the number had fallen to 1,600 (20 per cent).

[93] *Appendix to the Seventy-Seventh Report of the Commissioners of National Education, 1910-11*, [Cd. 6042] (H.C., 1911), Section I, p. 8.

[94] *Royal Commission on Trinity College Dublin and the University of Dublin.* 3382.

[95] 'Trinity and the Gael', *An Claidheamh Soluis*, 9 February 1907, p. 7.

[96] 'Irish Ireland and the University Question', *An Claidheamh Soluis*, 8 February 1909, p. 9.

[97] 'The New University: Irish Essential for Matriculation', *An Claidheamh Soluis*, 22 August 1908, p. 9.

[98] *Irish People*, 2 December 1908.

[99] 'After the Universities Bill', *The Leader*, 1 August 1908.

[100] *Ibid.*

[101] See Eoin MacNeill, *Irish in the National University of Ireland*. MacNeill was invited to sit on the Senate of the NUI in May 1908. See MS 10886 Irish Office in London to Eoin MacNeill, 5 May 1908, Eoin MacNeill Papers, NLI.

[102] *Freeman's Journal*, 2 January 1909.

[103] 'The Plague of B.A.s', *The Leader*, 18 December 1909.

[104] 'The University Commission Report', *An Claidheamh Soluis*, 28 March 1903.

[105] 'The University Question', *An Claidheamh Soluis*, 30 January 1904, p. 4. (emphasis in original).

[106] Cited in 'The University Question', *An Claidheamh Soluis*, 30 January 1904, p. 4.

[107] *Ibid.*

[108] 'The University Bill', *An Claidheamh Soluis*, 11 April 1908, p. 9. The reference is to Birrell.

[109] *Ibid.*

[110] These included Douglas Hyde and Mary Hayden – later an extern lecturer at St Enda's. See *The National University of Ireland. Act of Parliament Charter and Statutes*, X. The Senate (2), pp. 29–30 (HMSO, Dublin 1908). See also *The Leader*, 2 May 1908.

[111] 'Gaels and the University Bill', *An Claidheamh Soluis*, 25 April 1908, p. 9. Pearse's feminist sympathies remain unexamined. Certainly he was close to women such as Eveleen Nicolls and Mary Hayden, who held strong feminist views and on at least one occasion spoke at a meeting of the Irish Women's Franchise League, sharing the platform with Mr A.J. Nicolls, who spoke on 'Women and Social Reform.' See MS 21053, Hon. Secretary of Irish Women's Franchise League to Patrick Pearse, 28 July 1910 Pearse Papers, NLI.

[112] 'The New Dublin University: What We Want', *An Claidheamh Soluis*, 16 May 1908, p. 9.

[113] The accusation is uncited by Pearse. See 'The New University: Irish Essential For Matriculation', *An Claidheamh Soluis*, 22 August 1908, p. 9. Skeffington regarded the campaign for compulsion as 'an admission that the Gaelic League (had) failed to arouse the enthusiasm of the country … and that it must resort to the weapon of despair – coercion.' See in *The Irish People*, 26 December 1908.

[114] 'Irish as an Essential: The Why and the Wherefore', *An Claidheamh Soluis*, 19 December 1908, p. 9.

[115] 'The New University: Irish Essential For Matriculation', *An Claidheamh Soluis*, 22 August 1908, p. 9.

[116] 'The University and the Schools', *An Claidheamh Soluis*, 23 January 1909, p. 9.

[117] 'The New University: Irish Essential for Matriculation', *An Claidheamh Soluis*, 22 August 1908, p. 9.

[118] See 'Irish in the New University', *An Claidheamh Soluis*, 5 September 1908, *Ibid.*, pp. 205–7.

[119] 'The Issue Unchanged', *An Claidheamh Soluis*, 5 June 1909, *Ibid.*, p 232.

[120] William Delany SJ (1835–1924), prominent League member and President of University College, St Stephen's Green, Dublin had attended the Inaugural Meeting of the Irish Society at the Catholic College at St Stephen's Green on 29 November 1908. A paper by T.P. Nowlan entitled 'The Relation of Irish to the New University' was read in the absence of the author and concluded that Irish should be an 'integral part of any National University curriculum.' This claim was supported by a number of speakers. When Eoin MacNeill, who was presiding at the meeting, asked Father Delany if he wished to speak, he did so only in order that his silence might not be construed as supporting Nowlan's claim. See *A Page of Irish History: The Story of University College, Dublin 1883-1909*.

[121] See Thomas J. Morrissey SJ, *Towards a National University, William Delaney SJ*, p 329. Delany's view caused considerable controversy. *The Gaelic American* referred to him and 'other forces of Anglicisation' as representing those hostile to the language, who 'under the guise of religion and spurious utilitarianism' sought to 'hoodwink and rob the

Irish people of the blessings and benefits which would accrue from a truly Irish and National University'. Cited in *An Claidheamh Soluis*, 16 January 1909, p. 7, 'Press Opinions.'

[122] Thomas J. Morrisey SJ, *Towards a National University, William Delaney SJ*, p 330.

[123] Cited in Pádraig O'Fearaíl, *The Story of Conradh Na Gaeilge*, p. 35.

[124] *Ibid.*, p. 38.

[125] *Ibid.*, p 39.

[126] See Pádraig O'Fearaíl, *the Story of Conradh Na Gaeilge*, p 39.

[127] Pearse did, however, allow for the explanation, in English, of difficult points of grammar. See 'The Secondary School: Thoughts and Suggestions', *An Claidheamh Soluis*, 13 January 1906, p. 6. Presently the time allocated to Irish at senior cycle in Irish schools is approximately three hours and twenty minutes per week representing one forty-minute lesson each day for five days.

[128] 'The Secondary School: Thoughts and Suggestions', *An Claidheamh Soluis*, 13 January 1906, p. 6.

[129] *Ibid.*

[130] *Ibid.*

[131] *Ibid.* (emphasis in original).

[132] *Ibid.* In this Pearse reflected the position of Comenius who held that schooling should result in critical thinking and be 'conducted without blows'. Cited in Daniel Murphy, *Comenius, a Reassessment of his Work*, p. 93.

[133] Writing in *An Claidheamh Soluis* in January 1907 Pearse lamented 'A certain thoughtlessness in their (Irish children) treatment of weaker or more sensitive companions, as well as dumb animals, often amounting to positive cruelty.' He encouraged teachers to foster an 'all-embracing and consuming spirit of human kindnesses.' See 'The Formation of Character', *An Claidheamh Soluis*, 26 January 1907, p. 7. See also *An Macaomh*, Vol. I, No. 2, Christmas 1909, p. 56, 'Our Nature Study Log Book records that Milo MacGarry found a fine specimen of the Red Admiral Butterfly in the School Garden to-day. It was dead already (we are under a *geasa* not to kill wild

things), so Arthur Cole undertook to mount it for the Museum …' *Geasa* is
an Irish word implying prohibition but also a curse or spell. See also Margaret
Pearse 'Patrick and William Pearse', *Capuchin Annual*, May 1943 where
Margaret recorded that one boy was expelled from St Enda's for cruelty
to a cat. Ella Young recalled walking with Pearse in the grounds of The
Hermitage; 'Padraig Pearse took care not to trample on a wild flower. He has
tenderness for all living things' See Ella, Young, *Flowering Dusk*, p. 113.

[134] The timetable was 'not ideal' Pearse added, rather, 'conditioned by the
Programme of the Commissioners'. 'The Secondary School: Thoughts
and Suggestions, *An Claidheamh Soluis*, 13 June 1906.

[135] See Desmond Ryan, 'The Man Called Pearse,' *The Collected Works of
P.H. Pearse, St Enda's and its Founder*, p. 213.

[136] 'The Secondary School: Some Thoughts and Suggestions', *An Claidheamh Soluis*, 20 January 1906, p. 6.

[137] *Ibid.*

[138] 'The Secondary School: Some Thoughts and Suggestions', *An Claidheamh Soluis*, 20 January 1906, p. 6.

[139] *Ibid.*

[140] 'The Secondary School: Conversation Teaching', *An Claidheamh Soluis*,
3 February 1906, p. 6.

[141] *Ibid.* For examples of how schools advertised for new enlistments
see for example: *The Leader* 18 July 1908, 30 July 1910 & 17 September
1910. The last edition carries two advertisements that list the names of
pupils and the grades they achieved together with the relevant subjects.
St Flannan's College, Ennis, Co. Clare heads its list with the following:
'We find that the percentage of passes for all Ireland is 53.7, whilst that of
St Flannans reaches the high mark of 70 per cent.'

[142] 'The Function of a Text-Book', *An Claidheamh Soluis,* 27 January 1906, p. 6.

[143] *Ibid.*

[144] *Ibid.*

[145] 'Live Teaching in the Secondary School', *An Claidheamh Soluis*,
6 January 1906, p. 6.

[146] *Ibid.*

[147] *Ibid.*

[148] See D. Akenson, *The Irish Education Experiment*, pp. 378–80.

[149] *Ibid.*

[150] For an outline of bilingualism in Wales, see W.R. Jones, *Bilingualism in Welsh Education*, pp. 44–88. On the introduction of the Bilingual Programme generally see Thomas A. O'Donoghue, *Bilingual Education in Ireland, 1904-1922.*

[151] Pearse and his sister Margaret visited Belgium for six weeks, as part of the Fontenoy Group, organised by Major William Mc Bride in the summer of 1905. In 1943 Margaret recalled that they had enjoyed the trip. They visited Brussels, Malines, Antwerp, Ghent and Bruges. Pearse would visit schools in the morning and he and Margaret would spend the afternoon together touring the churches, museums and art galleries. Only in Antwerp did 'A friendly Inspector' invite her 'to accompany them'. See Margaret Pearse, Patrick and Willie Pearse, *Capuchin Annual*, May 1943, p. 87.

[152] 'Irish in the Schools' February 1900, published in *Guth na Bliadhna*, cited in Séamas O'Buachalla, *The Educational Writings of P.H. Pearse*, p. 311. On the intended limited applicability of the Bilingual Programme see below 2.2.2.

[153] 'Bilingual Education', *An Claidheamh Soluis*, 2 January 1904, p. 4.

[154] *Ibid.*

[155] *Ibid.*

[156] 'Bilingual Education', *An Claidheamh Soluis*, 16 January 1904, p.4

[157] See, the Bilingual Programme III. II. 1904, 'Programme for Infants in Schools Without Infant Departments, Object Lessons', in Hyland and Milne (eds) *Irish Educational Documents*, p. 164.

[158] 'The Bilingual Programme', *An Claidheamh Soluis*, 30 April 1904, p. 6.

[159] 'The Bilingual Programme', *An Claidheamh Soluis*, 7 May 1904, p. 6.

[160] 'The Bilingual Programme', *An Claidheamh Soluis*, 24 September 1904, p. 6.

[161] *Ibid.*

[162] See 'The Bilingual Programme in an Irish-Speaking District', *An Claidheamh Soluis*, 8 October 1904, p. 6.

[163] *Ibid.*

[164] *Ibid.*

[165] See 'Belgium and its Schools', *An Claidheamh Soluis*, 23 December 1905, p. 6.

[166] 'Belgium and its Schools', *An Claidheamh Soluis*,' 7 October 1905, p. 9.

[167] *Ibid.*

[168] 'Belgium and its Schools', *An Claidheamh Soluis*, 21 October 1905, p. 9.

[169] *Ibid.*

[170] *Ibid.*

[171] See *The Seventy-Second Report of the Commissioners of National Education 1905-1906*, [3154] (H.C., 1906), Irish, p. 21.

[172] *Ibid.*

[173] Pearse quotes a contemporary Belgian survey, which found 130 illiterates per 1,000 in the Belgian army as opposed to 8 per 1,000 in the Swiss, and 2 per 1,000 in the Danish armies. See 'Belgium and its Schools', *An Claidheamh Soluis*, 28 October 1905, p. 9.

[174] 'Belgium and its Schools', *An Claidheamh Soluis*, 18 November 1905, p. 9.

[175] *Ibid.*

[176] 'Belgium and its Schools', *An Claidheamh Soluis*, 25 November 1905, p. 9.

[177] *Ibid.*

[178] 'Belgium and its Schools', *An Claidheamh Soluis,* 17 February 1906, p. 9.

[179] *Ibid.*

[180] See 'Belgium and its Schools', *An Claidheamh Soluis*, 13 October 1906, p. 9. In an article in *An Claidheamh Soluis*, on 5 January 1907, Pearse noted that many teachers had contacted him for information about where to purchase *L'Image Animee*.

[181] 'Belgium and its Schools', *An Claidheamh Soluis,* 27 October 1906, p. 9.

[182] *Ibid.*

[183] On 'Position' see 'Belgium and its Schools', *An Claidheamh Soluis* 24 November 1906, p. 9.

[184] See 'Belgium and its Schools', *An Claidheamh Soluis*, 1 December 1906, p. 9.

[185] 'Belgium and its Schools', *An Claidheamh Soluis*, 16 February 1907, p. 9.

[186] See Maiéad Ní Chacháin (ed.), *Lúise Gabhánach Ní Dhufaigh agus Scoil Bhríde*, p. 1. See also John Hutchinson, *The Dynamics of Cultural Nationalism*, p. 163.

[187] 'Belgium and its Schools', *An Claidheamh Soluis*, 21 October 1905, p. 9.

[188] See *The Seventy-Second Report of the Commissioners of National Education 1905-6*, [3154] (H.C., 1906, Irish, p. 21; 'We recognise the educational necessity for instruction in Irish–speaking and bilingual districts …'

[189] See 'The Case for Bilingualism', *An Claidheamh Soluis*, 21 April 1906, p. 6.

[190] *Ibid.*

[191] 'The March of Bilingualism', *An Claidheamh Soluis*, 29 February 1908, p. 9.

[192] *Ibid.*

[193] *The Seventy-Second Report of the Commissioners of National Education 1905-6*, [3154] (H.C., 1906), pp. 21–22 states that: 'up to the present time the Bilingual Programme has been sanctioned in twenty-seven schools in the counties of Donegal, Mayo, Galway, Kerry and Cork.'

[194] 'Bilingualism', *An Claidheamh Soluis*, 20 June 1908, p. 9.

[195] *Ibid.*

[196] However, the Board had not sanctioned wholesale bilingualism. The rules for 1908–9 stated that 'Irish should be mainly the medium of instruction for the junior standards … and English mainly for the higher', *Ibid*, p. 199.

[197] Séamas O'Buachalla, *European Journal of Education*, Vol. 19, No. 1 (1984), p. 84.

[198] See Adrian Kelly, *Compulsory Irish*, p. 45.

199 On the American experience see E. Glyn Lewis, *Bilingualism and Bilingual Education, a Comparative Study* (1980), pp. 129–96.

200 See John Macnamara, *Bilingualism and Primary Education, a Study of Irish Experience*, p. 137 (Edinburgh University Press, 1966). It should be noted that the *Seventy-Second Report of the Commissioners of National Education, 1905-6*, [3154] (H.C., 1906), which officially sanctioned bilingual schooling, stated that the Programme would only be employed when the Commissioners were 'satisfied that instruction in the ordinary day school subjects will not be interfered with or hampered by the adoption of the Bilingual Programme …' See *Report*, Irish, p. 21.

201 John Macnamara, *Bilingualism and Primary Education, a Study of the Irish Experience*, p. 138.

202 'Live Teaching in the Secondary School', *An Claidheamh Soluis*, 6 January 1906, p. 6.

203 See Maureen Wall, 'The Decline of the Irish Language', pp. 88–9 in Brian O'Cuiv (ed.), *A View of the Irish Language*. See also Reg Hindley, *the Death of the Irish Language – A Qualified Obituary*, p. 14. Indeed even the Proclamation of Independence of 1916 was printed (and proclaimed) in English.

204 The estimated number of people learning Irish at schools belonging to the Christian Brothers, at Gaelic League courses and at night classes in 1904 was approximately 200,000. See Donnacha Ó'Súilleabháin, *Cath na Gaeilge sa Chóras Oideachais, 1893–1911*, p. 7.

205 The Four Masters College, Letterkenny, the Ulster College, Co. Donegal, the Connacht College, Co. Mayo, the Munster College, Co. Cork, the Ring College, Co. Kerry, the Belfast College, Co. Antrim and the Leinster College. *The Seventy-Sixth Report of the Commissioners of National Education, 1909-10*, [Cd. 5340] (H.C., 1910), Table 51, p. 40.

206 See *The Eighty-First Report of the Commissioners of National Education 1914-15*, [Cd. 8369] H.C. 1916, Table 55, p. 30, and *The Eighty-Sixth Report of the Commissioners of National Education, 1919-20*, [Cmd. 1476] H.C. 1920, Table 35, p. 29.

207 See *Saorstát Éireann, Census of Population 1926 Vol. VIII*. Irish Language, Dublin 1932, p. 1. Table 2: Irish Speakers as Percentage of Total Persons

in Each Province of *Saorstát Éireann* at Each Census from 1851–1926. However, the total number of Irish only speakers had fallen by 18 per cent since 1891.

[208] See Séamas O'Buachalla 'Educational Policy and the Role of the Irish Language form 1831–1981', in *European Journal of Education*, Vol. 19, No. 1. 1984, p. 85.

[209] *Ibid.*

[210] See Reg Hindley, *The Death of the Irish Language – A Qualified Obituary*, p 26.

[211] *Ibid.*, p. 37.

[212] Pádraig Ó'Riagáin, *Language Policy and Social Reproduction, Ireland 1893-1993*, p. 16. However, an article in '*An Camán*, in November 1932, cited a report by Thomas O'Derig who found that 'only four per cent of the national schoolchildren were being taught even two or three subjects through the medium of Irish. Of the 755 schools in the *Gaeltacht* of Donegal, Sligo and Mayo, 373 schools taught nothing through Irish as against 382 schools which were teaching the main part of the programme through Irish. In the *Breac-Gaeltacht* only one per cent of the schools taught through Irish.' The article concluded: 'it is apparent that the weapon of 'compulsory Irish' is not proving effective enough in this fight for the restoration of our national tongue.' See '*An Camán*, lml. I. *Uim*, a 22, '*Áth Cliath, Samhain, a* 12, 1932.

[213] Séan O'Catháin, SJ, *Secondary Education in Ireland*, p. 17.

[214] This tendency has continued, almost constantly, since 1851. In that year the percentage of Irish speakers in Leinster was 3.5 per cent, rising to 30.5 per cent by 1991. See, Pádraig Ó'Riagáin, *Language Policy and Social Reproduction, Ireland 1893-1993*, p. 146, Table 3.

[215] See Breandán S. MacAodha 'Was this a Social Revolution?' in Sean O'Tuama (ed.), *The Gaelic League Idea*.

[216] Cathair Ó'Dochartaigh, 'Irish in Ireland', in Glanville Price (ed.), *Languages in Britain and Ireland*, p. 27.

[217] See for example, Breandan S. MacAodha, 'Was this a Social

Revolution?' in Sean O'Tuama (ed.), *The Gaelic League Idea*; Reg Hindley, *The Death of the Irish Language, a Qualified Obituary*; Séan O'Lúing, 'The Present Position of the Irish Language', *Celtic Studies in Europe*.

[218] See Breandan S. MacAodha, 'Was this a Social Revolution?', in Sean O'Tuama (ed.), *The Gaelic League Idea*.

[219] Donal McCartney, 'Education and Language, 1938–51', in Kevin Nowlan and T.D. Williams (ed.), *Ireland in the War Years and After, 1939-1951*, p. 84.

[220] Committee On Irish Attitudes Research (1975) *Main Report*, cited in 'Educational Policy and the Role of the Irish Language from 1831–1981', Séamas O'Buachalla, *European Journal of Education*, Vol. 19, No. 1 (1984), p. 88.

[221] James, F. Lindsay, 'Irish Language Teaching: A Survey of Teacher Perceptions', *the Irish Journal of Education*, ix, 2 (1975), p. 103.

[222] *Ibid.* See Table II. p 89.

[223] *The Place of the Vernacular in Native Education*, (HMSO) London, 1925.

[224] See Clive Whitehead, 'The Medium of Instruction in British Colonial education: A Case of Cultural Imperialism or Enlightened Paternalism?' in *History of Education*, Vol. 24. No 1. 1–15 (1995), pp. 4–7.

[225] Gearóid Ó'Tuathaigh, the chairman of Údarás, remarked in 1998 that 'the linguistic basis for the *Gaeltacht* is fast eroding' with parents there relying upon schools to 'give Irish to their children' and that neither the state nor language enthusiasts could 'stop this erosion (nor) put in place a strategy to renew the language.' *The Irish Times*, 8 February 1998, cited in Cathair Ó'Dochartaigh, 'Irish in Ireland' in Glanville Price (ed.), *Languages in Britain & Ireland*, p. 11.

[226] 'For most of the past two hundred years, no one in Ireland would think of addressing a stranger in Irish and it is clear that in the private domain the spoken language will continue on the basis of social networks of those whose interests in Irish, which arise out of learning it, have brought them into contact with each other.' Cathair Ó'Dochartaigh, *Ibid.*, p. 33.

[227] Pádraig Ó'Riagáin, *Language Policy and Social Reproduction in Ireland 1893-1993*, p. 271.

[228] Even before Irish became obligatory for matriculation, the influence of university programmes upon school curricula was recognised. In his evidence before the Royal Commission on Trinity College, Dublin,

and the University of Dublin, 1906, T. W. Rollerston submitted that
'the curriculum of all the schools … work up to the University.' Eoin
MacNeill concurred stating that 'the kind of education given in Trinity
College affects the education given in a large number of secondary
schools throughout Ireland … the placing on a proper basis of Irish
studies in Trinity College would infallibly operate upon those schools.'
Royal Commission on Trinity College, Dublin, and the University of Dublin
1906, First Report of the Commissioners, Minutes of Evidence,
p. 212, 3,385.

Patrick Pearse, headmaster of St Enda's School 1908–1916.

St Enda's pupils at Cullenswood House, 1909.

Sзoιl Éanna, Rác Feaρnáιn : peιleaτóιρí (Sóιριρι), luċc buaιóce Cuρaτ-ṁιρ baιle Áċa Clιaċ, 1910-11.
St. Enda's College, Rathfarnham : Junior Football Team, Holders of Dublin Schools Cup, 1910-11.
p. bρeaċnaċ, R. Macaṁlaoιb, b. Ó Cuaċaιl, S. Mac Dιaρmaτa, S. Ó Dúnlaιnз, p. Ó Maolṁuaιτ, C. Mac Fιonnlaoιċ,
F. Ó Doċaρcaιз, S. Ó Duḟзaιll, b. Seoιзe, F. τe búρca (Caoιρeaċ), U. Ó Cúlaċáιn, b. Ó Cléιριз,
C. Ó Cléιριз, S. Ó Conċobaιρ.

Winners of the Dublin Schools Senior Cup, St Enda's, 1910-1911.

Desmond Carney as Giolla na Naomh in
An Rí, June 1912.

Boys at drill at St Enda's Rathfarnham. Photographs such as this were produced as postcards to
advertise the school.

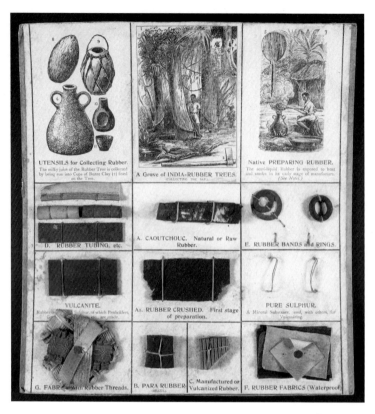

Teaching chart (the production of rubber), Pearse Museum, St Enda's, Dublin.

Boys at work in the school garden, Rathfarnham. The gardener, Michael Mac Ruaidhrí, later took part in the Easter Rising.

The study hall, St Enda's College.

The College chapel, St Enda's Rathfarnham.

'A worth home', the gardens at St Enda's Rathfarnham.

Pearse, Una O'Farelly, Eoin Mac Neill, Éamonn Ceannt and Douglas Hyde among others appear in this photography taken at the St Enda's Open Day, Rathfarnham, 1914.

Patrick and William Pearse at a public day at St Enda's in the summer of 1914. Desmond Ryan can be seen in the background.

From left to right, back row: Eamon Bulfin, Conor McGinley, Desmond Ryan, Fintan Murphy. Front row: Brian Joyce, Frank Burke and Joseph Sweeney as old men. This photograph was taken at the front steps of St Enda's in 1967 and the men stand in the same order as they did for a photo taken in 1916. Two members of the original group, Peter Slattery and Eunan McGinley, had died by the time this photo was taken.

Joseph Sweeney (aged eighteen) of 'E' Company, 4th Battalion in an Irish Volunteer's uniform. This photo was taken outside the front steps of St Enda's on Holy Thursday, 1916.

Patrick Pearse.

Four

Emmet's Ghost: The Boy Republic of St Enda's

THE IMPORTANCE OF PLACE

Pearse first opened St Enda's at Cullenswood House in September 1908 for an annual lease of £125. Three-quarters of a century earlier, in 1833, the proprietor Charles Joly had sold the premises to John Lecky, whose son John Hartpoole Lecky inherited it upon his father's death. Hartpoole Lecky's son, the historian William Lecky (1893–1903), was born at Cullenswood House and his *History of Ireland in the Eighteenth Century* (1896) reinterpreted English policy in Ireland in a manner more sympathetic to the Catholic position. In 1895 he was elected Member of Parliament for Trinity College, Dublin, and supported the establishment of the National University of Ireland. The connection with Lecky appealed to Pearse, who described the house as having 'a worthy tradition of scholarship and devotion to Ireland'.[1]

There was enough space at Cullenswood for five classrooms, which the inspectors who visited in 1910 described as clean and well heated.[2] The building was too small, however, to accommodate the number of students comfortably, and Pearse was forced to rent an adjacent house to provide sleeping quarters for the boarding pupils. The success of St Enda's meant that Pearse needed a larger premises and he moved

the school to The Hermitage, Rathfarnham in September 1910 while
Cullenswood House was reopened as a school for girls.[3] Even before
he became familiar with The Hermitage, Pearse wished to relocate to
'some beautiful place among the hills'.[4] This desire to become removed,
to find a less urban location, meant that he found The Hermitage
especially suitable but underlying the choice was the notion of removal,
a quasi-monastic aspiration that sprang from his interest in the early
hermit saints: '... we recall that Patrick built his first school on the
summit of the royal hill of Macha; that Enda fared across thirty miles of
stormy sea to find a rocky home in Aran; that Brendan built a monastery
on the tiny island of Inis Gluanie off the wild coast of Erris ...'[5]

Pearse also understood the importance of such a setting in competing
with established intermediate schools. In May 1910 he wrote to a friend
that if St Enda's was to 'hold [its] own' then it must have a 'beautiful'
home and compared the grounds favourably with Castleknock and
Clongowes College, two prestigious Catholic boarding schools.[6]

The Hermitage had originally been known as The Fields of Odin and
was first owned by Thomas Connolly of Castletown. In 1786 the freehold
was granted to Edward Hudson, a well-known Dublin doctor. Hudson
lived at The Hermitage until his death in 1827 when his son, William
Elliot Hudson (1796–1853), became the proprietor. William Hudson was
a lawyer with a keen interest in the new discoveries in Celtic archaeology taking place in the 1840s. He knew Thomas Davis personally and
was a patron of the Celtic and Ossianic Societies.[7] In particular, he was
interested in the preservation of early Irish manuscripts and in 1853
donated £500 to the Royal Irish Academy to assist in the publication
of its Irish Dictionary. The connection appealed to Pearse who wrote in
1910 that if ever there was 'money to spare' a bust of Hudson would be
placed in the school.[8]

There were yet more significant historical associations. Edward
Hudson's neighbour had been the lawyer John Philpott Curran,
a member of the Irish Parliament between 1783 and 1797. Curran had
supported Catholic emancipation and defended a number of the United
Irishmen after the failed rebellion of 1803. His daughter Sarah had been
secretly engaged to the patriot Robert Emmet (1778–1803).[9] The couple
often met in the grounds of The Hermitage and Pearse's declaration
that it was the spirit of Emmet that led him to Dublin foothills reflected
his growing preoccupation with the doomed leader. A number of large

Georgian houses in the vicinity of The Hermitage still maintained an 'aroma' of 'high courtesy and rich living'[10] and Pearse's desire to locate his school amongst them reflects that seeming tension between his wish to create something new and authentically Gaelic, and a finely honed Edwardian sensibility for all things respectable.[11] Yet Pearse was aware of the ambiguity of his feelings and while admiring their beauty noted that they belonged to a 'very definite phase' in Irish history; 'in such mansions as these' he mused 'lived those who sold Ireland'.

The estate was laid out in woods and copses and the closeness of the Dublin Mountains lent an atmosphere of openness. The grounds were home to a range of wildlife and the opportunity to have the boys learn from the natural environment was important in the move 'from the suburbs' to Rathfarnham.[12] The follies dotted about the estate were a final, flippant, attraction and included one known locally as Emmet's Fort.[13] Others included a dolmen, a circle of standing stones and a monk's cell or hermitage. Pearse understood the follies to be the indulgence of the Hudson's imagination, yet he was pleased that they were 'Irish in spirit'.[14] For him The Hermitage was a significant location. Its associations with the gaelic sympathies of Hudson, the more resonant connection with Robert Emmet; the beauty and scope of the estate and the civilizing effect it might have upon the boys meant that, for him, The Hermitage was not simply an adequate location but an integral element in the development of St Enda's.

St Enda's was among the first lay Catholic intermediate schools in Ireland.[15] Pearse understood that such a venture would require ecclesiastical support and hoped that the Revd William Walsh, Archbishop of Dublin, and 'some prominent Catholic laymen might be got as patrons'.[16] He was not the first to propose such an institution. In 1906, Thomas O'Nowlan, a former Jesuit priest and teacher at Mount Mellery Cistercian College in Co. Waterford, had approached Archbishop Walsh with a plan to establish an intermediate school for boys in Dublin. O'Nowlan was closely involved with the Gaelic League and indicated that Pearse should be the vice-president of the school. He did not receive the ecclesiastical support he requested and the school never materialised.

Both O'Nowlan and Pearse proposed founding schools against a backdrop of widespread clerical involvement in National and intermediate schools. The education system was denominational in character, if not in name, and clerics acted as patrons, trustees and visitors. Both the laity and clergy held often trenchant views on the issue. The *Peasant* newspaper, for example, was frequently critical of clerical involvement at managerial level while, at the other extreme, Revd Dwyer of Limerick had publicly declared that 'no laymen had the right to teach'.[17] Pearse therefore had to tread carefully and knew that his venture had little hope of success without support from the hierarchy. Once the school had moved to The Hermitage he sought permission to establish an oratory, as the walk to the parish church at Rathfarnham was some miles. Because the school was not associated with a religious order and no clergy served in a managerial capacity or had any involvement in its day-to-day operation, Pearse had to rely upon the willingness of local clergy to provide Mass and Confession. This did not present any significant difficulty and at different times clergy from Rathfarnham parish and priests from the Augustinian fathers at the nearby Orlath Grove served the needs of St Enda's. While the ethos of the school was explicitly Catholic, and Pearse went to great lengths to ensure that the boys' spiritual formation did not suffer in comparison with those attending schools run by religious orders, St Enda's was nonetheless a lay Catholic school, unconnected with the Dublin Diocese. It was operated, funded and owned by lay persons, reflecting a transition in the manner in which schooling could be conceptualised in early twentieth-century Ireland.

PEARSE AS TEACHER

The boys who attended St Enda's recall Pearse as an effective teacher with an arresting personality. Milo McGarry, who attended the school at both locations, remembered him as a 'splendid' teacher of histoy and languages.[18] It is difficult to establish, with certainty, which subjects Pearse taught. According to one past pupil, he taught French, arithmetic, history and Irish,[19] while another recalled that he taught 'mostly ... English, Irish and history' and was 'very educated in English and history'.[20] Certainly Pearse taught some of these subjects and while only O'Conaire mentions French, MacGarry records that he taught 'languages'.[21] He also recorded that Thomas MacDonagh was a keen Francophile and that he and Pearse shared an admiration for Napoleon.[22] MacDonagh had spent time in France and was responsible for the majority of French language teaching at St Enda's.[23] Michael

Smithwick taught higher mathematics and mathematical science. The Prospectus does not indicate Pearse's subjects but records his position as headmaster, Barrister at Law and 'Late Professor of Irish, University College Dublin'.[24] Given Pearse's work ethic, it is likely that he taught a number of subjects.

There is general agreement on his qualities as a teacher. Pádraig Óg O'Conaire remarked that it was 'as a teacher' that he should like to remember Pearse and that 'he was the favourite teacher' of some of the pupils.[25] In particular he recalled Pearse's ability 'to make time for each pupil'.[26] Brian Seoighe remembered Pearse as 'a super teacher ... along with being able to make the subject interesting ... he had great discipline'.[27] Frank Burke, a pupil and future headmaster of St Enda's, described Pearse as 'a very good teacher ... painstaking and very patient ... especially in his Irish classes'.

C.S. Andrews was unhappy at the school but not critical of Pearse. He particularly enjoyed the nature study lessons given by the headmaster in the grounds of The Hermitage[28] and recalled the walks there as 'the most pleasant experiences' he had at St Enda's.[29] However, he says nothing of Pearse's teaching. Mary Colum worked with Pearse at the school but in her autobiography makes no reference to his ability as a teacher.[30] She believed MacDara, the principle character in Pearse's play *The Singer*, represented Pearse's own aspirations: 'I felt it proud and wondrous to be a teacher ... I gave to the little lad I taught the very flesh and blood and breath that were my life'.[31] 'This was true of Pearse himself,' wrote Colum, 'he loved his pupils and his schools'.[32] Joseph Sweeney, a past pupil, recalled Pearse as 'a magnificent teacher, one of the two best teachers which I have met in my lifetime'.[33] 'Coilin', writing in 1917, claimed that Pearse was 'a highly gifted teacher' whose work at St Enda's was, 'in his own estimation, the most important work of his life'.[34] Desmond Ryan, past pupil and later teacher at St Enda's, recorded much of value about life at the school but little about Pearse's teaching. He noted that both he and MacDonagh 'kindled a love and appreciation of literature' and that Pearse resisted the idea of having to 'cover' so many texts in a given school year in order to prepare pupils for examinations.[35] Hence, as early as possible, he introduced his pupils to the 'classics of Irish and English literature'.[36] Ryan claimed that Pearse's success as a teacher was due to a combination of his personality and the use of pageant, drama, athletics and 'modern methods of language teaching'.[37]

He confirmed that Pearse rarely resorted to corporal punishment and
provided the only detailed account of the headmaster's typical day.[38]
The recollections of those who attended St Enda's reveal Pearse to have
been a patient man who worked hard. The consensus that he was a
naturally able teacher goes some way to explaining Pearse's assumption
that good teachers are charismatic and effortlessly able.

Pearse's teaching days were busy; he woke the boarding pupils at 7.30
and led morning prayers. At breakfast he sat with his colleagues and
the boys were permitted to talk – a liberty not common at the time.
Between the end of the lessons at 3.30 p.m. and the beginning of study
(5.50 – 10 p.m.), Pearse busied himself with personal or school matters.
According to Ryan he usually taught 'throughout the entire school day'
and 'supervised the minutest details of internal organisation'.[39]

While Ryan remembered a 'brilliant procession of teachers' at the
school, and Colum referred to Pearse's 'very modern methods'[40] past
pupil Sean Dowling held that St Enda's 'wasn't particularly good' as
a preparation for life.[41] Nonetheless, Ryan claimed that Pearse was 'a
born teacher … his exposition of any subject was always vivid, clear,
concentrated and energetic, arousing new interests, and opening up
new vistas to the listeners', he commanded respect yet was affable
and occasionally indulgent with pupils .[42] Ryan described Pearse as
'a slow and deliberate figure descending from the rostrum to tell us
the story of Fionn or Cúchulainn' or striding 'down the hurley field,
his black gown flying in the wind, to encourage the Scoil Éanna
players to beat some hostile team'.[43] Mary Colum recalled that he was
'full of humour and even whimsicality … never arrogant' and 'always
gentle'.[44] Marie Nic Shiubhlaigh recalled that 'to the casual observer'
the boys at St Enda's 'ran wild'.[45] The suggestion of an unruly school is
not repeated by other commentators, indeed Ryan recalled that Pearse
'could keep order with a look, or a word'.[46] Nic Shiubhlaigh remembered him as having an intimate knowledge of his pupils and, when in
their company, 'a sort of boyish enthusiasm which set him on a level
with all of them'.[47] The headmaster's school diaries show how accurate
her observation was. In these he noted their academic progress and
illnesses, his impression of how content they were at school, their
involvement in extra-curricular activities, and any personal aspect he
felt needed attention.[48] Pearse was often forthright in his appraisals.
He began one report to the parents of Edgar Colahan by declaring that

their son had 'no literary or scholastic ability of any kind' continuing, 'we believe that if he had been taken very carefully in hand while much younger he might have been made more of'.[49]

James Kilcullen, writing in 1962, believed that Pearse had many characteristics of the good teacher.[50] Unlike Dowling, Kilcullen believed that Pearse well understood the practical needs of boys who would soon have to make a living.[51] Milo Mac Garry recalled his first impression of St Enda's as a bustling place with Pearse at its centre, a 'big man dressed in black … his voice raised in greeting'.[52] In his biography of Pearse, Le Roux described him as 'a born educationalist' whose vocation to teaching was 'innate'.[53] When Joseph Sweeney arrived for the first time at St Enda's he and Pearse had a 'long conversation' about what subjects might best suit him.[54] Sweeney's recollections, published in 1982, support Thornley's remarks regarding Pearse's understanding of the relationship between educator and propagandist.[55] Sweeney recalled that he acquired a 'deep insight into history' and was 'very much' influenced by Pearse.[56] Sweeney later became a member of the Volunteers and fought in the Easter Rising.[57]

A number of the families that enrolled their sons at St Enda's were associated with the Gaelic League and several of the St Ita's girls had brothers there.[58] Stephen Gwynn was typical of the literary nationalists who sent their sons to the school. He enrolled his two boys, Owen and Denis, because he liked Pearse 'thoroughly and unreservedly' and believed that 'contact with such an idealist was as good a thing as could happen to them'.[59] Ryan recorded that there were boys from each province of Ireland and also Argentina (Eamon Bulfin) and America (Eugene Cronin, John Kilgallon and Kevin Heneghan), and most were from homes 'deeply akin to Pearse in hope and spirit'.[60] Maud Gonne also wished to send her son Seagan to the school.[61] Eoin McNeill's sons Niall and Brian were enrolled from the beginning.[62]

Pearse was aware that, beyond the immediate circle of sympathisers, his venture might be viewed with scepticism and in 1913 acknowledged his debt of gratitude to those who continued to support 'an ideal and a place which by many are still misunderstood and distrusted'.[63] Sean Dowling's family were committed Gaelic Leaguers but he believed that the school 'wasn't particularly good', adding that it would be 'splendid, if you were well off' but that the pupils of St Enda's 'didn't do particularly well'.[64]

Pearse did not seek out wealthy families and the original Prospectus
of the school pointed out that because the school had not been established 'with a view to personal profit', Pearse was able to fix the fees
'at a more moderate figure' than was customary.[65] The student body of
St Enda's were not 'a select group'.[66] Maire Nic Shiubhlaigh recollected
that the school 'attracted the children of some of the noblest families
in Ireland', although she does not identify these as being of nationalist
sympathy, or of being especially wealthy.[67] The labour leaders Jim Larkin
and James Connolly enrolled children at St Enda's and when Pearse was
criticised for accepting Larkin's children he retorted that he had 'done
more in six months than the politicians and ourselves with all our talk'.[68]
Ryan recorded that when a visitor to the school asked Pearse if it did
any good to have Larkin's boys there, he replied 'none whatever! But
here they stay'.[69] At the end of the 1910–11 school year Pearse reported
that Larkin's son James was a 'model of discipline … bright, cheerful and
apparently always happy'.[70]

The boys of St Enda's were encouraged to speak Irish as the first
language of the school. Ryan recalled that Pearse almost always spoke
Irish to both staff and pupils and when addressed in English would
respond by asking 'Ceard é?' ('What is that'?)[71] The boys were encouraged
to support the language in other practical ways. Less than two weeks
after the school opened they attended the Irish Language Procession
organised by the Gaelic League, in Dublin's Phoenix Park. These outings
became a part of school life.[72] In September 1909 the school made a
collection in aid of the Irish Language Fund and Pearse helped the
senior boys establish an Eire Óg (Young Ireland) branch of the League
under the presidency of senior boy Denis Gwynn, who later served on
the Western Front from 1916 to 1917. The boys marched in the language
procession in 1910 accompanied by the girls from their sister school
which had opened only six days previously. St Ita's was the only school
for girls to participate in the procession.

It is not surprising that the parents of the boys attending St Enda's
shared Pearse's ideals. But the experiences of Andrews and the comments
of Dowling demonstrate that not all pupils shared his vision, regardless
of their admiration for him. Indeed, the headmaster was disappointed
generally by the boys from the western *Gaeltacht* regions who, he
hoped, would be an encouragement to the other pupils to speak Irish.
Pearse expected the island boys to be closer to his notion of the Gael.

He spent many holidays in the Galway *Gaeltacht* region of Rosmuc
where he owned a holiday cottage and the schoolmaster at Gortmore,
Proinsias O'Conghaile, enrolled his son, also Proinsias, at St Enda's in
September 1908.[73] Two other boys from the area, Pádraig Óg Ó Conaire
and Colm O'Neachtain were also enrolled. Thomas MacDonagh told
W.B. Yeats that he found the boys from the *Gaeltacht* 'cold, dark and
reticent' yet 'merry, clever and talkative' when alone, or with the school
gardener Michael Mac Ruaidhrí, a native Irish speaker.[74]

The idealisation of the Aran and Blasket islanders as representative of a
purer and more authentically Irish way of life began only a few years after
Pearse's death. Pearse recognised, as others would later do, in particular the
English scholar Robin Flower (1881–1946), that the culture of the island
communities was precious and vulnerable. They represented, for Pearse,
the last living personification of the Irish-Ireland ideal. It was 'in the kindly
Irish west' that he felt he was 'in Ireland', to feel so in Dublin, he mused,
required 'a more rigorous effort of imagination'.[75] This idealisation of
the Gaelic peasant by urban Leaguers is typified by Pearse's friend Mary
Hayden. In 1903, she and Pearse holidayed in the western *Gaeltacht* in order
to improve their Irish. While visiting 'numerous cabins' around Recess, Go.
Galway, she discovered that indeed 'the pig *does* sleep in the living room'.[76]

THE STUDENT COUNCIL AT ST ENDA'S

Pearse's plea for freedom in schooling was most readily demonstrated
in the establishment of a student council at St Enda's. To help the boys
develop an understanding of the responsible use of freedom he wished
to grant a 'certain autonomy not only to the school but also to the
particular parts of the school: to the various sub-divisions of the pupils'.[77]
The council was inspired by a story told to Pearse by his aunt Margaret,
whereby the fosterlings of kings in ancient Ireland were allowed to
'make their own laws and elect their own leaders'.[78]

Each year, elections were held by the pupils to determine who should
sit on the council and who should act as school captain. Denis Gwynn
was the first captain with Eamonn Bulfin as vice-captain.[79] Other posts
at the school included librarian and school secretary.[80] In October 1909,
Denis Gwynn, who was then a first-year undergraduate at University
College Dublin, refused Desmond Ryan's nomination as school captain,

suggesting instead Eamonn Bulfin, who had also left school in the summer of 1909 to study at university. Both boys had returned to board at The Hermitage. Bulfin was also confirmed as captain of football and another past pupil, Frank Connolly, was elected school secretary. The student council for 1908–9 included Denis Gwynn, Desmond Ryan and Donal O'Connor, all past pupils who had returned to board. Eamonn Bulfin was again elected school captain in October 1910, thereby retaining the position for three years after leaving school.[81] In the third year, his vice-captain was Frank Burke, later the last headmaster of St Enda's.[82] Only in September 1912 did Bulfin think it 'better that boys still on the school roll should have the leadership'.[83]

Pearse does not appear to have interfered in the school elections and Bulfin was repeatedly elected, seemingly by virtue of his ability and popularity. But this would have suited Pearse. Bulfin was a capable organiser, shared Pearse's political credo and acted as spokesperson for the group of past pupils, known as 'Pearse's own' or 'E' Co. 4th Battalion, which took part in the Easter Rising. In 1912, Brian Seoighe was elected captain of hurling; he too fought in the Rising and later returned to St Enda's as a teacher.

Desmond Ryan remembered the council as being a means of encouraging the boys to speak Irish, helped with the internal organisation of the school and was 'elected with great excitement annually by the boys themselves'.[84] Le Roux suggests that the council was a means of inculcating a sense of responsibility in pupils.[85] Fifty years after the founding of St Enda's, Desmond Ryan wrote that Pearse had 'made his school a Republic for his students'.[86] The institution outlived Pearse. Séan Sheridan, who was enrolled at St Enda's in 1917, recalled that the council was an 'unusual feature' and contributed to the 'democratic and happy' atmosphere there.[87]

Like Thomas Arnold, Pearse wanted to operate his school using a code of honour informed by the principle of freedom.[88] Joseph Sweeney recalled that Pearse ran the school on this principle and pupils were encouraged to admit to and take responsibility for their misdemeanours.[89] Every year, new boys would enrol who 'didn't understand this and who didn't want to understand' and Sweeny recalled 'four or five of us bigger fellows' taking a recalcitrant boy to Pearse's office where they 'flung him in and closed the door behind him and he had to explain himself to Pearse'.[90]

Self-regulation, however, is not always, if ever, to be relied upon. C.S. Andrews, who came from the traditionally working–class Summerhill area of Dublin, found himself the victim of bullying because of his accent and dislike of Gaelic games.[91] In his autobiography he conceded that he provoked an amount of this and following a fight that resulted in his being plunged into the school lake, he left St Enda's.[92] Certainly, Pearse would have abhorred such behaviour but the incident sheds light on Nic Shiubhlaigh's recollection that 'inside the school gate' the pupils had 'an empire of their own, administered by themselves'.[93] While Andrews 'loathed' the school he does not blame Pearse for his experiences there or his departure.[94]

Despite Pearse's disapproval of corporal punishment he occasionally employed it for misdemeanours. Andrews recorded that he once received a 'mild lecture and four not very hurtful slaps with a cane'.[95] Pádraig Óg O'Conaire recalled that he only punished one boy who 'deserved it for what he did'.[96] The boy was Ó'Conaire, who stole a cake from the kitchen. The incident was no doubt disappointing for Pearse as he was one of the boys from the West Galway *Gaeltacht*.

In a time when corporal punishment was common, it is possible that Pearse's reluctance to employ it lent the school a certain air of liberty rather than license.[97] It was his policy to accept a pupil's word as the truth. He abhorred lies, lamenting in 1907 that Irish children had too little 'veneration for the truth' and his willingness to wait for moral maturity was striking.[98] Kenneth Reddin recalled that there were no prefects at St Enda's, 'you were not watched, or kept under constant observation' rather:

> … you were put on your honour … on your first transgression Pearse called you into his study; you gave your word not to offend again, and you usually kept your word. If you didn't, you knew … that you were doing something shabby on the Ard-Mhaighistir, that you were letting him down, letting St Enda's down, and letting yourself down too … The discipline at St Enda's was good and we mostly told the truth.[99]

Alfred Dennis recalled that the boys did not lie to Pearse 'because he believed every word they said'.[100] Another commentator recorded that he had a 'genius' for 'control', remarking that 'the discipline was good, and it was maintained not by threat of physical punishment, but by trusting them, by putting them on their honour'.[101] After Pearse's death, a newspaper article claimed that 'perhaps he was prone to trust too much to honour, and pretty often he was deceived, but his very trustfulness appealed to the lads: "It was no fun to tell lies to Pearse, he always believed you" said one young culprit'.[102]

Ryan recorded that on several occasions Pearse had correctly trusted the word of a boy, despite evidence to the contrary.[103] Boys he believed were 'proverbially honourable in their dealings with one another; our achievement has been to bring the masters within the magic circle, and thus give a new extension to "schoolboy honour".'[104] Sweeney, who recollected that 'if something happened you were supposed to stand up and admit it', supports this.[105] The boys' trust was returned. Pearse made a point, for example, of not reading the letters they sent home.[106] The same willingness to trust the word of pupils informed the practice of Mary MacSweeney who modelled her school, also called St Ita's, upon Pearse's schools. According to her niece, MacSweeney believed that:

> … children were not basically liars and that she could turn anyone [sic] to
> speak the truth in time … 'the truth always' this was her teaching … my
> aunt would take a child who would come from another school who would
> be lying, because it seemed to have been the norm and she said 'the way you
> train a child is that the child's word is her honour and you accept it and if
> the child says she didn't do it you accept that as the truth' and within weeks
> a child who had been lying would be telling the truth …[107]

SCHOOLING IN FREEDOM

The principle of freedom informed all aspects of life at St Enda's; freedom for the boys to contribute to the operation of the school and to learn how to accept responsibility for their actions. Equally Pearse insisted that the school remain unburdened by the demands of the Intermediate Examination and create courses of study that met the needs of its particular student body. This way, no pupil would be 'forced into a groove of study for which he evinced no special talent or inclination'.[108] Hence, Pearse did not prepare pupils for the Intermediate Examinations unless requested by parents but he advised them that 'in no instance will a course or programme of the Board be allowed to interfere with the pursuit of the distinctive ideals of the school'.[109]

In March 1909 he wrote that 'At Scoil Éanna we take the view that we alone, in consultation with our pupils and their parents, have the right to decide what subjects we shall study, what books we shall read'.[110] Senior pupils, however, were prepared for the new matriculation examination for the National University of Ireland.[111]

Pearse believed that a good teacher could teach with any or no programme but this view did not permeate all his educational thinking. His pronouncement regarding the Intermediate Examinations of 1909 was carefully worded: 'Where parents so desire, pupils will this year be sent forward for the examination of the Intermediate Board'.[112] The reason for the proviso 'this year' was explained in a letter to William Bulfin, father of Eamon, a pupil at St Enda's, in which Pearse conceded that 'we meant to have it [the examination] from the start ... but held back last year because there was no oral inspection and we knew we should not get credit for our viva voce teaching'.[113] He continued, 'now all that is changed ... really it is the abuse of the Intermediate System and not the use of it that has worked havoc. The Programme itself is a magnificent one' and concluded that St Enda's should be able to participate in it 'without being led away into a scramble for honours or into "cramming" our boys'.[114] Indeed, twelve boys secured entrance to the NUI between 1910 and 1913, three on scholarships.

Pearse's willingness to prepare boys for an examination to which he was fundamentally opposed was informed by the same principle of freedom. He disliked the public examinations but accepted that others did not share his views. Although his letter to Bulfin admits that he would like to have had the Intermediate Programme 'from the start' he could not avail of it while no system of oral inspection was available. Pearse explained: 'We decided last year ... to hold aloof from the intermediate. The establishment of a system of oral inspection by the Intermediate Board has brought about a new state of affairs which makes it possible for us to avail of the Board's grants, without sacrificing any of our principles ...'[115]

He could not ignore the potential income results fees would generate and was anxious that the dissenting character of the school be maintained.[116] Indeed, he repeatedly proclaimed that it was for the Intermediate System to follow the example of St Enda's, rather than the other way around.

PUPILS' VIEWS OF PEARSE

Pearse's personality was not complex but elements of it appear contra-
dictory. While possessed of great energy and usually working at an
intense pace, he still managed to often exude an air of distant, even aloof,
solitude. He appears to have acted differently with children than with
adults. Frank Burke recalled that his headmaster 'wasn't a good mixer'
and that while 'very talkative with the boys … with grown up people
he seemed to be more or less stand-off-ish', although Burke is the only
pupil to make such a statement.[117] Ryan recorded that deputations from
the pupil body requesting half-holidays for special occasions were usually
met with 'affable and laughing surrenders'.[118] When the pupils presented
him with an umbrella as a birthday present, Pearse, 'in one of his rare
bursts of self-revelation, spoke to us of his friendships with pupils past
and present'.[119] Certainly, he was a shy man and admitted this openly.
In a letter to the father of John Kilgallon, written aboard the *Baltic* as
he returned from America in May 1914, he thanked the family for their
hospitality, remarking that 'I am not a very sociable or talkative person,
but I did feel intimate and at home in your circle'.[120] In a 1912 epistle to
himself he wrote: 'Pearse you are a reserved person! You do not associate
with Gaels. You shun their company. On the occasions when you join
them, a black cloud accompanies you, which as it were settles over them.
Those who were talkative before your arrival grow silent and those who
were merry become gloomy. I wonder if it is the English blood in you
which is responsible for that?'[121]

A press article of 1916 described him as 'silent and reserved except
with very intimate friends' and a man who 'rarely revealed his deeper
feelings'.[122] The school diary recorded that, at one *céilidhe*, 'the headmaster sat silent', although it is possible that this simply referred to his
not joining in the singing.[123]

Pearse was always conscious of his role as the headmaster of a school
in which he hoped to create a domestic atmosphere and referred to the
pupils and staff as a 'family' presided over by his mother, Mrs Pearse.[124]
Brian Seoighe recalled her greeting him on his arrival at St Enda's: 'She
… kissed me and put her arms around me'.[125] C.S. Andrews recalled
her as a 'grand old lady'.[126] Three of the four Pearse family members
living at The Hermitage taught in the school. Indeed, before the establishment of St Enda's, Margaret had established a small kindergarten at

Cullenswood House.[127] Mrs Pearse carried out some domestic work and Margaret taught music, religion and French to the Preparatory Grade and oversaw the Junior School.[128] William taught art, and Mary Brigid, who did not live at the school, taught music using a harp Pearse had bought for her.[129] Marie Nic Shiubhlaigh, who knew the family personally, recorded that she met Pearse frequently but 'never knew him very well – not so much as an individual as a member of a family'.[130] McGarry recollected that, overall there was an 'atmosphere of intimacy'.[131] It was common, for example, for the masters and boys to participate in games together; Willie Pearse, in particular, played handball and football with the senior teams. Chess and billiards were also played between pupils and masters.

The relationship between Pearse and his pupils was critical in the creation of this friendly atmosphere. If he wrongly accused a pupil he would apologise, hoping that his pupils would recognise that it was as important to be good as to be learned.[132] It appears that Pearse's affection for the pupils was reciprocated. The boys 'came to him with all their troubles' and Pearse 'found by experience that he could always trust them'.[133] Ryan believed he won their 'sympathies and affections' and recounts an incident that demonstrates not only the loyalty of some senior boys but also the atmosphere at St Enda's in 1916. Upon hearing a rumour that Pearse was to be arrested, four 'armed senior boys' left the school to meet him as he walked home.[134] These were the past pupils then boarding at The Hermitage while attending university. Four past pupils had, in fact, been sworn into the Irish Republican Brotherhood eighteen months before their old teacher.[135]

Edwards claims that each night Pearse sat on the bed of one or other of the boarders 'chatting to him and getting to know him, as an individual whose mind he might influence',[136] but there is no evidence that this ever happened. Only Joseph Sweeney makes reference to Pearse and the boarders, recording simply that he would call them every morning for prayers and breakfast – the normal duty of a dean at the period. Recollections of Pearse are unanimously generous. Even Eugene Cronin, who had come from America to board at St Enda's and repeatedly complained of homesickness, was never critical of Pearse or the school.[137]

Pearse was sensitive to the impact of boarding school life on new pupils. A report on David Sears written in 1911 notes that he 'probably felt a little isolated at the beginning' but was soon 'quite at home'.[138] Writing to Michael Cronin in May 1914, Pearse assured him that when his son Eugene returned to St Enda's he would be placed 'in the special charge of my mother and sister'.[139] He was quite confident that 'as soon as he settles down with his new friends and fits into the homelike surroundings ... there will be nothing like loneliness'.[140] Writing to the Cronin family in 1915 he remarked that 'the return to school after Christmas is always the hardest on a boy ... but we have had one or two little treats for [them] in the evenings'.[141] The reception Pearse received upon returning to St Enda's from America in May 1914, when the pupils prepared a welcoming party complete with bunting and music, testified to his popularity.[142] Elizabeth Countess of Fingall was in the company of General Blackadder on the evening of Pearse's courts-martial. The General described passing sentence upon Pearse as 'the one of the hardest tasks I have ever had to do' and described him as 'one of finest characters I have ever come across', musing 'I don't wonder that his pupils adored him'.[143]

THE TEACHING STAFF AT ST ENDA'S

Pearse surrounded himself with like-minded colleagues. The most notable of these was Thomas MacDonagh whose father, also Thomas, had been a teacher and trained at Marlborough Street College. MacDonagh's mother was a convert to Catholicism, as Pearse's father had been, and had opened a school in Cloughjordan, Co. Tipperary, in the 1860s. MacDonagh had attended Rockwell College and later taught at St Kieran's College, Kilkenny and St Coleman's in Fermoy. According to his son, Donagh MacDonagh, he chanced upon Irish after he had left school when 'he and some other boys had gone to a meeting of the Gaelic League in the hope of a laugh'.[144] He left St Coleman's to take a post at St Enda's, where he acted as assistant headmaster, later recalling that the school had been started 'with more headshakes than handshakes'.[145] Like William Pearse he was a painter and both men had studied art in Paris. His home, on the Grange Road, Rathfarnham, was close to The Hermitage and became the meeting place for many of Dublin's literati, such as Padraig Colum and James Stephens.[146] Its proximity meant that 'the boys of St Enda's used to find one of their greatest sources of amusement in discussing MacDonagh's latest love affairs'.[147] He lent the school a spirit of high culture so valued by Pearse.[148] He was a painter, poet, literary critic and committed Gaelic League enthusiast. Sean Dowling remembered him as a good teacher but 'easily distracted'.[149]

Another pupil remembered him as 'a wonderful character' and certainly easily sidetracked: 'we used to start him off by asking him a question when he came into the class ... and he would go off talking and he wouldn't stop until the bell rang for the next class'.[150] At university MacDonagh was a popular lecturer whose classes attracted even students who were not studying his course.[151] He was critical of the running of the school, espoused the liberal humanist tradition of education and, like Pearse, treated the pupils as 'equals'.[152] Maire Nic Shiubhlaigh recalled that he was 'a gifted teacher ... deeply interested in his work'.[153] Donagh MacDonagh described him as teaching with 'such laughing ease that the pupils regretted the bell which silenced his discourse'.[154] The contrast of personalities may have been beneficial and MacDonagh acted as a spur to Pearse's more sombre disposition, joking that Pearse had opened the school only so that he might make speeches.[155] He was a more outspoken nationalist than Pearse and openly discussed his hopes for independence with the pupils.[156] According to Ryan, he was 'in the strictest sense of the word, a master', possessing 'the power of stimulation and suggestion'.[157]

Ryan points to the assistance Pearse received from MacDonagh and the 'brilliant procession of teachers who passed through the school' remarking that, in their hands, 'only very unsusceptible and unpromising material ... would not have yielded highly successful results'.[158] Even allowing for Ryan's hyperbole, the teaching staff at St Enda's appear to have been committed and hardworking. Mary Colum, who worked at St Enda's for a time, recalled that Pearse 'acquired an interesting group as teachers ... not all of us, I am very sure, were equal to what he wanted, but at least we responded to his ideas'.[159] Her autobiography provides a valuable insight into the mood of young Irish Irelanders at that time:

Almost everything significant in the Dublin of that period was run by the young; youth, eagerness, brains, imagination, are what I remember of everybody. There was something else that was in all of them: a desire for self-sacrifice, a devotion to causes; everyone was working for a cause, for practically everything was a cause.[160]

Pearse, then, was of his time, a serious, dedicated young Irish Irelander, like so many of his friends and associates. Le Roux sheds light on Colum's remarks, noting that while 'apostolic souls and minds' may have been a rarity under the National System, the staff at St Enda's were of a 'different stamp', their task being to turn out pupils as 'good citizens and subjects convinced that life has a more useful purpose than utilitarianism'.[161] Certainly, Pearse thought highly of MacDonagh and described his teaching as 'distinguished' by 'ripe scholarship and a fine literary sense'.[162] He 'created in his pupils an enthusiasm for literature and for ideas', his influence at St Enda's was 'inspiring and bracing,' as a teacher he 'combined mastery of the teacher's technique and an authoritative manner'.[163] MacDonagh immersed himself in the life of St Enda's with the same zeal as Pearse. A close associate of Edward Martyn and Joseph Plunkett, he devoted much of his time to the dramatic performances at the school.[164]

William Pearse shared MacDonagh's interest in drama, acted in a number of amateur theatrical productions and was the driving force behind the dramatic presentations that took place at St Enda's.[165] Historically, William has received little attention and his influence upon Pearse is uncertain. As children and adults the brothers were inseparable. He had studied at Dublin's Metropolitan School of Art under Oliver Sheppard RHA and later in London and Paris.[166] Upon the death of James Pearse, he and Patrick assumed control of a business neither had any interest in. They sold it and invested in Cullenswood House. Like Pearse, Willie was an ardent Irish-Ireland sympathiser. He learned Irish and gave a number of Irish classes while a student at the Metropolitan School of Art. He began teaching art at St Enda's in September 1908 but it was not until 1913 that he became a regular member of staff.[167] Upon MacDonagh's departure to the National University he became, in effect, the assistant headmaster of St Enda's.[168] Louise Gavan Duffy claimed that, after 1914, Pearse's involvement in the IRB meant that he devoted less time to the school while William assumed more responsibility at a time when the school was in decline.[169] In the years 1915–16 there were only twenty-eight pupils enrolled at St Enda's.[170]

Ryan recalled that William was 'painstaking' in his teaching method[171] but Sean Dowling recollected that he: 'Took us for art classes but in a very desultory way ... I don't remember him as being a good teacher, or a bad teacher ... very genial and easily moved to laughter, he was a very nice person, very gentle'.[172] C.S. Andrews remembered 'seeing him once in a smock and carrying a chisel' but 'nobody took very much notice of him … a gentle-looking fellow'.[173] MacGarry's memories were of a similarly indifferent art teacher.[174] Yet David Sears remembered him as an 'excellent' teacher who by 'taking their … ideas seriously' won the affection of his pupils.[175] He was disarming in debate, a skilful teacher of imaginative essay writing and possessed of a 'tolerably keen insight into the character of boys, except that he was inclined to see only their good points'.[176] In 1913 an open letter in *An Scoláire* praised William for his patience, for having 'played many parts well' and 'chiselled many lasting works of art'.[177] Certainly the pupils liked him and gave him 'a rousing welcome' on his return from visiting Paris in October 1909.[178]

Mabel Gorman, a pupil at St Ita's, modelled regularly for William and, though she was considerably younger than he, it was rumoured that he became 'deeply attached' to her.[179] William showered her with gifts and they carried out a prolonged written correspondence. Mabel contracted tuberculosis and died while still in her teens. Numerous letters testify to William's attention to her, although it is difficult to see in these anything other than a type of paternal affection or perhaps simply the veneration of young girls so characteristic of the late Victorian and early Edwardian period.[180] Mabel's letters reveal that as she grew to adolescence she was less inclined to spend time at The Hermitage. Her letters and those of her family to William are courteous and affectionate throughout but the content of sWilliam's epistles is unknown, as none have survived. Eileen Byrne, a pupil of Margaret Pearse, also modelled for William.[181]

William's importance, however, lay less in his teaching than in the other areas of his involvement at St Enda's. He was a keen sportsman and would regularly join in the school football and hurling games.[182] His most significant contribution to the life of the school was his promotion of drama. He was involved in every school production, often assuming an acting part.[183] He was a devotee of Dickens, Ibsen and Tolstoy, and his interest in the arts must have contributed to the cultured ambience that Pearse sought to create at The Hermitage; a tone he hoped would be enhanced by the collection of paintings that adorned the school.[184] He produced work for sale in Dublin and London craft shops along with other artists belonging to a small group known as the Irish Art Companions.[185] He criticised Pearse when necessary and would occasionally spend 'hours' arguing with him over some aspect of school business.[186] Ryan recalled that Pearse did 'as he liked' until William 'lisped his fierce word',[187] although Nic Shiubhlaigh felt that William was 'overshadowed' by his brother, agreeing 'with his every decision' largely, she believed, due to their 'having similar views on all subjects'.[188] Ruth Dudley Edwards points out that William's criticisms were valuable because 'made from a position of unquestionable loyalty'.[189] It was William who 'made the young idea wipe its boots on the mat and keep its fork in its left hand and answer all bells promptly. It was he who managed plays and pageants and guided clumsy fingers round circles and curves in the drawing class'.[190]

A yearly plan of teaching work drawn up by William shows that his lessons included: sculpture, design, object drawing, drawing from nature, freehand drawing, geometrical design and casting.[191] He shared Pearse's conviction about the importance of nature and the role of beauty in enhancing the experience of life. Notes he made for a lesson reveal that he believed 'art' could not be taught but pupils could become skilful if they paid keener attention to their surroundings:[192] '... you will help me and yourselves greatly by looking about you when you are out, observe how many petals the dog rose has ... and when you are in the garden looking up at the apples, remember something *more* about them than the taste ...'[193]

William's nationalism was almost entirely cultural.[194] It is undoubtedly true; however, that had William not been executed in 1916 'he would have been unknown to succeeding generations'.[195] His loyalty to both Pearse and St Enda's were sincere, speaking of the probability of an insurgent's death he remarked that 'I should not care. I should die for what I believed. Beyond my work in St Enda's I have no interest in life'.[196]

The third permanent member of staff at St Enda's was Thomas MacDonnell. He had taught Irish at the Connaught College of Irish, Mount Partry and at the Gaelic League's Leinster College of Irish in Dublin.

The assistant, or part-time teaching staff, included Michael Smithwick, a well-known Gaelic League supporter. Smithwick had taught mathematics at Rockwell College, Cashel, where Thomas MacDonagh had been a pupil. J.P. Henry, the principal of the Leinster College of Irish, taught Irish. T.P. O'Nowlan, lecturer in Ancient Classics and Irish at University College Dublin and St Patrick's College, Maynooth and lecturer in Irish at Carysfort Training College, taught Classics.[197] Owen

Lloyd and Vincent O'Brien gave music lessons in harp, violin, piano and singing and were joined in 1910 by Margaret Pearse.[198] Joseph Clarke taught manual instruction. John Glinch, chief accountant with Messrs Geo. Perry & Co. Ltd, Dublin taught commercial subjects. William Carrol taught gymnastics and drill at St Enda's and St Ita's. The tone Pearse wished to engender at St Enda's is touched upon in a letter to Séamas Hampton in July 1908. He wanted to employ Hampton as part-time gymnastics instructor but reminded him that he required someone who was a 'Gael' and knew 'some Irish'.[199]

The following taught on an occasional basis: Agnes O'Farrelly and Eamon O'Neill (Irish language and literature), Eoin MacNeill (Irish History and Archaeology), Mary Hayden (English language and literature), Helena Concannon and C.P Curran (French and German literature), Revd R. O'Daly PhD (Phonetics), Dr Conn Murphy D.Ph (philosophy) and Alphonsus O'Farrelly (physical science).[200] Margaret Pearse was the headmistress of the Junior School assisted by Gertrude Bloomer who later became headmistress of St Ita's. The Junior School initially accepted girls, but this was discontinued in 1909 and Margaret and Miss Bloomer 'joined the staff of Scoil Éanna proper'.[201] There were also a number of medics 'on call' to the school.[202]

In September 1909 Padraig Colum took a part-time post as teacher of English literature and composition to Middle Grade and Matriculation classes.[203] The inclusion of such a well-known cultural nationalist added significantly to the Irish-Ireland tone of the school. Visitors occasionally observed bilingual lessons and both Pearse and Thomas MacDonnell gave sample lessons in October 1909.[204] MacDonagh and MacDonnell left St Enda's during the summer of 1909, the former to study for university examinations.[205] Three new members joined and quickly became 'part of the St Enda's family'.[206] Within a week of their arrival the new masters were participating in school *céilidhes*.[207] Before joining St Enda's in 1910 Frank Nolan, a fluent speaker of Irish, taught classics at Loreto College, St Stephen's Green. He was keenly interested in teaching methodology and in 1911 attended a course in educational science at University College, Dublin. His use of the Direct Method to teach Latin interested the National School inspectors who visited St Enda's in 1910.[208] They also observed Nolan teach geography and mathematics through Irish.[209] Kane left in December 1910 to become an inspector.[210] Also in the summer of 1910, Thomas MacDonagh left to take up a post as lecturer in English at University College, Dublin.[211] In a letter to Gertrude Bloomer, he confessed that he was 'dissatisfied with certain things in the teaching and the staff' but added reassuringly that he had not 'lost faith in St Enda's', indeed, it was 'the best school for boys in Ireland' founded by 'the noblest man'.[212]

Two of the first staff to join Pearse had left the school and he later noted that their days working together had been 'the most spacious in our history'.[213] Eamon O'Toole, who had been the school dean of discipline since 1910, also left at the end of 1912. However, Thomas MacDonnell, who had left the school a year earlier, returned as Junior Resident Master.[214]

Captain Con Colbert (physical drill) joined the school in 1913. Colbert, like MacDonagh and the Pearse brothers, was later executed for his part in the Rising.[215] The appointment of David Houston, professor of zoology at Trinity College and biology at the College of Surgeons, reflected Pearse's conviction of the value of learning by doing. Houston lived very close to The Hermitage where he taught biology. His sons, Cyril and Walter, attended the school and both he and MacDonagh were closely associated with the Irish Theatre.[216] He was nicknamed 'creeping-out' by the boys who enjoyed his penchant for teaching out of doors.

Pearse's wish to employ Gaelic Revival supporters limited his choice of teachers. He struggled, in particular, to find a drill instructor who was not a retired British Army soldier. The financial burden of permanent staff in a school that was founded on antipathy to the Intermediate Programme added to Pearse's difficulties. He knew that in moving to The Hermitage he would lose a significant number of pupils and the loss of fees made it more difficult for him to meet the staff salary.[217] His goddaughter, Sighle Bairéid, recalled that he 'didn't pay the staff, Thomas MacDonagh always had great difficulty in getting money out of him ... even when he was getting married'.[218] Certainly, the frequent changes in staff meant that it was difficult for Pearse to create a stable environment at the school.[219]

A wide range of visiting speakers complimented the succession of teachers. St Enda's would be the new Eamhain Macha and its boys would sit at the feet of the 'heroes and seers and scholars' of early twentieth-century Ireland.[220] Visitors to the school included Douglas Hyde, Countess Markievicz, Roger Casement, Maud Gonne McBride, Eoin MacNeill, Standish O'Grady and Padraig Colum.[221] Pearse wanted the boys to be addressed by those representing the highest 'thought and achievement in any sphere of welcome endeavour'.[222]

When Douglas Hyde addressed the school in October 1909 he told the boys that the eyes of Irish-Ireland were upon St Enda's, that 'the enemies of true national education were watching it with no less interest' and that the school must provide an example for others to follow.[223] He emphasised that the pupils should take pride in their own language, telling them that on a recent visit to England a boy had mocked him for his 'Irish brogue' to which Hyde had replied that, whereas the boy had only one language, he had two: 'I am twice as good a man as you, for you have only one language'.[224] 'That,' he commented, 'was the way to talk to Englishmen. You must stand up to them and give them blow for blow.'[225] Hyde urged the boys to unmake the last two generations of Irish history and return Ireland to an Irish-speaking nation. St Enda's was a true school, unlike the 'West British' colleges which he did not name, although he and his listeners 'knew where they were'.[226] In thanking Hyde, Pearse assured him that he and the boys were 'humble privates' in the 'army that was fighting for Ireland's intellectual independence'.[227]

St Enda's had many such visitors during its first two years. In one day (21 January 1909) for example, three visitors made separate addresses. One of these was Father Landers who became the school chaplain.[228] In February the Hon. William Gibson, accompanied by the mother and aunt of T.P. O'Nowlan, addressed the school.[229] Like Hyde, Gibson advised the boys of the 'philosophical and literary' superiority of the Irish language.[230]

Mary Hayden introduced the boys to *Beowulf* in a 'very animated' lecture entitled 'Anglo-Saxon Literature'.[231] Although they 'liked' the character, they thought him 'a barbarian beside Cúchulainn'.[232] Agnes O'Farrelly also delivered a lecture on 'Early Irish Literature'.[233] Séamus MacManus, a friend of Pearse, told the boys, in May 1909, that 'though young' they were citizens of 'no mean country' and to keep the 'high ideal of duty and honour before them'.[234] The following day, the Lord Abbot of Mount Melleray Abbey, the Rt Revd Maurus Whelan, told the boys that they were the heirs to the monastic tradition of learning that had been broken by the Tudor Dissolution of the Monasteries.[235]

Frequently the lectures given at the school touched upon the issue of language and national sovereignty. In November 1910, Father Fitzgerald, a friend of the Pearse family, gave an illustrated talk entitled 'A Tour around the Orient and Australia'.[236] Speaking about India, he drew their attention to the 'gigantic mistake, from its own point of view' the British had made 'in giving education to the Hindoos' because, he suggested, an educated people cannot be ruled against their will.[237] He pointed also to the Maoris of New Zealand, 'self-governing' and 'retaining their own language'.[238] The previous year a visitor had spoken to the boys during a lecture on 'Geography and How to Study It' of the 'struggle of the Georgians for their language and nationality'.[239]

Pearse and his guests also gave lectures of cultural or academic interest. Helen Laird's first talk, 'Plant Life', was reinforced by the distribution of seeds which, when dampened, expanded or contracted.[240] Pearse gave occasional lectures on the flora and fauna of Ireland.[241] David Huston's talks on zoology were particularly popular and on at least one occasion some of the boys found him 'in high disputation' with Micheál Mac Ruadhraí on the 'momentous theme of vegetable marrows'.[242] He gave two whole-school lectures at St Enda's, speaking to the boys about native plants, the formation of bogs and the various ways in which seeds were carried and scattered. Huston's ability to make his subject inter-esting was such that, on one occasion, a group of boys abandoned their hurling game to listen to a lecture he was giving to a group of science students in the school grounds.

A number of these speakers also visited St Ita's, where Pearse delivered 'rousing addresses' every two weeks.[243] The girls were addressed, for example, upon the 'Social Position of Catholics' and the role of the Irish language in schools. A Father Sherwin, who visited the school in October 1910, told the pupils that the future of the language depended upon Ireland's 'women and girls' although none of the first pupils to enrol at St Ita's were fluent speakers and few knew Irish.[244]

These lectures and talks were an important part of the social and intellectual life of St Enda's. They were usually a pleasant diversion for the boarding pupils and introduced them to personalities from political, academic and artistic communities. Certainly, exposure to personalities such as Hyde and MacNeill helped to create an intellectually stimu-lating environment, a quality attested to by the inspectors who visited the school in 1910. At least one boy, Denis Gwynn, disagreed with the views of these speakers and joined the British Army at the outbreak of the First World War.[245] He evidently decided against the version of history presented at St Enda's, and upon hearing of his decision, Thomas

MacDonagh remarked that it was wholly consistent with the spirit of patriotism Pearse and he had tried to foster in their pupils.[246] Pearse's desire to foster a sense of duty was not simply limited to duty to Ireland. It is worth noting that in the often cited dream of the martyred pupil he wrote of the boy dying for 'some august cause' not necessarily Ireland's.[247]

FOOTBALL AND FOOTLIGHTS

There were three aspects of extra-curricular life at St Enda's: lectures, sport and drama. These pursuits encouraged school spirit and bonds of mutual friendship and responsibility. Extra-curricular activities were particularly important for the boarding pupils, providing them with entertainment and social interaction with children outside the school. Many of these were standard school activities, such as visits to museums in Dublin and the Botanic or Zoological Gardens. As The Hermitage was situated at the foothills of the Dublin Mountains frequent hikes were taken to local scenic spots, such as the Hell Fire Club or Bride's Walk. The pupils visited city art galleries and in March 1909 some boys attended a talk by Pearse at the Metropolitan School of Art.[248]

The Hermitage hosted a number of *céilidhes* and social evenings. These were occasionally attended by the St Ita's girls and their teachers and on 1 November 1910 the boys looked forward to a fancy dress party to be held at that 'distant Tir na nOg, St Ita's'.[249] The girls made their own costumes and prizes were awarded for the most original. Many dressed as Queen Medb and other female figures from Celtic mythology. Dancing lasted until midnight although the St Enda's School diarist wistfully recorded that 'we could have danced till morning'.[250] Frank Connolly, a past pupil of St Enda's, later joined the school dancing class: 'A thing he had persistently refused to do' while a pupil.[251] Social inter-action between the schools was not uncommon.[252] One week before the fancy dress party the entire school and its staff had visited St Enda's. They toured the grounds; some of the younger girls climbed to the top of Emmet's Fort, and evening tea was followed by a *ceilidhe* and songs.

Interaction between the schools reflects Pearse's concern that the pupils learn the skills of social interaction, ensure familial contact and provide the type of enjoyable outlet so important for pupils of that age group. While it is tempting to think of these occasions in terms of A.S. Neill's observation that dance served 'as an excellent outlet for unconscious sex interest' in young adults, it is unlikely that such a motive can be attributed to Pearse.[253] Yet these gatherings continued to be a feature of life at The Hermitage during the lifetime of St Ita's, and relatives of boys in St Enda's continued to be involved in dramatic productions and occasional social functions after St Ita's closed. The editors of *An Scoláire* commented upon these occasions in characteristic manner. In 1913, for example, St Ita's was described as 'guarded by an iceberg dame, one Bloomer ... and lesser dames about whom the least [sic] said – the better'. The same article gently teased one of the boys, who, unable to give up their company, walked a group of girls to the end of the school driveway where they departed for St Ita's.[254]

After sport, drama was the most important extra-curricular activity at St Enda's. Pearse and William invested considerable time and effort in productions at the school and regularly brought the boys to the fledgling Abbey Theatre.[255] The nationalist rhetoric of Thomas MacDonagh's *When the Dawn is Come*, which they saw in October 1909, sent the 'younger boys' home 'yearning for rifles'.[256] The following month the pupils were again at the Abbey, this time to see *The Flame on the Heath* and *The Turn of the Road*, both produced by the Theatre of Ireland.[257]

In February 1909, Pearse informed the boys that the feast day of St Enda (21 March) would be celebrated by the performance of two plays at the school – Douglas Hyde's *An Naomh ar Iarraidh (The Lost Saint)* and *The Coming of Fionn*, written by Standish O'Grady. O'Grady's scholarship was renowned. W.B. Yeats considered that his *History of Ireland: The Heroic Period* (1878) had heralded the beginning of the Literary Revival. Preparations for the production began on 6 February and senior boys were awarded the leading parts.[258] Later that month the school attended a production of Lady Gregory's *Kincora*, a re-telling of the Battle of Clontarf.

Preparations for the St Enda's Day plays took up a great deal of time and William, assisted by his nephew Alfred McGloughlin, oversaw much of the work. Standish O'Grady attended the first full dress rehearsal and gave the boys 'many useful hints on speaking and acting'.[259]

The plays, performed between 21 and 22 March, were praised in *An Claidheamh Soluis* for capturing 'the spirit of the ancient heroes'.[260] According to the paper, St Enda's was providing its pupils with a chance to become familiar with myths and legends they would not usually have been exposed to, otherwise they would have known only 'Tom Brown', 'Dick Turpin' and 'Crusoe'.[261] 'We want more colleges like St Enda's,' the review concluded, 'to bring back the Fianna and give courage and hope to young Ireland'.[262] Sinn Féin recorded that 'the performance of *An Naomh ar Iarraidh* gave one the impression that the play could never be better produced'.[263] Press coverage such as this provided St Enda's with valuable publicity. The plays were staged in the school gymnasium and more than 100 people attended on the evening of 20 March.[264] The following night, a 'brilliant literary audience' included Eoin MacNeill, W.B. Yeats, D.P. Moran and Padraig Colum. Countess Markievicz and Standish O'Grady attended the final performance on 22 March 22nd.[265]

In April the boys performed Hyde's play again as part of the Dublin Feis, and older pupils continued to visit the Abbey Theatre. Encouraged by the success of the St Enda's Day performances Pearse proposed an end-of-term pageant based on the boyhood deeds of Cúchulainn.[266] The pageant was performed in the school grounds on 22 June 1909 before an audience of 500 guests although Pearse recorded that the staff were unhappy with the event.[267] While acknowledging that good reviews appeared in *Sinn Féin*, the *Irish Nation* and *An Claidheamh Soluis*, he admitted to having a 'grievance against the reporters for leaving before the speeches'.[268] They were 'only speeches at a school fete', he conceded, but in a remark that revealed his exaggerated opinion of the work being done at the school, fumed that 'they contained things that were better worth recording than all the news that was in the newspapers the next day'.[269]

Pearse planned to stage his own play *Iosagán* and Padraig Colum's *The Destruction of the Hostel* at Christmas 1909. *Iosagán* focused upon innocence and redemption. Pearse wrote it for performance 'in a particular place and by particular players'.[270] Set among the common people of rural Ireland and infused with Catholic piety, the piece was staged at the school on St Brigit's Day 1910. 'Whatever beauty it had,' Pearse wrote the following December, was due to 'a beauty altogether of interpretation, to the young actors who played it'. The boys performed both plays in the Abbey Theatre in April 1912. During Easter Week of 1911 they performed Pearse's *Passion Play*. Maire Nic Shiubhlaigh recalled that the performance created 'a minor sensation' and praised it as 'probably the first really serious piece of gaelic dramatic writing produced' in Dublin.[271] Pearse had hoped to stage the play every three years but it was not staged again after 1916. The following June, his *An Rí (The King)* was performed in the open-air thaetre at The Hermitage and again at the Abbey Theatre in 1914. These performances made considerable demands on Pearse and his staff but did much to enhance the reputation of St Enda's. In particular they attracted free publicity. They were also accomplished performances. Marie Nic Shuibhlaigh recalled that the results achieved 'were remarkable' and that 'the acting was of a high standard'.[272]

While Pearse could justifiably take pride in the achievements of St Enda's upon the Dublin stage, sport remained the most important extra-curricular activity at the school. In keeping with its spirit, hurling, Gaelic football and handball were the core games.[273] Pearse's preference was for hurling, a game he believed to be authentically Gaelic.[274] From September to December 1910 the boys 'practised hurling morning, noon and evening'.[275] He believed that football was 'against Scoil Éanna tradition' but happily supported it.[276]

The Gaelic Athletic Association, founded in 1884, was doing much to spread an interest in games and many League members and sympathisers were involved as players and organisers in local branches. At the beginning of the century Gaelic games were associated with nationalism and existed in opposition to the Irish Athletic Association, a Protestant organisation that had promoted a ban on playing sport on Sundays. Dublin children of the period typically followed the fortunes of English football and cricket teams, trading cigarette cards of their sporting heroes. The promotion of hurling and Gaelic football at St Enda's, therefore, reinforced the school's difference and emphasised its nationalist aspirations.

Whenever possible, English was dispensed with at games as Pearse recognised that they represented an informal learning opportunity. Instruction in drill and gymnastics was also given through Irish. The school Prospectus of 1909 listed hurling, football, handball, drill and gymnastics. Irish dancing was offered as part of the 'ordinary curriculum' and chess was encouraged as an indoor game.[277] When the school opened, the programme of games was impeded by the pupils' lack of familiarity with them, many having previously played rugby, soccer or cricket.[278] The initially modest enrolment at Cullenswood House made it difficult for Pearse to organise teams capable of competing with other schools.[279] Access to local playing fields was not secured until January 1908. For much of the first year, school games were played between the pupils and the first competitive fixture did not take place until June 1909. A resounding and important victory for St Enda's over the local St Kevin's School gave the boys confidence and signalled their sporting worth to other schools.[280] The first competitive football match took place in October 1909 against St Lawrence O'Toole Club. St Enda's lost but avenged their defeat the following month. This victory was important for the boys because 'O'Tooles' were the leaders of the Minor School League. In 1910 the junior hurling team, captained by Frank Burke, were ranked top of the Dublin Schools Juvenile League. Burke maintained a lifelong interest in Gaelic games and was playing football at Croke Park on Bloody Sunday 1920 when the British Irregulars (Black and Tans) killed twelve people.[281]

St Enda's boys played fixtures almost weekly between September and December 1910. Some of these games were significant victories and helped create those teams that would be so successful in the following year.[282] In 1910, the under XVIII football team reached the School's Championship Final, a remarkable achievement for a small school barely two years old. They were heavily defeated but Pearse knew that to reach that stage of the competition had been 'itself an achievement'.[283]

In April 1910 the senior hurling team played local rivals 'Crokes' for the League Championship. St Enda's were awarded the match when their opponents were disqualified for entering over-aged players. In the same year, the senior hurlers lost the Senior Hurling Final, but St Enda's won the Schools Junior Hurley League, having been granted a walkover.[284] Typically these games took place at Croydon or Phoenix Park, Dublin, on Sunday mornings and were occasions when the boys would find common cause supporting their school, thereby fostering 'that spirit of comradeship and of interest in the school, cherished at Scoil Éanna'.[285] St Enda's greatest sporting victories took place in 1911 when the Junior Hurling Team won the Dublin Schools' Championship for the second time and the Junior Football Team won the Schools' Football Championship. These were considerable achievements for a school that was founded only three years previously. St Enda's was making a name for itself as an exponent of a new type of school rooted in strident cultural nationalism.

It was, perhaps, a surprise therefore when, in 1913, a senior boy called James Rowan proposed that cricket be allowed as a summer sport.[286] Rowan argued that while some believed it an 'English sport', the sons of 'modern patriots' also played the game.[287] Rowan was not hostile to the ethos of St Enda's. A poem he submitted to *An Scoláire* called on Ireland's boyhood to 'Avenge ... your slaughtered saints, whose bones / lie scattered on the Wexford plains so cold'.[288] His proposal provoked a hostile reaction from another senior boy, D.P. O'Connor, who argued that the cricket-playing sons of modern patriots were not necessarily themselves patriotic.[289] Echoing Pearse's reasoning, he opposed cricket not because it was English, but because it was not Irish and called on the school to oppose the 'pernicious proposal'.[290] Rowan's suggestion provoked an animated debate. Tennis was suggested as a compromise but the issue was eventually referred to Pearse, who turned to the pupil council which determined that Rowan's proposal should be voted on by the school body. A vigorous campaign ensued with the boys being canvassed by supporters of both positions and finally the proposal was defeated by vote.

The event illustrates a number of important features about life at St Enda's. The boys were free to propose additions to the life of the school, even if those additions were quite at odds with its ethos and culture. Indeed, the school atmosphere was such that Rowan, at any rate, felt no inhibition in making such a proposal. The event further shows that the pupils' magazine operated as a vehicle for the free dissemination of opinion and a forum for debate. A body existed that could arbitrate on contentious issues, an atmosphere existed in which such debates could take place, a structure was in place that allowed the boys to democratically exercise choice and by doing so learn the responsibilities demanded of citizenship. Freedom was accorded to the pupil body to propose, debate and decide matters they deemed to be important. Thus St Enda's represented what Pearse sometimes referred to as, a 'child-republic'. While it would be disingenuous to suggest that Pearse habitually exposed the boys to views profoundly contrary to his own, it is nonetheless true that, along with Bertrand Russell, he instinctively believed that 'one of the most important things to teach in the educational establishments of a democracy is the power of weighing up argument, and an open mind which is prepared in advance to accept whichever side appears the more reasonable'.[291] Pearse's neutrality in the cricket debate is all the more interesting when we recall that in 1905 he had proposed that foreign sports that competed with Irish games should be prohibited in schools.[292]

THE INSPECTORS

Pearse wrote that he established his school in order to bring about a revolution in Irish education. St Enda's was to serve as an exemplary model of defiance and change but it also had to operate as an ordinary school. Therefore, good standards of teaching and learning were important. We have already noted the views of past pupils in this respect, but in May 1910 St Enda's, then still at Cullenswood House, was visited by three intermediate school inspectors.[293]

Intermediate oral examinations had been instituted in 1909 and Pearse believed this allowed St Enda's to avail of the Board's grants without any sacrifice 'of principles' as use of the Direct Method would be officially recognised.[294] The Report affords an invaluable insight into the workings of the school and crucially provides a detailed portrait of Pearse's as a practising teacher.

Table 3. Enrolments and Age Profile at St Enda's School, May 1910

Age	10–13	13–19	Over 19
Day Pupils	22	14	0
Boarding Pupils	7	28	1
Total	29	42	1

Source: *Report of the Commissioners of Intermediate Education for the Year 1910*, London, 1911.

Seventy-two boys were enrolled at the time of the inspection. (Table 3.)[295] The school library contained 2,000 volumes of 'Irish, English and general literature'.[296] Lessons began at 9.30 a.m. and ended at 3.30 p.m. with one break of forty-five minutes. Evening study began at 5.30 p.m. and ended at

7.30 p.m. with a period from 9 p.m. to 9.30 p.m. for senior boys. The Report noted that discipline was 'bad' in 'some classes' although no record of transgressions or penalties was kept and instances of corporal punishment, which staff were at liberty to administer, were reported to the headmaster.[297] While the school Prospectus of 1909 described hurling, football and handball as the 'chief' games the inspectors' noted that they were compulsory.[298] The observation that sports were organised by a 'committee of the boys' is unhelpful because we cannot know if this merely means that freely elected committees were organising compulsory activities.[299]

All teachers present on the day of the inspection were observed. Dr Doody taught Greek to Senior and Middle Grade, which comprised three pupils. One of these was Denis Gwynn, although he is not named. The inspector, E. Ensor, concluded that Doody knew 'little Greek prose and nothing of Greek verse'[300] but was impressed by Denis Gwynn describing him as 'probably the best Greek student that I have seen' noting that he had learned many Odes from Horace for pleasure 'no repetition being enforced in the school'.[301] The sole student in Middle Grade was 'below Pass standard'.[302]

Ensor also observed Doody's Latin lessons. He described the Senior Grade lesson as 'worthless' and 'ridiculous' and Dr Doody's ignorance of Latin as 'even more glaring than in Greek'.[303] His written corrections were 'a farce' and the pupil's work 'full of ridiculous errors'.[304] Ensor's criticisms cannot be accounted for. Doody may have been an ineffective teacher, but he was the only staff member to possess a PhD, so it must be assumed that his knowledge of Greek and Latin was hardly as poor as the inspector recorded. Indeed, Ensor's remarks are out of tune with the general tone of the Report.

Thomas MacDonagh's teaching of French was generally good, although the inspector, C.E. Wright, found that the boys were unable to answer questions concerning grammar.[305] He also recorded that translation in Junior Grade was 'very poor'.[306] MacDonagh also taught Senior and Junior Grade English and Ensor noted that because the boys had translated parts of Lamb's *Essays* into both Irish and French they had acquired a better knowledge of the text. He also recorded that composition was 'unusually strong', due largely, he thought, to the availability of such a well-stocked school library.[307]

MacDonagh's teaching of Latin to Junior Grade was careful and competent but he was less effective in teaching mathematics. The two boys to whom he taught geometry produced untidy and careless work.[308] In his Preparatory Grade class only one boy out of sixteen could offer the correct definition of a right-angle and the inspector submitted that if the 'nonsense' offered by this group of boys was the result of bilingual teaching, it would be better 'not to waste time on geometry'.[309] Ensor's views are in striking contrast to the recollections of past pupils and associates of MacDonagh already outlined.

Michael Smithwick's teaching was uneven although Michael McDermott, who had only recently joined the staff in his first post, was found to be an impressive addition.[310] Richard Feely's algebra class received an unfavourable report [311] although Thomas McDonnell's work was praised as 'satisfactory' in 'every department'.[312]

Initially, Margaret Pearse taught French to Preparatory Grade and when the Junior School closed Pearse assumed this duty. Inspector C.E. Wright, who observed Pearse's lesson pointed to the lack of whole-class teaching which, he believed, resulted in boys being examined individually and then being 'left alone' for the remainder of the lesson, a practice he noted as 'widespread in Irish schools'.[313] Pearse was also observed teaching Irish and English by Joseph O'Neill who wrote glowingly of the rapidity with which the boys were becoming fluent in the former. He recorded that Pearse was meticulous in his corrections, thorough in his teaching and employed the Direct Method with impressive results. He noted in particular that Pearse began a lesson by drawing the figure of a horse on the blackboard which stimulated conversation – a method Pearse had observed in Belgium. 'In general,' O'Neill concluded, the work done by Pearse in Irish was 'very effective'.[314] C.E. Wright observed Pearse teaching Preparatory Grade algebra 'almost' entirely through Irish. He noted that Pearse began the class by reading aloud the correct answers to the homework set the previous day. He did this very slowly. Wright assumed this to be because some boys may not have understood him; 'several' he recorded, 'betrayed uncertainty'.[315] Only eleven of the sixteen boys had attempted the homework in its entirety and Wright found the work in this class 'careless', 'untidy' and 'dirty'.[316] The inspector set an exercise for the boys but only one finished it correctly, although four boys claimed to have done so. Wright found that on three occasions that pupils falsely claimed to have completed work correctly and suggested that teaching through Irish was a possible cause of confusion in the class.

Ensor observed Pearse teaching English, history and geography. The English class comprised only six pupils and the lesson on Goldsmith was 'somewhat' over their heads.[317] He gave history lessons in English and geography through Irish although both were taught through Irish in the Preparatory Grade, presumably to facilitate the acquisition of Irish at the earliest possible stage. Ensor recorded that Pearse had 'excellent manner and method'; praise indeed from the usually less than generous inspector.[318]

The school debating society was the first the inspectors had encountered.[319] Ensor held that the talks given by visiting speakers, the school library and various societies contributed to the high standards in the school and concluded that the 'experiment of a bilingual school' was a success due to the 'intelligence and originality of its masters'.[320] Though the Report pointed to some significant weaknesses in the teaching at St Enda's, it was generally very favourable, an outcome that must have pleased Pearse greatly.

FUNDING ST ENDA'S

In 1910 The Hermitage was available at an annual rent of £300 or could be bought for £6,000. Pearse was anxious to secure the property and confident that 'all friends of education in Ireland' would financially support the school, but his confidence was misplaced.[321]

Initially Pearse had hoped to buy the building by raising £10,000 to cover purchase and furnishing. Failing this he hoped to lease the premises with the option of later purchase and therefore decided to form a company to oversee the project.[322] He had initially hoped to raise the money by donations which he would later repay. The donors would remain free from any financial responsibilities, their donation not representing an investment. Failing to secure sufficient funding through donations however, he was later forced to sell shares in the schools. While many invested and waived any claim to share in any future profits, others did not and disgruntled creditors later caused considerable difficulties. To begin with, Pearse only raised sufficient funds to meet the initial deposit on the premises but not to begin alterations.

The conditions of the lease meant that a number of modifications were required. The proprietor, William Woodbyrne, insisted that boarding pupils should not have access to the house between rising and bedtime and that only limited admittance be granted to day pupils. The house was to be used as a family residence only, with a limited number of rooms made available for school activities. Pearse, therefore, undertook to construct classrooms and a dormitory adjoining the building. The dormitory was never built and with Woodbyrne's permission, a number of rooms at the top of the house were converted for the purpose.

Pearse was to assume tenancy on 1 July 1910 but by the end of June he was still trying to raise funds to allow him begin building work. By mid-July he had installed the most essential furnishings. The school opened as planned, on 11 September, while Cullenswood House became home to St Ita's. Because almost half the pupil body did not make the move to Rathfarnham, Pearse suffered a significant loss of revenue. The Hermitage was on the outskirts of Dublin, a considerable distance from Ranelagh.[323] Sighle Bairéid recalled that: 'It was a ridiculous thing to have moved … he thought that the people from Ranelagh and all those places would … cycle out to Rathfarnham. There were no facilities by way of buses or even trains … that's where he made the mistake, if he had stayed in Ranelagh and expanded the school there, it would have been a huge success.'[324]

Séan Sheridan, who attended St Enda's in 1917, incorrectly recalled that there was a tramline 'to the gates' of The Hermitage. Indeed, in 1910 the estate would have been considered quite isolated.[325] Pearse persevered, convinced of the importance of his venture. An announcement in *The Irish Times* on 3 September 1910 reminded readers of the school's 'distinctly Irish complexion' and emphasised its new, 'more suitable premises'.[326] The smaller enrolment at The Hermitage suggested that Pearse could not depend upon the loyalty of the St Enda's parents, and a meeting of those who had subscribed to the school was called on 3 December 1910 so that he might formalise his relationship with them and discuss ways of raising further capital. It was decided that he would have executive control of the schools; bear sole financial responsibility; that an easier system of subscription be set up and that school patrons be sought. These should form a consultative committee which would audit the school accounts, receive a quarterly report from Pearse (now 'Director') and submit an annual progress report. Pearse submitted that St Enda's needed £1,500 immediately to allow him continue building work and a memorandum to this effect was circulated in January 1911.

Pearse was only able to meet part of the initial building cost. The patron scheme failed to raise sufficient funds and the consultative committee proved ineffectual. At the suggestion of George Gavan Duffy, Pearse decided to form a limited company.[327] Duffy suggested appointing a collector of subscriptions (shares). In October 1911 Pearse explained the scheme to Joseph Dolan, a principle benefactor of the school. He would establish a limited liability company and a network of collectors organised from amongst supporters of the school would sell shares in St Enda's at £1. Dolan accepted Pearse's invitation to become a director of the school and Pearse also approached Alex Wilson, Mary Hayden, Eoin MacNeill and Douglas Hyde.[328] In October he wrote to Gertrude Bloomer, the headmistress of St Ita's, explaining the proposed limited company. It was, he admitted, 'the one hope of placing the financial affairs of the College on a sound financial basis'.[329] He arranged a meeting with Bloomer to draw up a balance sheet for St Ita's but confessed that he was 'full of anxiety as to the immediate future'.[330]

While neither of the schools was making a loss, Pearse was hard pressed by debts incurred by the building work at The Hermitage. Other creditors were also pressing for payment. In October 1919, for example, Clery's & Co. of Dublin, threatened to resort to their solicitors for the satisfaction of unpaid bills. They wrote again in March 1911 to say that their 'collector' would call to St Enda's to collect monies he had undertaken to pay on the ninth of that month. A letter later that month expresses surprise that Pearse had not paid as promised, adding that they 'would regret any unpleasantness which would arise in the collection of the a/c but we cannot wait any longer for payment'.[331] In the same month, the Dublin publishing house Gill & Sons, which supplied St Enda's with school texts, threatened legal action to recoup unsettled accounts. Between March and September 1911 the company wrote to Pearse on at least nine occasions seeking full or part payment of outstanding debt. On three occasions they threatened to refer the matter to their solicitor. Yet they were prepared to be patient and justifiably claimed in September 1911 that Pearse had treated them 'very badly and for no other reason than' that they had 'been too lenient'.[332]

Pearse was forced to approach friends and supporters for payment for shares in advance of their issue. He was anxious to convince a wide range of supporters to become directors in the new company, but by November 1911 had only persuaded Stephen Barret (Bairéid), Joseph

Dolan, Alex Wilson and Michael Smithwick. Many of those he hoped would be actively supportive declined to become involved and sales of shares were slow.[333] Other supporters were more forthcoming. The editor of *An Claidheamh Soluis*, Stiofán Bairéid, for example, bought seven shares in the company. In January 1912, Seán T. O'Ceallaigh accepted the job as collector of shares but by this time the debts of the schools stood at £2,666 while only £200 had been raised by share sales.[334] On 27 January 1912 the directors met and decided that it was not viable to continue the company unless £500 was raised. The situation of St Ita's was perilous. By May, Pearse was unable to meet salaries and wrote to Mary Maguire (later Colum) that there was 'not a single penny in the treasury of St Ita's' and he 'daren't draw on the all too scanty resources of St Enda's'.[335] The following month he told Gertrude Bloomer that the finances of St Ita's had reached a 'desperate stage'.[336] A number of creditors were pressing for payment and Boland's Flour Mills had served a writ on him for the amount of £37.[337] As early as March 1910, seven months before St Enda's was to leave Cullenswood House, the company wrote to him complaining that the school account was 'so long overdue that it had come under the special notice of the Board' and requested that the amount be 'reduced substantially by the end of this month'. Six weeks later the company wrote again demanding 'an immediate settlement of the balance to the end of March last'. The following month they wrote again, saying that while they appreciated the payment of £10, they must have £25 'by next Tuesday if the account [was] to continue'. Pearse's personal income was insignificant and he was aware that if his difficulties became public knowledge, suppliers would decline further credit. Parents, staff and pupils would become unsettled. Pearse and Bloomer took out a joint personal loan in order to pay off the most pressing debts.

At the end of June, Pearse wrote to Alex Wilson, estimating expenditure to date of approximately £5,000. He explained that 'no statement of the revenue and expenditure of St Ita's is at present available' but that Louise Gavan Duffy had offered to lease the school for £180 per year for three years and was prepared to pay down £360 in advance.[338] She had also offered to accept sole financial responsibility for the venture. Wilson believed that Pearse had underestimated the expenditure by approximately £3,000 and suggested that the costs were closer to £8,000. He advised that unless £3,000 could be raised it would not be possible for the schools to open in the autumn.[339]

Pearse faced a financial crisis. If he accepted Gavan Duffy's proposal it would allow him to clear St Ita's debts and concentrate upon St Enda's, which was now meeting its costs. It had assets of £650 including unpaid fees (£250) and monies owed by the Department of Intermediate Education (£250).[340] The school's income for the year 1911–12 was £2,550 (see Table 4).

Table 4. Statement of income and expenditure of St Enda's College for the year ending 1912

	£	s	d
Fees	2,200	0	4
Grazing rents	82	0	0
Sale of Vegetables	45	12	7
Sale of Livestock	22	10	10
Grants from Intermediate	0	0	0
Board and Dept. of Agr.	200	0	0

Source: Ms 5051, Pearse Papers, NLI.

Pearse's problem, therefore, remained the outstanding debts incurred in the building works at The Hermitage and the ongoing running expenses of St Ita's. The directors remained unconvinced of the viability of the schools and in the summer of 1913 the company went into liquidation. Pearse proposed buying back Scoil Éanna Ltd from the liquidator while agreeing with the creditors that he would pay them 2s in every pound on condition that they not press for further payment until 31 August 1913, by which time he expected to have secured fees for the new school year. A donation of £300 from Alex Wilson allowed him to initiate the re-purchase of the company. By August, Gertrude Bloomer had resigned as headmistress of St Ita's. She was owed £170 in unpaid salary and expenses. She explained that she could not sustain any further loss and Pearse conceded that she could not be expected to.[341] The loan from Wilson and other donations allowed him to reopen the school and he was now free from the pressure of creditors until August 1914.

In February 1914, he departed for America on a fundraising tour. The trip was organised by Bulmer Hobson, who swore Pearse into the Irish Republican Brotherhood (IRB) before his departure.[342] In America he met Joseph McGarrity, who organised his itinerary and introduced him to ex-patriots who might be of assistance.[343] Pearse's American audiences, however, were more interested in the activity of the Volunteers than in St Enda's. He addressed gatherings in Boston, Philadelphia, New York and Springfield, Massachusetts. While insisting upon the importance of his work at The Hermitage he couched it in terms he knew his audience would relish: 'Our work is radical: it strikes at the root of Anglicisation ... the whole experiment of Irishising education in Ireland must stand or fall with St Enda's'.[344] On 19 April he addressed a crowd of 2,500 at Celtic Park, New York, at what was officially designated 'St Enda's Field Day.'[345] Pearse was in constant communication with The Hermitage, sending regular notes for William to read to the pupils. He left America on 7 May 1914 having raised $3,000, far short of the $10,000 he had hoped for.[346] This would allow him to satisfy some of the most pressing creditors and to reopen the school in September, beyond that, the future was uncertain. Pearse returned 'somewhat richer in purse and much richer in memories'.[347]

During the summer of 1914 he was occupied with work both within the Irish Republican Brotherhood and at The Hermitage. He had managed to avoid closure, but, as in America, the public were becoming more interested in Pearse's nationalist oratory than his educational endeavours.[348] His time was increasingly taken up by the Volunteers and the internal battle between the Redmonites and Separatists.[349] Writing to Joseph McGarrity in September 1914, he admitted that there were fewer boys than in previous years, possibly due to his 'political opinions', which were 'looked upon as too extreme and dangerous' and made parents 'nervous'.[350] He also pointed out that the economic inflation caused by the war meant that there was less money available for private schooling.[351] His personal liabilities at the end of 1914 were almost £6,000. Gertrude Bloomer was still owed £152 but there was 'no money available to reduce any of the liabilities of St Enda's or St Ita's' and the struggle to keep the former open was 'harder than ever'.[352] Pearse understood his position and his assessment was realistic. St Enda's was 'losing every year' but his 'instinct and honour cried out against' closing the school.[353] Again, to do so would remove the only asset upon which he might secure future funds.[354] Yet his assertion that he had 'done the right thing in keeping on for the past two and a half years' is questionable.[355] Many creditors were exasperated. A note from Boland's Mills was not untypical, referring to an offer to begin repaying his debt by 2s in each pound it stated: 'The position appears to be that your friends will provide 2/– in the £ but that you yourself will undertake nothing. Looking to our experience of you, we submit that such a proposition on your part goes beyond all reason. We have nothing to add.'[356]

Pearse reassured Gertrude Bloomer that if he were able to return to America for six months in the autumn, he could raise enough money to clear his debts. Given his work within the IRB at this time, the rapidly changing political climate and the perilous position of the schools, he cannot have believed this to be a realistic course.

Upon returning from America, Pearse found that he faced an income tax demand of £150 on 'profits of trade, etc'.[357] He was furious and argued that as the school was losing 'about £200' annually and that as he had 'no other source of income of any sort' he could not be liable for income tax. He could not afford the cost of legal expenses to prove this and called the demand 'grotesque', adding that he was 'obviously a pauper'.[358] In 1941 Alfred Dennis recalled visiting The Hermitage one evening and finding Pearse's study in darkness 'because he had not enough money to pay the bill'.[359]

The school year opened in September 1915 against the backdrop of an unusual event. The owner of The Hermitage, William Woodbyrne, had died in 1913. Since then, Pearse had corresponded with Woodbyrne's solicitor, Sir John R. O'Connell. In September 1915, the Lord Chancellor had spoken to O'Connell of Pearse being in a 'very dangerous position'.[360] Pearse presumed this was a reference to his political, rather than financial activities. O'Connell had consulted with J.C. Meredith, a Redmondite, who had been removed from the Executive of the Volunteers. Following this conversation, O'Connell issued a writ against Pearse for £288 representing the rent for one year on The Hermitage. Usually Pearse paid rent in two instalments, he had been late on occasion, but always met the expense in full. Clearly he could not meet the demand and was convinced that it represented a plot to discredit him. He turned again to Joseph McGarrity, who had already donated £800 to the school.[361] Failure to pay would 'smash St Enda's' and 'impair, most seriously if not fatally' Pearse's 'public influence and utility'.[362] If he could not pay the demand by 8 September, St Enda's would close and he would be declared bankrupt. 'I am down and out,' he conceded, 'my fall now will discredit the whole cause'.[363]

Joseph McGarrity lodged £300 and the crisis was averted. Pearse wrote to thank him and added 'we have a bigger school than last year ... I am full of hope'.[364] In fact, there were only thirty boys enrolled at St Enda's in 1915–16. The attendance register for drawing classes dated 1 August shows that in William Pearse's second year Junior art class there were only seven pupils, there were five boys in the Middle Grade class and two in the senior class.[365] Irregular pupil attendance reflects the atmosphere of uncertainty that must have prevailed at at this time. A pupil named William Collins, for example, attended school for only one week in September 1915 and two days in January 1916, while another, Cecil Bertha-Hill, did not return to school after 25 November 1915.[366] We do not know why some boys left St Enda's, but in September 1915 a Volunteer military-type drill took place in the school grounds that included shooting competitions and a demonstration of field manoeuvres by Cumann na mBan. The change of emphasis from Cúchulainn pageants to an event such as this could not have gone unnoticed by parents.[367]

Upon death, Pearse's gross debts were reckoned at £2,075.[368] The amount available to be divided among creditors was £140. The debt remained to the Pearse family. Writing to Eamonn De Valera in October 1941, Margaret Pearse explained that while she was experiencing difficulties meeting 'the rates' on The Hermitage, he could be assured she would do so in future, adding that she was 'nearly clear of the school debts'.[369] While the school may have incurred debts after 1916, this letter, written a quarter of a century after Pearse's death, reveals the legacy of debt left to St Enda's.

The move to Rathfarnham caused serious financial difficulties and the decision to lease a property, much of which Pearse was prohibited from using and in need of significant structural alterations, seems rash. He had not realised the benefits of the Cullenswood House location. Moving to The Hermitage resulted in an unsustainable loss of pupil numbers and income and without the generosity of friends such as McGarrity and Dolan the school could not have remained open. While the move had obvious advantages in terms of space and grounds it is difficult to understand Pearse's unwillingness to consider its impact upon enrolments. Obviously he hoped that Irish-Ireland would send their children or at least contribute financially. Certainly, he exhausted every possibility of raising funds. In this he suffered some ill luck.

His tour of America in the spring of 1914, for example, coincided with that of others who were canvassing for funds for the nationalist movement in Ireland. But Pearse usually persisted in the face of difficulties. A press article written around the time of his execution referred to his ability to 'ignore complications'.[370] Alfred Dennis recalled that 'in his military career ... he did not burden his brain with the complex routing of military detail'.[371] This aspect of Pearse's behaviour is important in understanding his personality; indeed his own description is the most accurate: 'There are some adventures so perilous that no one would ever go into them except with the gay laughing irresponsibility of a boy ... one does one's deed without thinking ... such an adventure, I think, has been St Enda's.'[372]

Such cavalier rhetoric would have found little sympathy with Pearse's creditors and his inability to meet their demands lessens the achievement of St Enda's. The school never recovered from the move to The Hermitage and he was not prepared to allow St Enda's develop in its own time and at its own pace. Pearse seems never to have considered a future St Enda's in which he was not involved. As a consequence he was not prepared to look beyond the immediate project. There is no indication that he ever considered relocating the school, even when enrolments were unsustainably low in the two years before 1916. Pearse was unable, rather than unwilling, to meet his debts and his genuine attempts to establish financial equilibrium always omitted the possibility of relocation; the one radical move that might have reinvigorated St Enda's and laid a secure foundation for what might have been a successful school.

NATIONALISM AT ST ENDA'S

Pearse was always a separatist. At his trial in 1916 he explained how, as a child, he had prayed that he might, one day, play some part in winning Irish independence.[373] Repeatedly he called for the connection with Britain to be broken. While in America in 1914 he proclaimed that 'we, and ours, the inheritors of this idea [separatism] have been at age-long war with one of the most powerful Empires on the Earth'.[374] His commitment was publicly articulated in his orations on Emmet and Tone and the articles published in *Irish Freedom* between June 1913 and January 1914.[375] He had always insisted that education, correctly understood, had to do with the making of good men and women. A good citizen was, by definition, a good Irish man or woman, in other words, a patriot. His reasoning was simple: 'You cannot make an Irish boy a good Englishman or a good Frenchman'.[376]

Because schooling was concerned with helping to make good Irishmen and women it followed that it should have an Irish inflexion. Pearse was committed to the creation of a 'Gaelic' school of the type 'not known or dreamt of in Ireland since the Flight of the Earls'.[377] As early as 1909 he wrote about the pupil body of St Enda's belonging to families 'out of which nations are made'.[378] The school should be 'worthy' of Ireland and be the 'most Irish of Irish schools', it must recreate the 'knightly' tradition of the macradh of Eamhain Macha, 'dead at the Ford ... in the beauty of their boyhood'.[379] Pearse repeatedly drew attention to the notion of sacrifice and duty, citing the credo of Cúchulainn: 'I care not though I were to live but one day and one night, if only my fame and my deeds live after me' and Colmcille's fabled aspiration that if he should die, let it be from 'the excess of the love I bear the Gael'.[380]

The figure of Colmcille does not present any serious moral ambiguity. Pearse was interested in the monastic communities as a model and metaphor for his work at St Enda's, rather than in the life of the saint. Cúchulainn, however, presents a more uncertain model and later Emmet and Tone represented more contentious figures still. For Pearse, figures such as St Enda of Aran, Colmcille and Cúchulainn exemplified desirable virtues; a belief reinforced by the dramatic productions at St Enda's. A review of *The Coming of Fionn* in March 1909, noted that the 'heroic spirit had entered into' the pupils' 'hearts and minds'.[381] The 'spirit' of the evening was not 'something isolated', rather 'a natural continuation of that and many other evenings when the spirit of Fionn and his heroic comrades had been instilled into their minds'.[382] Fionn and the other figures had become 'part of the mental life' of the teachers and pupils at St Enda's.[383] Padraig Colum noted that 'the art was here not rootless, it came out of belief, work and aspiration'.[384] These commentators were not sentimentalists but experienced critics. Their response reflected Pearse's own hope that by ending the school year with a performance of the Cúchulainn pageant he would send the boys home with the hero's 'knightly image ... in their hearts'.[385]

Central to the type of nationalism expounded at St Enda's was the notion of sacrifice. As articulated by Pearse, the concept of sacrifice meant the voluntary relinquishing of personal desires or possessions for a greater good. Since coming to adulthood he had devoted himself to causes and campaigns. He had consciously made personal sacrifices and, as he matured, the concept acquired a profound personal significance. Indeed, W.B. Yeats described him as 'a dangerous man' who suffered 'the vertigo of self-sacrifice'.[386] He emphasised the notion of sacrifice in the character of Cúchulainn and the lives of the saints and the theme was a recurring one in school productions. Pearse repeatedly held the figure of Cúchulainn before the boys as an exemplar and it served as the school emblem. Ryan recalled that, every day, after religious instruction, Pearse would continue telling the Cúchulainn saga and that the mythical hero eventually became an important if invisible member of the staff.[387] His influence permeated the life of the school, as did that of the Fianna. Boys were encouraged to be truthful as Pearse held before them the boast of the Fianna that 'falsehood was never imparted to us'.[388] Clearly Cúchulainn was an apposite model – youthful, loyal, courageous, a master hurler and a figure that was embraced by the revivalist movement as iconically Celtic.[389]

Sacrifice is at the heart of the Cúchulainn myth; his death represented loyalty to his clan and defiance of their foe and Pearse had transformed the figure into a near reality. In playing the character on stage, Frank Dowling perfectly captured Pearse's own 'high ideal of the child Cúchulainn, shy and modest with a boy's aloofness, grave earnestness' and 'irresponsible gaiety'.[390] The significance of the figure and the tradition of sacrifice that it represented, led Pearse to wonder if the 'inspiration and tradition' he tried to give the pupils would be articulated in some, more significant, manner: 'Sometimes I wonder whether, if ever I need them for any great service, they will rally, as many of them have promised to do'.[391]

The concept of sacrifice was most strikingly detailed in Pearse's play An Rí (The King).[392] Its setting is an ancient monastery. The Abbot explains to a group of boys that the King is suffering successive defeats at the hands of his enemies because he has 'forsaken God'.[393] The Regent admits his unworthiness and calls upon the Abbot to lead his army but the Abbot and his monks decline, citing their own sinfulness. Finally, one of the boys, Giolla na Naomh (The Servant of the Saints), is elected to lead the armies as he is 'the most innocent' among them.[394] The boy dies in the ensuing battle but the King's enemies are defeated. The relationship between sacrifice and freedom is central to the piece but so too is the notion that this freedom could be achieved only by the death of the innocent: 'Do not keen this child,' the Abbot says, finally, 'for he hath purchased freedom for his people' rather 'let shouts of exultation be raised'.[395] Hence the death of the child (and the innocent) redeems the people.

Desmond Ryan recalled that 'Robert Emmet's memory haunted Pearse … he seemed to see him tapping his cane along the Rathfarnham roads, rambling through the Hermitage grounds'.[396] At The Hermitage, Pearse was surrounded by the physical history of Emmet. Unlike Cúchulainn, Emmet represented a historic, rather than mythical, example of sacrifice. The 'white sacrifice' of the saints coupled with the 'red sacrifice' of figures such as Emmet and Tone would inspire the 'new heroic age', indeed the boys could have no 'finer inspiration'.[397] This concept of abandon, of joyfully sacrificing life in pursuit of a cause, became central to Pearse's thinking on nationalism. At St Enda's he tried to 'keep before' the pupils 'the image of Fionn during his battles – careless and laughing … Emmet when he mounted the scaffold in Thomas Street, smiling'.[398] The 'exhilaration' of fighting had 'gone out of Ireland' and only by sacrifice like that of Giolla or Emmet could it be rekindled.[399]

In May 1913 Pearse told a number of the boys about a dream he had had some four years previously.[400] A pupil of the school stood on a gibbet before a large 'indifferent' crowd awaiting execution for 'some august cause'.[401] The boy was 'proud' and 'joyous' and Pearse recalled feeling the scene to be more poignant because the crowd regarded the boy as foolish, rather than as a 'martyr … doing his duty'.[402] Another pupil stepped forward, embraced the first boy and tied a kerchief about his eyes, an act of 'brotherly loyalty' that went some way to compensate for the indifference of the crowd.[403] When Pearse recounted the dream 'at a school meeting' some days later, the boys wondered which of them had been its subject and Pearse recollected that he did not think he had given the secret away.[404] He told the group that he could not wish for them 'a happier destiny than to die thus in defence of some true thing' and recorded that 'they did not seem in any way surprised, for it fitted in with all we had been teaching them at St Enda's'.[405]

This dream and the manner in which it was recounted are striking – and troubling – for a number of reasons. Pearse recollected that it was the 'only really vivid dream' he had had since childhood.[406] It is note-worthy that the cause for which the boy dies is not specific; the 'great service' remains vague.[407] The subject of the dream, however, is very vivid. Pearse recalls noticing the hair on his forehead stirred by the wind, as he had often seen it when the boy was hurling.[408] He could not recollect if he 'gave away' the secret of which boy had been the subject of the dream, in other words he may have indirectly indentified him. Finally, Pearse recorded that the boys 'did not seem' surprised at his revelation as it corresponded naturally with the spirit of the school. Indeed, 'what we had been teaching them at St Enda's' was that death for a 'true' cause was a noble act and citing J.M. Barrie's Peter Pan he mused that 'to die will be a very big adventure'.[409] The St Enda's boys were 'always allowed … to feel that no one can finely live who hoards life too jealously'.[410] Because Pearse had had the dream four years previously, that is, around 1909, it belongs not to the period at The Hermitage but to the beginnings of St Enda's. Pearse's dream is deeply troubling to a modern reader. Even the excesses of propaganda aimed at British schoolboys in this pre-war period pale by comparison. What is more remarkable is that there is no record of it other than Pearse's own account and it is not unreasonably to assume that his pupils simply omitted it from their memoirs in the hope that their headmaster's telling would, in time, be forgotten.

The School Prospectus of 1908–9 explained that the school staff 'directs earnest efforts towards the awakening of a spirit of patriotism and the formation of a sense of civic and social duty'.[411] The Irish version of the same Prospectus, however, stated that the school would attempt to foster in pupils the desire to 'spend their lives working zealously for their fatherland and, if necessary, to die for it'.[412] Even those who were enrolled at St Ita's at Cullenswood House, after the boys had moved to The Hermitage, were 'full of eagerness to attempt something … if need be, to suffer something' and this, Pearse held, was 'the right spirit in which to begin making history'.[413]

The effect of this attempt to awaken the 'spirit of patriotism' was evidenced in the pages of An Scoláire.[414] While the magazine is notably free of overt militancy, an anonymous poem of May 1913 includes: 'Now Fenian proud, lift high your head / 'Twas vows and now 'tis blows instead / For Vengence, for our Martyred Dead /For Freedom and for Ireland.'[415]

Another issue contained an anonymous article that promised 'on the day (Ireland) unsheathes the sword laughingly … grimly her foes will be scattered'.[416] Unquestionably the notion of separatism and militancy hung upon the air at St Enda's and was reinforced by the convictions of its staff, four of whom were later executed for their part in the Rising, representing almost one-third of the total executions. The insurgent Con Colbert taught drill at St Enda's while Tom Clarke gave instruction in code signalling. A past pupil recalled that he and other boys assisted Mr Slattery, the chemistry teacher, in making explosives: 'I used to be sent downtown to Bolieau & Boyd to get all the right chemicals. We ground them up with pestle and mortar and he mixed them and weighed them … I used to test them occasionally on the grounds of the school.'[417]

Donagh MacDonagh recalled Con Colbert, Sean Heuston and Liam Mellows coming to the school 'to train the boys … and into the ranks of the Fianna went many who later fought for Ireland both in 1916 and later'.[418] St Enda's hosted occasional military displays by the Irish Citizen Army.[419] A letter from Eugene Cronin to his aunt in New York, noted that 'we are learning how to drill here, how to use a rifle and practising skirmishing'.[420] While this form of drill and display were not unusual at the period they had a distinctly nationalist attitude at The Hermitage. Pearse kept a small museum at the school dedicated to the history of rebellion in Ireland. The collection included: a cannonball from the Siege of Limerick, pikes from the 1798 Rising, items belonging to the 'Wild Geese', a sword once belonging to Lord Edward Fitzgerald, the death mask of Emmet and the block upon which the patriot reputedly stood at his execution.[421] These were reminders of glorious but distant resistance. The present age, Pearse lamented, had compromised with 'respectability'.[422] Men were concerned with being 'dapper' rather than strong.[423] What was needed again was strength because the 'reign of force' had not passed.[424]

This belief lay at the heart of Pearse's thinking. By 1913 his writing was replete with the vocabulary of conflict: 'battle', 'soldier', 'enemy', the need for 'every child to be an efficient soldier, efficient to fight, when need is, his own, his peoples', and the world's battles, spiritual and temporal'.[425] The work of St Enda's, in this respect, was the preparation of its boys to fight the battles in which they chose to engage but given the spirit fostered there it was probable some would choose the cause of Irish separatism.

BOY SOLDIERS?

Denis Gwynn condemned Pearse for using the school 'as the instrument to provide himself with the nucleus of a band of young politicians who would follow him to the scaffold'.[426] If this was so, Pearse was very much disappointed. Less than twenty past pupils were involved in the Rising and the number may have been as low as twelve. Four, at least, had joined the Irish Republican Brotherhood before Pearse and all were surely also influenced by factors other than their former headmaster. Countless insurgents of all ages, who had no contact with St Enda's, or Pearse, were influenced by the spirit of the times.[427] Yet some boys 'came very much under the influence of Pearse'.[428] Joseph Sweeney received his entire post-primary schooling at St Enda's and recorded that he and most of the older boys 'were committed completely to the idea of separation, the old Wolfe Tone definition of freedom – to break the connection with England'. Upon finishing school, Sweeney began studying engineering at University College, Dublin while living at The Hermitage, where Pearse swore him into the IRB in 1915. In the months leading up to Easter 1916, Sweeney ran messages for Pearse, mostly to other leading IRB members and occasionally transported munitions. On Easter Monday morning 'E' Company 4th Battalion, or 'Pearse's Own', a group of past pupils, assembled outside the Yellow House pub in Rathfarnham before making their way into Dublin to join the insurrection.[429]

The number of past pupils who took part in the Rising is uncertain. Mrs Margaret Pearse insisted that it was no more than 'sixteen or seventeen'.[430] Frank Fahy, speaking in 1918, thought the number to be seventeen.[431] Eight of those who joined Pearse at the General Post Office were later interned at Frongoch Prison Camp in Wales, they were: Eamon Bulfin, Joseph Sweeney, Frank Burke, Desmond Ryan, John Kilgallon, Fintan Murphy, Brian Joyce (Seoighe) and Joseph O'Connor. Micheál Mac Ruadhraí and Patrick Donnelly, another employee at The Hermitage, were also imprisoned at Frongoch. David Sears, who was a senior boy at St Enda's from 1914–1916, may also have taken part in the Rising.[432] Le Roux held that only twelve 'ex-pupils' participated.[433] In a letter penned from the General Post Office to Mrs Pearse, on Wednesday 26 April, Pearse assured his mother that the 'St Enda's boys' who had been on duty with him, were 'all in excellent spirits'.[434] On 1 May, these were taken to Richmond Barracks, as was William Pearse. Patrick was taken to Arbour Hill and believed that 'E' Company 4th Battalion was also there. In his final letter to his mother on 3rd May he expressed his hope that 'the St Enda's boys (would) be safe'.[435]

Le Roux insisted that Pearse knew that teaching the boys the 'history of the Conquest' he would make them 'rebels, felons, martial spirits, resolute and devoted men who should rapidly win rank as patriots'.[436] Clearly, Pearse taught the boys that duty to country, in whatever form it was articulated, was the responsibility of the good citizen; citizenship and Irishness became interchangeable and the example of nationalists, such as Emmet, served to help pupils identify the characteristics of patriotic behaviour. Pearse had seen his pupils 'moved inexpressibly' by the story of Emmet or Anne Devlin and had found it 'legitimate' to make use of that reaction for 'educational purposes'.[437]

Clearly this is problematic. It is difficult to see what 'educational purposes' Pearse is referring to. He may have wanted the people of Ireland to be rebels, but unlike the boys of St Enda's, they were not a captive audience at The Hermitage.[438] Yet if Denis Gwynn was correct in condemning Pearse for leading boys into the insurrection, the small number that took part suggests that, in reality, his influence was limited. The St Enda's boys who joined Pearse at the General Post Office were past pupils and made choices, not as schoolboys, but as adults, and Pearse cannot justifiably be held accountable for those choices, even if the part played by him in their education cannot be wholly disregarded.

Indeed, the issue of influence is not uncomplicated. The Minutes of the Commissioners of National Education, 27 July 1916, recorded that allegations had been made that the Rising was fermented 'by the careful instilling of revolutionary principles in the teaching of many … primary schools'.[439] This was not an uncommon view. The leaders of the Rising had surely 'found a soldiery apt to carry out their behests; brought up on a sort of gospel of hate … in too many of the National Schools' indeed 'several prominent instigators were teachers'.[440] But the Report of the Commissioners, published the following year, attested that 'no evidence has been adduced which would warrant the conclusion that seditious teaching in the National Schools exists to any appreciable extent'.[441] Finally, the notion that Pearse took advantage of the times to ferment militant separatism in his pupils should be tempered by the knowledge that 'it wasn't like 1916 in 1916'; participants acted within a context that has been refined by history and out of motives which, ultimately, we cannot know.[442]

Pearse's work at St Enda's might be described as pedagogically sound and politically suspect. This is not to judge his politics, rather, to condemn his using the school to promulgate them because once the syllabus becomes politicised, its content is jeopardised and vulnerable. For example, Pearse characterised the school system of the period as a vast 'machine', 'shaping and moulding', grinding 'night and day' and 'devoid of understanding, of sympathy, or imagination' but this is ungenerous and untrue.[443] His criticism regarding the lack of emphasis upon Irish history in schools at the beginning of the twentieth century is interesting when considered in the light of Giroux's argument that conservative educational ideology is concerned to establish 'a society without a history of protest'.[444] However, this does not excuse his presenting history in an uncritical and anecdotal way.[445] Unquestionably he presented specific historic incidents as 'liberating remembrance.'[446] In effect, he understood the teaching of history as a 'resource for reconstructing an ethics of politics and possibility from the conflicts ... and stories of those who chose to resist and reverse the mechanisms of ... domination'.[447] Pearse's use of history is troubling and finds a place within Giroux's advocacy of 'radical historical traditions', offering models of 'responsible defiance and action'.[448] He offered subversive historical narratives that were intended to become 'part of the dynamic of renewal and transformation central to the politics and pedagogy of democracy'.[449] Importantly, Giroux qualifies this position by insisting that 'defiance' be 'responsible'. The term, however, remains undefined and therefore allows a multitude of interpretations, although any understanding that promotes the use of history as a 'resource', which provides the educator with 'stories', that can 'serve' as 'subversive historical discourses' is ultimately unsatisfactory and should be rejected.[450] While incidents in the past may help us better understand contemporary political struggles we must be cautious in seeking solutions that worked in a quite different historic moment.[451] For historians, learning about the past should supersede learning from it. The past, in other words, has an inherent integrity.

Yet, for Pearse, pedagogy was always political. This is not to admit, however, that St Enda's did not provide a generous and pedagogically sound educational experience. The inspectors who visited in 1910 were evidently impressed with what they witnessed. At the heart of Pearse's project was the desire to provide a new model, a different type of schooling. Certainly its outward form was similar to most other schools,

Dublin was not ready for a radical educational experiment in 1908, yet Pearse's very prescient insight was that old forms could act as vehicles for new ideas. Hence, St Enda's, while dressed in the trappings of a standard intermediate school, sought to invert the whole political order by demonstrating that schooling could be employed as a cultural antidote. Pearse was among the first to realise and articulate this notion several decades before the advent of better-known radical educators and theorists.

Notes:

[1] 'By Way of Comment', *An Macaomh*, Vol. I, No. 1, Midsummer 1909.

[2] The inspectors who visited the school in May 1910, noted the dimensions of the rooms as follows: classroom I. 21ft by 21ft, classroom II. 11ft 15ins by 12ft, classroom III. 15ft by 12ft, classroom IV. 25ft by 11ft (used as a science room), classroom V. 30ft by 18ft (used as an art room). See 'Report on St Enda's College' *The Report of the Commissioners of Intermediate Education 1910*.

[3] Parents of pupils attending St Enda's had suggested the establishment of a sister-school. When the school moved to The Hermitage, St Ita's (Scoil Íde) was opened in Cullenswood House.

[4] *Ibid.*

[5] MS 21094 Pearse Papers, NLI.

[6] Patrick Pearse to Canon Arthur Ryan, 2 May 1910, in Séamas O'Buachalla (ed.), *The Letters of P.H. Pearse*.

[7] The Celtic Society (founded 1840) – an amateur archaeology and philology association, merged with the Irish Archaeological Society in 1845. The Ossianic Society was founded in 1853 to preserve manuscripts from the Fionn mythological cycle.

[8] 'By Way of Comment', *An Macaomh*, Vol. I, No. 2, Christmas 1909.

[9] *Ibid.* Robert Emmet (1778–1803); leader of the United Irishmen rebellion of 1803, later executed.

[10] *Ibid.*

[11]   See p. Cooke, 'P.H. Pearse: Victorian Gael', in Higgins and Ui Chollatain (ed.) *The Life and Afterlife of P.H. Pearse.*

[12]   *Ibid.*

[13]   Emmet's Fort was constructed quite a distance from the main house
and part of the structure incorporates the estate boundary wall. Follies
were built on the grounds of many estates in Ireland in the eighteenth
and nineteenth centuries in keeping with the fashion for the mock
medieval and castellated buildings. See James Howley, *The Follies and
Garden Buildings of Ireland*, p. 40 & p. 105. Mary Emily McGloughlin,
Pearse's step-sister, was later granted accommodation in this building
when abandoned by her husband Alfred McGloughlin while Mrs Pearse
and her two daughters occupied The Hermitage.

[14]   The attraction of these was such that Pearse mentioned them in a
letter to a family friend: 'There are woods, a little lake, an old hermitage,
a cromlech, an *ogham* stone, on the land.' Patrick Pearse to Canon Arthur
Ryan, 2 May 1910, Séamas O'Buachalla (ed.), *The Letters of P.H. Pearse.*

[15]   Writing to Eoin McNeill, Pearse pointed to the unique nature of
his planned school, explaining that there was 'no Irish High School in
Ireland' nor 'High School(s) for Catholic boys conducted by laymen
in Ireland.' Patrick Pearse to Eoin McNeill 24 February 1908, Séamas
O'Buachalla (ed.), *The Letters of P.H. Pearse.*

[16]   *Ibid.*

[17]   Séamas O'Buachalla (ed.), *The Letters of P.H. Pearse*, p. 126, source
uncited. Ruth Dudley Edwards correctly points out that in planning
St Enda's Pearse was anxious to avoid any 'odour of anti-clericalism – of
which he was so often accused', *Patrick Pearse: The Triumph of Failure*,
p. 114. However, such accusations came in the wake of the Dr Hickey
controversy in 1909. See below.

[18]   See Milo MacGarry, 'Memories of Scoil Éanna', *Capuchin Annual*
(1930), p. 36.

[19]   Pádraig O'Conaire, interviewed by Proinsias O'Conluain, in 'This
Man Kept a School', RTÉ April 1979. Pearse studied French at University
College between 1899 and 1901, where he took his Degree with
Honours. Professor Edouard Cadie, recommended him as 'an earnest

student who always did his work to my satisfaction …' MS 211050, Pearse Papers, NLI. Pearse was not listed as teaching arithmetic in the *Prospectus* of 1908–09, see *The Prospectus of Scoil Éanna (1909)* although he taught algebra to Preparatory Grade in 1909–1910.

[20] Brian Seoighe, interviewed by Proinsias O'Conluain, 'This Man Kept a School', RTÉ April 1979. Ryan records that his literary tastes were orthodox: Shakespeare, Milton, Wordsworth, Yeats and Chesterton. See 'The Man Called Pearse', *The Complete Works of P.H. Pearse, St Enda's and its Founder*, Desmond Ryan (ed.), pp. 232–3.

[21] Milo MacGarry, Memories of Scoil Éanna, *Capuchin Annual* (1930), p. 33.

[22] *Ibid.*, p. 36. Edgar Holt recorded that Pearse possessed a lock of Napoleons hair (see *Protest in Arms*, p. 50), while Ruth Dudley Edwards considered that he was possessed of a 'Napoleonic complex' (see *Patrick Pearse, the Triumph of Failure*, p. 342).

[23] *Ibid.* See also *An Cosantoir*, Vol. V, No. 10, October 1945. Margaret Pearse also taught French.

[24] This is not to imply that Pearse was employed on a full-time basis by the NUI.

[25] Pádraig O'Conaire, interviewed by Proinsias O'Conluain, 'This Man Kept a School', RTÉ, April 1979.

[26] *Ibid.*

[27] Brian Seogihe, interviewed by Proinsias O'Conluain, 'This Man Kept a School', RTÉ, April 1979.

[28] 'Todd Andrews talks to Padraig O Raghallaigh', RTÉ November 1974, Andrews began attending the school in September 1910 when it re-located to The Hermitage. See *An Macaomh*, Vol. II, No. 3, Christmas 1910, p. 74.

[29] C.S. Andrews, *Dublin Made Me*, p. 44.

[30] Mary Catherine Gunning, journalist and critic, relocated to America with Padraic Colum whom she married in 1912.

[31] 'The Singer', *The Complete Works of P.H. Pearse, Plays, Poems, Stories.*

[32] Mary Colum, *Life and the Dream*, p. 152.

[33] See Griffith and O'Grady, (ed.), *Curious Journey, An Oral History of Ireland's Unfinished Revolution*, p. 37 (hereafter *Curious Journey*).

[34] See 'Coilin', *P.H. Pearse, a Sketch of His Life*, pp. 6–7. The name employed by the anonymous author belongs to the central character in Pearse's play 'The Keening Woman'. See *The Collected Works of Padraig H. Pearse, Plays, Stories, Poems*, p. 193.

[35] See 'The Man Called Pearse', in Desmond Ryan (ed.), *The Complete Works of Padraig H. Pearse, St Enda's and its Founder*, p. 214. In 1906, Pearse published a sample timetable for the teaching of Irish but added: 'one or two unprescribed texts should be read in class…', *'The Secondary School: Thoughts and Suggestions, An Claidheamh Soluis*, 13 January 1906. p. 6.

[36] *Ibid.*

[37] *Ibid.*

[38] *Ibid.*, p. 215.

[39] *Ibid.* Patrick and Margaret Pearse had taught catechism at Westland Row church. See Senator Margaret M. Pearse, 'Patrick and Willie Pearse', *Capuchin Annual*, May 1943. These times changed over the years. The Inspectors' Report of 1910, for example, records study as ending at 9 p.m.

[40] *Ibid.*

[41] Sean Dowling, interviewed by Proinsias O'Conluain, 'This Man Kept a School', RTÉ, April 1979. In the Intermediate Examinations of 1909 Dowling won an Exhibition in the Modern Literary course (Junior Grade), qualified for a Prize in the Science course and won a Composition Prize in Irish. See *An Macaomh*, Vol. II, No. 3, Christmas 1910, p. 75, entry for 17 September.

[42] See 'The Man Called Pearse', in Desmond Ryan (ed.), *The Complete Works of P.H. Pearse, St Enda's and its Founder*, p. 177 & p. 179.

[43] *Ibid.*, p. 179.

[44] See Mary Colum, *Life and the Dream*, p. 152.

[45] See Maire Nic Shiubhlaigh *The Splendid Years*, Edward Kenny (ed.), p. 148. A letter from Mr R.J. McKennan, who lived in the building

adjoining Cullenswood House, throws light upon this remark. Having
contacted Pearse on previous occasions, he complained, in a letter to
Pearse in March 1910, of the 'want of control exercised by you over the
lads attending your school'. Boys entering his garden 'again and again'
to retrieve footballs aggrieved McKennan in particular. One pupil,
having been confronted by Mrs McKennan reacted 'with language
and a demeanour' which her husband preferred 'not to describe'.
McKennan's greenhouse had been damaged and he complained of
the boys climbing the boundary wall 'and their conduct while there,
making offensive, impertinent and unprovoked remarks to my wife and
children.' He reminded Pearse that he had complained 'of the noise' on
past occasions, concluding that it had been 'beyond anything that should
be possible in a civilised country'. MS 21053 R.J. McKennan to Patrick
Pearse, 8 March 1910, Pearse Papers, NLI. It is possible that Pearse forsaw
this difficulty. In August 1908 he had received an estimate for proposed
work on a ball alley at Cullenswood House which would include raising
a new brick wall 'on top of the old' wall for a sum of five pounds. MS
21052 Estimate from J&R Thompson Ltd, Builders & Contractors,
13 August 1908, Pearse Papers, NLI.

[46]   See Desmond Ryan, 'St Enda's – Fifty Years After', *University Review*,
Jubilee Issue, Vol. II. 3 &4, p. 84.

[47]   Marie Nic Shiubhlaigh, *The Splendid Years*, p. 148.

[48]   These entries were drafts of end of year reports to be sent to parents
and guardians. Draft Reports, MS 21086 Pearse Papers, NLI, *passim*.

[59]   *Ibid*.

[50]   James Kilcullen, 'Appreciation, Headmaster of St Enda's', *Eire-Ireland*,
Summer, 1962.

[51]   *Ibid*.

[52]   See Milo MacGarry, 'Memories of Scoil Éanna', *Capuchin Annual*
(1930), p. 35. Pearse's physical stature was considerable. Brian Seoighe
remembered him as 'over six feet' and 'broad'; Brian Seoighe, interviewed
by Proinsias O'Conluain, 'This Man Kept a School', RTÉ, April 1979.
Mary Colum recalled that he was 'tall' and 'somewhat heavily built', Mary
Colum, *Life and the Dream*, p. 152. All sources agree that he habitually
dressed in black or dark clothing.

[53] See Louis N. Le Roux, *Patrick H. Pearse*, Desmond Ryan (trans.), p. 97.

[54] Griffith and O'Grady (eds), *Curious Journey*, recollection of Joseph Sweeney, p. 37.

[55] In his essay, 'Patrick Pearse: The Evolution of a Revolutionary' Thornley describes Pearse's version of Irish history as 'scarcely the view of modern historical scholarship'. While it demands much of Pearse's grasp of history when viewed through the demands of scholarship some half century later, it seems certain that his reading and exposition of Irish history was unscholarly. See David Thornley, 'Patrick Pearse: The Evolution of a Revolutionary' in F.X. Martin (ed.), *Leaders and Men of the Easter Rising: Dublin 1916*.

[56] Griffith and O'Grady (ed.), *Curious Journey*, recollection of Joseph Sweeney, p. 38. Michael Hayes recorded that Pearse had 'close associations' with University College, St Stephens Green, where between 1900–02 he gave a course in Irish History 'of a popular sort'. See Michael Hayes, 'Thomas MacDonagh and the Rising' in F.X. Martin (ed.), *The Easter Rising 1916 and University College Dublin*, p. 38.

[57] He later became the youngest member of the first Dáil.

[58] See Mairéad Ní Ghacháin (eds), *Lúise Gabhánach Ní Dhufaigh agus Scoil Bhríde*, p. 3

[59] Stephen Gywnn, *Experiences of a Literary Man*, p. 284.

[60] See Desmond Ryan, 'St Enda's – Fifty Years After', *University Review* (1958), Vol. III. 3&4 Double Issue, p. 83.

[61] See Nancy Cardozo, *Maud Gonne, Lucky Eyes and a High Heart*, p. 274. See also Janis and Richard Londraville (eds), *Too Long A Sacrifice: The Letters of Maud Gonne and John Quinn*, p. 149. See also Anna Mac Bride (ed.), *The Gonne – Yeats Letters 1893-1938, Always Your Friend*, letter 304, pp. 352–3.

[62] See *St Enda's Roll Book 1908-9*, 1 August 1908, Pearse Museum. See also Michael Tierney, *Eoin MacNeill, Scholar and Man of Action 1867-1945*, p. 119.

[63] See *The Complete Works of P.H. Pearse, St Enda's and its Founder, P.H. Pearse, the Story of a Success*, p. 83. See also Donagh MacDonagh, 'Thomas MacDonagh,' *An Cosantoir*, Vol. V, No. 10, October 1945, p. 527.

[64] Sean Dowling, interviewed by Proinsias O'Conluain, 'This Man Kept a School', RTÉ April 1979. See also Martin Daly *Memories of the Dead*, p.18: 'It must not be forgotten that some of the most distinguished people of Ireland trusted their boys to St Enda's methods [*sic*] we shall hear much more yet of St Enda's boys in the life of the country and it will be found that the very idealism of their training under Pearse has put an edge on their minds that will leave a mark … on the coming generation.'

[65] See *Prospectus of Scoil Éanna, (1909)*. Séan Sheridan, who enrolled at St Enda's in 1917, recollected that 'the fees of forty pounds per year was quite a substantial amount in those days…', see Séan Sheridan, *What if the Dream Come True?*, p. 40. (James Kelly, Dublin, n.d.). Pearse customarily tried to tailor fees to suit the financial situation of those wishing to send a child to St Enda's.

[66] Séamas O'Buachalla, interviewed by Proinsias O'Conluain, 'This Man Kept a School', RTÉ April, 1979.

[67] See Maire Nic Shiubhlaigh, *The Splendid Years*, p. 147.

[68] 'The Man Called Pearse', in Desmond Ryan (ed.) *The Complete Works of P.H. Pearse, St Enda's and its Founder*, p. 242.

[69] Desmond Ryan, 'St Enda's – Fifty Years After', see *University Review*, 1958 Vol. II. 3 & 4 Double Issue, p. 85. See also F.X. Martin (ed.), *Leaders and Men of the Easter Rising: Dublin 1916*, p. 129.

[70] Draft Reports, MS 21086 Pearse Papers NLI.

[71] See 'The Man Called Pearse', in Desmond Ryan (ed.), *The Complete Works of P.H. Pearse, St Enda's and its Founder*, p. 149. Joseph Sweeney recalled that if you wanted any privileges from Pearse you had to ask in Irish, adding that 'you hadn't a hope of getting anywhere if you asked in English'. See Griffith & O'Grady, *Curious Journey*, pp. 37–8.

[72] See *An Macaomh*, Vol. II, No. 2, Christmas 1910, p. 57, entry for 19 September.

[73] Pearse built the cottage on a parcel of land overlooking Loch Eileabrach that he had purchased for £10 in 1905. The building was not complete until 1909 and he sold it to his sister Margaret for the same sum in 1912 to help offset some of the debt incurred by St Enda's. He continued to use it as a holiday retreat until 1916. The cottage was

later extensively damaged by the British Army. Margaret Pearse sued for compensation in 1923 and was awarded £200 in 1925. MS 21059 Reddin & Reddin Solicitors to Margaret Pearse, 16 August 1923, Pearse Papers, NLI.

[74] See W.B. Yeats, *Autobiographies* (Macmillan London 1955). Mac Ruaidhrí was the school gardener and 'handy-man'. While evidently the *Gaeltacht* boys were at ease with Mac Ruaidhrí, others found him intimidating. Alfred Dennis recalled that he and his companions 'dreaded … Micheál Mac Ruaidhrí of the Lodge'. See Alfred Dennis, 'A Memory of P.H. Pearse', *Capuchin Annual*, December 1941, p. 260. He lived in the gate lodge at The Hermitage, to which he returned with his wife in January 1912 without having told anyone of his plans to marry. Mac Ruaidhrí was a combatant in the Easter Rising. See also Desmond Ryan, *The Popes Green Island*, p. 297.

[75] 'Education in the West of Ireland', *Guth na Bliadhna*, 11 April 1905.

[76] See Mary Hayden Diaries, 2 January 1903, NLI (original emphasis).

[77] See 'Association of Pupils with Administration', *The Prospectus of Scoil Éanna, (1909)*: 'the pupils are as far as possible actively associated with the administration of the school.'

[78] Patrick Pearse, 'The Story of a Success', in Desmond Ryan (ed.), *Collected Works of Padraig H. Pearse, St Enda's and its Founder*, p. 32.

[79] See *An Macaomh*, Vol. I, No. 1, Midsummer 1909, p. 80, entry for 11 September.

[80] *Ibid.*, p. 84.

[81] *An Macaomh*, Vol. II, No. 3, Christmas 1910, p. 76.

[82] *An Macaomh*, Vol. II, No. 2, May 1913, p. 48. See also, Patrick Pearse to Mrs Burke (n.d.) MS 21086 Pearse Papers, NLI.

[83] *Ibid.*

[84] See Desmond Ryan (ed.), *Collected Works of Padraig H. Pearse, St Enda's and its Founder*, V – A Retrospect, p. 100.

[85] See Louis N. Le Roux, *Patrick H. Pearse*, Desmond Ryan (trans.), p. 149.

[86] See Desmond Ryan, 'St Enda's – Fifty Years After', *University Review*,

Vol. III. 3 & 4, Double Issue (1958), p. 84. Pearse and the pupils often employed the term 'republic' to refer to St Enda's. See for example *An Macaomh*, Vol. II, No. 3, Christmas 1910, pp. 74–5, entries for 13 and 22 September.

[87] Séan Sheridan, *What if the Dream Come True?*, p. 42.

[88] See for example: J.G. Hardy, *The Public School Phenomenon, 1597-1977*, V. Ogilvie, *The English Public School, Thomas Arnold on Education: A Selection of his Writings.* Thomas Arnold (1795–1842) headmaster of Rugby school, England.

[89] See Griffith and O'Grady (eds.), *Curious Journey*, recollection of Joseph Sweeney, p. 37.

[90] *Ibid.*

[91] In this respect the observations of Stephen Gwynn, who sent two sons to St Enda's are noteworthy. Contrasting the English public boarding school with similar institutions in Ireland he believed the latter to be superior because the boys were more closely supervised. Supervision made 'serious bullying impossible … the idea that it is good for a boy to be knocked about without stint is foreign to Irish ideas.' See Stephen Gwynn, 'Irish Education and Irish Character', *Irish Books and Irish People*, p. 72.

[92] See C.S. Andrews, *Dublin Made Me*, p. 43.

[93] See Maire Nic Shiubhlaigh, *The Splendid Years*, p. 148.

[94] 'From the word go I loathed the place … except one thing, I loved the grounds,' 'Todd Andrews talks to Padraig O Raghallaigh', RTÉ, November 1974.

[95] See C.S. Andrews, *Dublin Made Me*, p. 44.

[96] Padraig Óg Ó'Conaire, interviewed by Proinsias O'Conluain, 'This Man Kept a School', RTÉ, April 1979. See also Milo MacGarry, 'Memories of Scoil Éanna', *Capuchin Annual* (1930), p. 35.

[97] On the legacy of Pearse regarding corporal punishment see Andree Sheehy Skeffington, *Skeff, the Life of Owen Sheehy Skeffington 1909-1970*, p. 179.

[98] See 'The Formation of Character', *An Claidheamh Soluis*, 26 January 1907, p. 7

[99] Kenneth Reddin, 'A Man Called Pearse', *Studies*, June 1943. It is not impossible that some boys may have gone to Pearse to admit transgression rather than face the self-policing antics of peers such as Sweeney.

[100] See Alfred Dennis, 'A Memory of P.H. Pearse', *Capuchin Annual*, December 1941, p. 261.

[101] See 'Coilin', *P.H. Pearse, a Sketch of His Life*, p. 10.

[102] Scrapbook of press cuttings (n.a. / n.d.) MS 32695 / 1 (3) NLI.

[103] See 'The Man Called Pearse', in Desmond Ryan (ed.) *The Complete Works of P.H. Pearse, St Enda's and its Founder*, p. 177.

[104] *Ibid.* 'Coilin' claimed that Pearse's ability to win the confidence of his pupils lay in his 'natural gifts of sympathy and understanding.' See *P.H. Pearse, a Sketch of His Life*, p. 4

[105] See Griffith and O'Grady (eds.), *Curious Journey*, recollection of Joseph Sweeney, p. 37.

[106] In a letter to a parent Pearse explained that he was not aware of the extent of their sons homesickness as he did 'not read the letters which the boys send home, although it is done in most schools ... ', see Patrick Pearse to Michael Cronin, 23 May 1914, Pearse Collection, Pearse Museum, KGA.

[107] Máire Bruagh (Nic Shuibhlaigh), niece of Mary MacSweeney, interviewed by author. MacSweeney opened St Ita's in September 1916.

[108] See *The Prospectus of Scoil Éanna, (1909)*, 'Selection of Course'.

[109] *Ibid.*

[110] 'The Tyranny of Programmes', *An Claidheamh Soluis*, 27 March 1909, p. 9. See also 'Irish Education', *Irish Freedom*, March 1913. This feature of the school was recorded in the Report of the Inspectors 1910. See Report on St Enda's College 'English', *The Report of the Commissioners of Intermediate Education for the Year 1910*.

[111] See *An Macaomh*, Vol. II, No. 2, May 1913, 'Of Studies', p. 48.

[112] *The Prospectus of Scoil Éanna (1909)*, 'Selection of Course'.

[113] Patrick Pearse to William Bulfin, 14 September 1909, in Séamas O'Buachalla (ed.), *The Letters of P.H. Pearse*. Eamon Bulfin had been enrolled at St Enda's from its establishment. He was a school-captain and combatant in the GPO during Easter Week. The praise heaped upon the Programme is possibly due to Pearse's delight in the appointment of Joseph O'Neill as an intermediate inspector. O'Neill was from the Aran Islands and was one of the three inspectors who reported on St Enda's in the spring of 1910. Pearse understood the importance of the results fees arising from connection with the Intermediate System. Writing to Edward Martyn (1859–1923) in 1908 he conceded the necessity of considering some connection but 'without materially interfering with the Irish character of the school.' Patrick Pearse to Edward Martyn, 27 February 1908, Séamas O'Buachalla (ed.), *The Letters of P.H. Pearse*.

[114] Patrick Pearse to William Bulfin, 14 September 1909, in Séamas O'Buachalla (ed.), *The Letters of P.H. Pearse*.

[115] 'By Way of Comment', *An Macaomh*, Vol. I, No. 2, Christmas 1909.

[116] Alfred Dennis, a past-pupil of St Enda's recalled that Brother Carey of Synge Street who knew Pearse as a pupil there and spoke highly of St Enda's, 'withdrew his recommendation when he heard Pearse had been forced to take up the Intermediate.' Alfred Dennis, 'A Memory of P.H. Pearse', *Capuchin Annual*, December 1941.

[117] Frank Burke, interviewed by Proinsias O'Conluain, 'This Man Kept a School', RTÉ, April 1979.

[118] 'The Man Called Pearse', Desmond Ryan (ed.), *The Complete Works of P.H. Pearse, St Enda's and its Founder*, p. 179. An example of such an occasion occurred when the boys won a Dublin Juvenile Hurling Competition. See *An Macaomh*, Vol. II, No. 3, Christmas 1910, p. 76.

[119] See *An Macaomh*, Vol. II, No. 3, Christmas 1910. The umbrella is on display at the National Museum, Dublin.

[120] Patrick Pearse to Mr John Kilgallon, 14 May 1914, Pearse Collection, Pearse Museum, KGA. Pearse was returning from his fundraising trip in America.

[121] *An Barr Buadh* (The Trumpet of Victory) was a paper established by Pearse in 1912. It ran to only few editions. Ryan failed utterly to

appreciate the value of this piece, commenting in 1924 that in it Pearse inquires 'why he inspires his friends with silent awe …' See Desmond Ryan (ed.), *The Complete Works of P.H. Pearse, St Enda's and its Founder, The Man Called Pearse*, p. 249.

[122] See scrapbook of press cuttings MS 32695 / 1 (3). NLI.

[123] See *An Macaomh*, Vol. II, No. 3, Christmas 1910, p. 74, entry for 16 March. Some years later, Pearse recorded his warm recollections of the last night of his return trip from America aboard the SS *Campania*, when he 'recited in Irish '*m'óchón agus móchón ó*' at the end of voyage party. This appears to have been a very jovial affair as passengers wedged themselves between furnishings to avoid stumbling about due to very rough seas. MS 21084 'The Voyage of Patrick', Journal of Patrick Pearse on SS *Campania*, 15 September 1914, Pearse Papers, NLI.

[124] *An Macaomh*, Vol. I, No. 2, Christmas 1909, p. 55.

[125] Brian Seoighe, interviewed by Proinsias O'Conluain 'This Man Kept a School', RTÉ, April 1979. *Ibid.*

[126] 'Todd Andrews talks to Padraig O Raghallaigh', RTÉ, November 1974.

[127] Margaret Pearse, interviewed by Proinsias O'Conluain 'This Man Kept a School', RTÉ, April 1979. Margaret Pearse explained: 'I had a private school in Cullenswood House, I had boys and girls in it, I got on very well, and he [Pearse] used to come and do the Irish for me and he said to me one day, "What will you say if this is all ended some day and I start a school of my own?" I said "I want *my* school!" and he says "I think I'll be starting a big school" so not long after that we left Marlborough Road and he started school in Cullenswood House.'

[128] See C.S. Andrews, *Dublin Made Me*, p. 44: 'Miss Margaret Pearse, taught religion. She looked, and was, very cross.' Junior School refers to those classes of pupils that were of National school-going age.

[129] The whereabouts of this instrument is now unknown. A harp on display at the Pearse Museum is not considered to be the original, which may have eventually found its way to the Cork School of Music.

[130] Maire Nic Shiubhlaigh, *The Splendid Years*, p. 148.

[131] Milo MacGarry 'Memories of Scoil Éanna', *Capuchin Annual* (1930), p. 35.

[132] *Ibid*. See also 'By Way of Comment', *An Macaomh*, Vol. I, No. I, Midsummer 1909.

[133] Desmond Ryan, *Remembering Sion, a Chronicle of Storm and Calm*, p. 159.

[134] *Ibid.*, p. 176.

[135] See F.X. Martin (ed.), *Leaders and Men of the Easter Rising*, p. 157. The four were collectively known as 'The Dogs', they were: Desmond Ryan, Frank Burke, Eamon Bulfin and John Sweeney. Billy Moore (Liam Ó' Mordha), who attended the school between 1920–21, recalled Pearse's surprise when, one evening, he discovered these past pupils in a group of Volunteers whom he was about to address. Second Interview with Billy Moore, 9 August 1992, Pearse Museum.

[136] Ruth Dudley Edwards, *Patrick Pearse, The Triumph of Failure*, p. 130.

[137] See: Eugene Cronin to Michael Cronin, 19 May 1914; Eugene Cronin to 'Father and Mother, 21 January 1916; Michael Cronin to Theresa Howard (Aunt Theresa), 10 March 1916, Pearse Collection, Pearse Museum, KGA.

[138] Draft Reports MS 21086, Pearse Papers, NLI.

[139] Patrick Pearse to Michael Cronin, 1 May 1910, Pearse Collection, Pearse Museum, KGA. Cronin was a regular contributor to the Gaelic League. See List of Subscribers to Gaelic League MS 11574 NLI (n.d.).

[140] *Ibid*.

[141] Patrick Pearse to Michael Cronin, 14 January 1914, Pearse Collection, Pearse Museum, KGA.

[142] See Desmond Ryan (ed.), *The Complete Works of P.H. Pearse, St Enda's and its Founder*, A Retrospect, p. 109.

[143] See Elizabeth Countess of Fingall, *Seventy Years Young*, p. 375.

[144] See 'Thomas MacDonagh', Donagh MacDonagh, *An Cosantoir*, Vol. V, No. 10, October 1945, p. 527.

[145] MS 8903 Thomas MacDonagh to Gertrude Bloomer, 17 June 1910, Thomas MacDonagh Papers, NLI.

[146] See Michael Hayes, 'Thomas MacDonagh and the Rising' in F.X.

Martin (ed.), *The Easter Rising, 1916 and University College, Dublin*, p. 39.

[147] See Donagh MacDonagh, 'Thomas MacDonagh', *An Cosantoir*, Vol. V, No. 10, October 1945, p. 528.

[148] 'During a few hours he had strayed into innumerable by-paths of knowledge where Cúchulainn elbowed Dante and Catullus walked down arm-in-arm with Canon O'Leary'. See Desmond Ryan (ed.), *The Complete Works of P.H. Pearse, St Enda's and its Founder*, V – A Retrospect, pp. 91–2.

[149] Sean Dowling interviewed by Proinsias O'Conluain, 'This Man Kept a School', RTÉ, April 1979.

[150] *Ibid.* See also Michael Hayes, 'Thomas MacDonagh and the Rising', in F.X. Martin (ed.), *The Easter Rising, 1916 and University College, Dublin*, p. 39.

[151] *Ibid.* See also, Ulick O'Connor, *The Troubles*, p. 73.

[152] See Milo MacGarry, 'Memories of Scoil Éanna', *Capuchin Annual* (1930), pp. 34–5.

[153] Maire Nic Shiubhlaigh, *The Splendid Years*, p. 155.

[154] Donagh MacDonagh, *P.H. Pearse*, MS 33 694/G, NLI.

[155] 'The Man Called Pearse', in Desmond Ryan (ed.), *The Complete Works of P.H. Pearse, St Enda's and its Founder*, p. 186. See also Marie Nic Shiubhlaigh, *The Splendid Years*, p. 155.

[156] See Desmond Ryan, 'St Enda's – Fifty Years After', in *University Review* (1958), Vol. II, 3 & 4, Double Issue, p. 38. See also Michael Hayes, 'Thomas MacDonagh and the Rising' in F.X. Martin (ed.), *The Easter Rising, 1916 and University College, Dublin,* p. 39.

[157] See 'The Story of a Success, V – Retrospect', in Desmond Ryan (ed.), *The Complete Works of P.H. Pearse, St Enda's and its Founder*, p. 91.

[158] *Ibid.*, p. 217.

[159] See Mary Colum, *Life and the Dream*, p. 153.

[160] *Ibid.* Shane Leslie recalled that: 'The intellectual uprising of Dublin was then at its height, and masters and boys entered into it not only as students but as performers.' See Shane Leslie, *The Irish Issue in its American Aspect*, p. 83.

[161] Louis N. Le Roux, *Patrick H. Pearse* Desmond Ryan (trans.), p. 139.

The delineation 'subjects' is baffling.

162 'Application of T. MacDonagh M.A. for appointment to the Chair of History, English Literature and Mental Science, University College Galway.' MS 10855 Testimonial by Patrick Pearse, 10 February 1913, Thomas MacDonagh Papers, NLI.

163 *Ibid.*

164 Edward Martyn (1859–1923), playwright and Gaelic Revivalist. Joseph Plunkett (1887–1916), poet and social reformer, accompanied Roger Casement to Germany in 1915 to seek funding for Dublin rising. Executed in 1916.

165 See 'The Man Called Pearse', in Desmond Ryan (ed.), *The Complete Works of P.H. Pearse, St Enda's and its Founder*, p. 195.

166 *Ibid.*, p. 192. A letter from Padraic Colum, seeking a position for his brother at the National Museum in Dublin, states that he 'could get recommendations from Mr Oliver Shepherd and Mr Willie Pearse.' MS 10862–3 Padraic Colum to The Directors, National Museum, Dublin, 10 May 1910, Count Plunkett Papers, NLI.

167 See *An Macaomh*, Vo. I, No. 1, Midsummer 1909, p. 81, entry for 22 September.

168 Desmond Ryan, 'A Retrospect', *The Complete Works of P.H. Pearse, St Enda's and its Founder*, p. 95.

169 Mairéad Ní Ghacháin (ed.), *Lúise Gabhánach Ní Dhufaigh agus Scoil Bhríde*, p. 3.

170 See MS 3497 Roll Book of St Enda's 1915–16, Pearse Papers, NLI.

171 Desmond Ryan (ed.), *The Complete Works of P.H. Pearse, St Enda's and its Founder*, A Man Called Pearse, p. 198.

172 Desmond Ryan, interviewed by Proinsias O'Conluain 'This Man Kept a School', RTÉ, April 1979.

173 C.S. Andrews, *Dublin Made Me*, also 'Todd Andrews in conversation with Pádraig Ó'Rathallaigh', RTÉ, November 1974.

174 See Milo MacGarry, 'Memories of St Enda's', *Capuchin Annual* (1930), p. 32. MacGarry records only that William could 'draw well'.

[175] David Sears, 'Some Impressions of William Pearse', in *Memories of the Brothers Pearse*, p. 27. The Pearse Commemoration Committee. Pearse Collection, Pearse Museum.

[176] *Ibid.*

[177] *An Scoláire*, Vol. I, No. 6, 18 May 1913, p. 2.

[178] See *An Macaomh*, Vo. I. No. 2. Christmas 1910, p. 58, entry for 5 October.

[179] Pádraig Ó'Snodaigh, 'Willie Pearse: Artist', in *Leabhrán Cuimhneacháin ar an Fhoilsiú ar Ocáid Bronnadh Eochair Scoil Éanna ar Uachtarán na hÉireann, Eamonn De Valera*, 23 April 1970. See also Ruth Dudley Edwards, *The Triumph of Failure*, p. 120. Mabel Gorman attended St Enda's School when it opened in 1910. See *An Macaomh*, Vol. I, No. 1, Midsummer 1909, p. 76. She is mentioned in the school diary as having been at the fancy dress party held on 1 November. See *An Macaomh*, Vol. II, No. 3, Christmas 1910.

[180] See Catherine Robson, *Men in Wonderland: The Lost Girlhood of the Victorian Gentleman*.

[181] Two statues for which Eileen Byrne is reputed to have modelled are stored at the Pearse Museum, Rathfarnham. The biographer of Evelyn Nicolls, Micheál O'Dubhshláine, refers to Mabel Gorman as '*cailín* Willie' (William's girl) but the existence of such a relationship is speculation. See *Oighan Uasal Ó'Phríomhchathair Eirann*, p. 90. Eileen Byrne lived at Oakley Road, where the Pearse family resided before moving to The Hermitage in Rathfarnham.

[182] See Desmond Ryan, 'A Retrospect', *The Complete Works of P.H. Pearse, St Enda's and its Founder*, p. 96.

[183] William took the part of Pilate in the production of the *Passion Play* which was performed by the St Enda's boys and the girls from St Ita's, in the Abbey Theatre in 1911. For partial notes on teaching drama made by William Pearse, see MS 21086 (1) Pearse Papers, NLI.

[184] See Ruth Dudley Edwards, *The Triumph of Failure*, p. 117. Beatrice Lady Glenavy recollected that her allegorical painting of Mother Ireland had been bought by Maud Gonne and presented to St Enda's. Some years later she met a past-pupil who remarked that 'this picture had inspired

him to 'die for Ireland!' I was shocked at the thought that my rather banal and sentimental picture might, like Helen's face, launch ships and burn towers!' See Beatrice Lady Glenavy, *Today We Will Only Gossip*, p. 91. James Pearse had collected Hogarth prints, a number of which are held at the Pearse Museum, Rathfarnham.

[185] Regarding the Irish Art Companions see *Leabhrán Cuimhneacháin Aran Fhoilsiú ar ócáid Bronnadh Eochair Scoil Éanna ar Uachtarán na hEireann*, Eamon De Valera, 23 April, 1970, p. 18, 'William Pearse, Artist', Pádraig Ó'Snodaigh.

[186] See 'The Man Called Pearse', in Desmond Ryan (ed.), *The Complete Works of P.H. Pearse, St Enda's and Its Founder*, p. 202.

[187] Desmond Ryan, *Remembering Sion, a Chronicle of Storm and Calm*, p. 126.

[188] Maire Nic Shiubhlaigh *The Splendid Years*, p. 150.

[189] *Ibid.*, p. 193

[190] Desmond Ryan, *Remembering Sion, a Chronicle of Storm and Calm*, p. 114.

[191] See teaching notes for drawing by William Pearse MS 21072 (1), Pearse Papers, NLI.

[192] *Ibid.*, 1–4.

[193] *Ibid.*, 10. (emphasis in original). The document is marked '1st Year' by the author.

[194] See 'The Man Called Pearse', in Desmond Ryan (ed.), *The Complete Works of P.H. Pearse, St Enda's and its Founder*, p. 203. Lesson notes for history classes covering the period 1400–1689, possibly made by William, are utterly uncontentious. See notebooks on Irish history, MS 21068 Pearse Papers, NLI.

[195] *Ibid.*, p. 205.

[196] See 'The Man Called Pearse', in Desmond Ryan (ed.), *The Complete Works of PH. Pearse, St Enda's and its Founder*, p. 191.

[197] J.P. Henry was the author of *A Handbook of Modern Irish* which was widely used by the Gaelic League in its Irish language classes. His work at St Enda's was largely confined to teaching advanced Irish to senior pupils.

O'Nowlan was a scholar of repute and Pearse thought highly of him. In a letter of recommendation he described him as 'a ripe scholar, a genuine student, a man of wide culture and an Irishman of fine character.' MS 21088 Patrick Pearse to Dr Coffey, December 1911, Pearse Papers, NLI.

[198] Patrick Pearse to Mrs Humphreys, 24 September 1910, Séamas O'Buachalla (ed.), *The Collected Letters of P.H. Pearse.*

[199] Patrick Pearse to Séamas Hampton 10 July 1908, Séamas O'Buachalla (ed.), *The Collected Letters of P.H. Pearse.*

[200] *An Macaomh,*Vol. I, No. I, Midsummer 1909, p. 71.

[201] *An Macaomh,*Vol. I, No. II, p. 55.

[202] The medical attendants were: Dr J.J.Touhy, physician and surgeon, Dr M.F. Cox, consulting physician and surgeon, Dr J.P. Henry, Ophthalmist, P.J. Birmingham, dentist. See *An Macaomh,*Vol. I, No. I, Midsummer 1909, p. 71.

[203] See *An Macaomh,*Vol. I, No. 2, Christmas 1909, p. 57 & 60. Padraic Colum (1881–1972) playwright, novelist and folklorist.

[204] See *An Macaomh,*Vol. II, No. 3, Christmas 1910, pp. 77–8.

[205] Thomas MacDonagh studied part-time at University College, Dublin from 1909–11 after which he submitted his MA thesis, *Thomas Campion and the Art of English Poetry* (pub. 1913).

[206] *An Macaomh,*Vol. I, No. 2, Christmas 1909. They were Mr Kane who taught French and Mr Nolan who taught geography, Latin, Irish and mathematics. There is no record of the subjects taught by Eamon O'Toole.

[207] *Ibid.,* p. 75.

[208] *Ibid.,* pp. 77–8. These inspectors were from the Gaelic League Leinster College of Irish. An article in the *Freeman's Journal* in March 1908 explained that the college was providing a series of lectures on the Direct Method of teaching 'intended for the benefit of Inspectors and Organisers of National Schools, and is the outcome of the representations made some time ago to the National Board by the Committee of the College as to the necessity of having school classes which had been taught on the 'Direct Method' inspected on similar lines. The Education Office

acknowledged the justice of the demand, and in response to an offer by the College Committee, the Board granted facilities 'to such Inspectors and Organisers as were desirous of attending the present course of lectures.' See the *Freeman's Journal*, 10 March 1908.

[209] See *An Macaomh*, Vol. II, No. 3, Christmas 1910, p. 78.

[210] *Ibid.*, p. 79.

[211] *An Macaomh*, Vol. II, No.2, May 1913, p. 48.

[212] MS 8903 Thomas MacDonagh to Gertrude Bloomer, 17 June 1910, Thomas MacDonagh Papers, NLI.

[213] *An Macaomh*, Vol. II, No. 2, May 1913, p. 48.

[214] *Ibid.*

[215] Con Colbert (1886–1916) nationalist and combatant in Easter Rising, executed May 1916.

[216] Thomas MacDonagh, Edward Martyn and Joseph Plunkett formed the Irish Theatre in late 1914. The company was short-lived but Maire Nic Shuibhlaigh opined that it was 'probably the most important of all the theatrical companies which appeared in Dublin in the years immediately before 1916 ... it indicated the path which MacLiammóir and Edwards later took when they founded the Dublin Gate.' Both Martyn and Plunkett frequently visited St Enda's and were friends of the Pearse brothers. Martyn was a member of the school's academic council. William in particular knew Martyn and Plunkett well through their shared interest in the theatre and was a member of the Irish Theatre. Willie and Margaret Pearse also founded the short-lived Leinster Stage Society and they and Maire Nic Shuibhlaigh, performed adaptations from the works of Dickens in Dublin and Cork. See Maire Nic Shuibhlaigh *The Splendid Years*, p. 151. The Society earned an unenviable reputation, the *Cork Echo* reporting that during one tour in Cork an '*Echo*' boy refused a free pass in farmyard language ...', MS 21092 Pearse Papers, NLI.

[217] In *The Story of A Success III* – 'Adventures', Pearse added as a footnote that 'by coming out to Rathfarnham we lost our day boys, who were half our number.' See 'P.H. Pearse', in Desmond Ryan (ed.), *The Complete Works of P.H. Pearse, St Enda's and its Founder*, p. 49. Yet writing to his friend Canon Arthur Ryan in May 1910 Pearse had confided

that by moving 'we stand to lose half of our day-boys ... but some of our best day-boys will come to us as boarders ... moreover, we are convinced that we could do far better work if we had more boarders and fewer day-boys. The latter interfere with our work at many points.' See Patrick Pearse to Canon Arthur Ryan, 2 May 1910, in Séamas O'Buachalla (ed.), *The Letters of P.H. Pearse*.

[218] Sighle Bairéid, interviewed by Proinsias O'Conluain, 'This Man Kept a School', RTÉ, 1979. Sighle Bairéid was Pearse's godchild. Her father, Stiofán Bairéid, was the treasurer of the Gaelic League and a close friend of Pearse. He assisted his purchase of Cullenswood House by standing as guarantor for a loan of £275.

[219] See 'Coilin', *Patrick H. Pearse, a Sketch of His Life*, p. 11.

[220] 'By Way of Comment', *An Macaomh*, Vol. I, No. 2, Christmas 1909. Brighid Lyons Thornton recalled the affection in which the boys held Countess Markievicz. On a visit by the Countess at which Thornton was present she was struck by the way the boys 'rallied 'round her and 'the emotion and enthusiasm' they displayed. See Griffith & O'Grady (eds) *Curious Journey*, recollection of Brighid Lyons Thornton, p. 39.

[221] Standish James O'Grady (1846–1928) historian and antiquarian, author of *History of Ireland: The Heroic Period* (1878).

[222] 'By Way of Comment', *An Macaomh*, Vol. 1, No. 2, Christmas 1909.

[223] *An Macaomh*, Vol. I, No. 2, Christmas 1909, p. 50.

[224] *Ibid.*, p. 51.

[225] *Ibid.*

[226] *Ibid.*

[227] *Ibid.*

[228] *An Macaomh*, Vol. I, No. 1, Midsummer 1909, p. 83.

[229] *Ibid.*

[230] *Ibid.*

[231] *Ibid.*

[232] *Ibid.*, p. 85.

[233] *Ibid.*, p. 83.

[234] *Ibid.*, p. 88.

[235] *Ibid.*

[236] *An Macaomh*, Vol. II, No. 3, Christmas 1910, pp. 70–1.

[237] *Ibid.* When McDermott left St Enda's he went to teach in north-west India. The editors of *An Macaomh* commented in 1910 that 'doubtless he has already made hurlers of the Hindoos.' *Ibid.*, p. 74.

[238] *Ibid.*

[239] *An Macaomh*, Vol. I, No. 1, Midsummer 1909, p. 82.

[240] See *An Macaomh*, Vol. II, No. 3, Christmas 1910, p. 52.

[241] For example see *An Macaomh*, Vol. I, No. 1, Midsummer 1909, p. 84.

[242] *Ibid.*

[243] *An Macaomh*, Vol. II, No. 3, Christmas 1910, p. 80.

[244] *Ibid.*

[245] Denis Gwynn, son of Stephen Gwynn, was senior boy and school captain in 1908–9. He won a Classical Scholarship to study at University College, Dublin and was later lecturer in history at University College, Cork. He made the decision to join the British Army while studying at University College Dublin.

[246] Donagh MacDonagh, *P.H. Pearse*, MS 33694/G NLI, p. 5. Dongah MacDonagh agreed with his father's view but commented that a youth 'trained to love of liberty' could easily be deceived 'by talk of Poor Little Belgium and the freedom of small nations.'

[247] 'By Way of Comment', *An Macaomh*, Vol. II, No. 2, May 1913.

[248] See *An Macaomh*, Vol. I, No. 1, Midsummer 1909, p. 82 & 88.

[249] *An Macaomh*, Vol. II, No. 3, Christmas 1910, p. 77, entry for 1 November.

[250] *Ibid.*, p. 82.

[251] *Ibid.*, p. 77. Connolly was one of the past pupils who resided at The Hermitage while studying at university.

[252] *Ibid.*

[253] A.S. Neill (1883–1973) founder of Summerhill School, England. See *Summerhill, a Radical Approach to Education*, p. 71.

[254] See 'Secret History of Scoil Éanna …' *An Scoláire*, Vol. II, No. 2, May 1913, p. 3.

[255] Founded in 1899 by W.B. Yeats, Lady Gregory and Edward Martyn.

[256] *An Macaomh*, Vol. I, No. 1, Midsummer 1909, p. 82.

[257] Founded by Edward Martyn, later became the Irish Theatre, of which William Pearse was a member.

[258] *An Macaomh*, Vol. I, No. 1, Midsummer 1909, p. 87.

[259] *Ibid.*, p. 85. Alfred McGloughlin was the son of Emily Pearse, the daughter of James Pearse by his first marriage with Emily Susanna Fox and step sister of Patrick Pearse.

[260] 'The Return of the Fianna', *An Claidheamh Soluis*, 27 March 1909, p. 11.

[261] *Ibid.*

[262] *Ibid.*

[263] 'Plays and Books' *Sinn Fein,* 27 March 1909.

[264] This was a modest corrugated construction, a photograph of which is reproduced in *An Macaomh*, Vol. I, No. 1, Midsummer 1909, p. 83. Maire NicShiubhlaigh referred to it as 'A little corrugated iron shed.' See *The Splendid Years*, p. 148.

[265] *Ibid.*, p. 86.

[266] *Ibid.*, p. 87.

[267] *An Macaomh*, Vol. I, No. 2, Christmas 1909.

[268] *Ibid.*

[269] *Ibid.*

[270] *Ibid.* When writing drama, Pearse would tailor his characters to the characteristics of those who he had selected to play them. See Maire

NicShiubhlaigh, *The Splendid Years*, p. 149.

[271] Maire NicShiubhlaigh, *The Splendid Years*, p. 146.

[272] *Ibid.*

[273] A handball court was built at The Hermitage in 1910.

[274] *An Macaomh*, Vol. I, No. 1, Midsummer 1909, p. 62; 'We play football, but we are emphatically a hurling School' (*sic*).

[275] *An Macaomh*, Vol. II, No. 3, Christmas 1910, p. 62.

[276] *An Macaomh*, Vol. II, No. 2, May 1913, p. 49.

[277] *The Prospectus of Scoil Éanna (1909)*, 'Physical Culture.'

[278] See *An Macaomh*, Vol. I, No. 1, Midsummer 1909, p. 90. Billy Moore (Liam Ó'Mordha) was enrolled at St Enda's in 1921. He recalled that he did not know how to play hurling as he had only played rugby and cricket at his former school, Roscrea College. Second interview with Billy Moore (Liam Ó'Mordha, 2 August 1992, Pearse Museum).

[279] *Ibid.*, p. 87. On 20 April 1909 there were sixty boys enrolled.

[280] St Kevin's, who had issued the challenge, were beaten 11 goals and 9 points to 1 goal and 9 points in a hurling match, *Ibid.*, p. 89.

[281] The shootings were in reprisal for the actions of the IRA who, on 21 November, killed fourteen British secret service agents. On Frank Burke's involvement see Seán Sheridan, *What if the Dream Come True?*, p. 43.

[282] For fixture details see *An Macaomh*, Vol. II, No. 3, Christmas 1910, pp. 63–8.

[283] *Ibid.*, p. 65.

[284] *Ibid.*, p. 68.

[285] *Ibid.*, p. 62.

[286] See *An Scoláire*, Vol. I, No. 2, 20 April 1913, p. 6.

[287] *Ibid.*

[288] *Ibid.*, p. 9.

[289] *Ibid.* Vol. I, No. 3, 26 April 1913, p. 3.

[290] *Ibid.*

[291] Bertrand Russell, *Why I Am Not A Christian*, p. 138.

[292] See 'About the Intermediate', *An Claidheamh Soluis*, 9 December 1905.

[293] C.E. Wright, E. Ensor and J.J. O'Neill.

[294] 'By Way of Comment', *An Macaomh*, Vol. I, No. 2, Christmas 1909.

[295] Report on St Enda's College, *The Report of the Commissioners of Intermediate Education for the Year 1910*, 'General Description of Schoolhouse.'

[296] *Ibid.* (5) (6) & (16). A charge of five shillings per annum was added to school fees to support the 'compulsory extras' of 'school museum and library'. A similar charge was levied for 'games and gymnasium'. See *The Prospectus of Scoil Éanna, (1909).*

[297] Report on St Enda's College, *The Report of the Inspectors of Intermediate Education for the Year 1910.*

[298] See *Prospectus of Scoil Éanna, (1909)*, 'Physical Culture. And also Recreation'. It is possible that this meant only that these were the only games available, therefore pupils wising to play team sports had to choose from these.

[299] Report on St Enda's College, *The Report of the Commissioners of Intermediate Education for the Year 1910.* 'Recreation'.

[300] *Ibid.* 'Greek, Senior Grade.'

[301] *Ibid.*

[302] *Ibid.* 'Greek, Middle Grade.'

[303] *Ibid.* 'Latin, Senior Grade.'

[304] *Ibid.*

[305] 'French, Junior and Preparatory Grades – Mr MacDonagh', Report on St Enda's College, *The Report of the Commissioners of Intermediate Education 1910.* The attitude of Wright and Ensor toward Irish is ambiguous. That of Ensor is possibly implied by his reference to Irish as one of the 'four foreign languages' taught at St Enda's. Also, he failed to note, or notice, that Spanish was also taught.

[306] *Ibid.* 'Junior Grade.' An undated document (*c.* 1911) in Pearse's hand records details of examinations at the school. Seven boys failed in French. Pearse recorded that 'the results would have been good only for French'. See MS 21094 Pearse Papers NLI.

[307] Report on St Enda's College, *The Report of the Commissioners of Intermediate Education 1910.* 'English, Senior Grade – Mr MacDonagh.'

[308] *Ibid.* 'Mathematics, Geometry, Senior Grade – Mr MacDonagh.'

[309] *Ibid.* 'Mathematics, Geometry, Preparatory Grade – Mr MacDonagh.'

[310] *Ibid.* 'Mathematics, Geometry, Middle Grade – Mr McDermott.' It was noted, however, that McDermott's Junior Grade mathematics class 'showed no interest' and worked 'mechanically and unintelligently'. *Ibid.* McDermott had spent some years at the Catholic Seminary at Maynooth but had not taken holy orders. He applied for a post at St Enda's in June 1909. At that period he was preparing to take a Masters of Arts Degree in classics at the Royal University of Ireland. He had taken his degree in Latin and Greek and during his first year had studied mathematics. While at Maynooth he had also studied Irish and in his letter of application expressed the hope that he would be vouched an opportunity to teach 'at least Preparatory and Junior classes.' MS 21053 Michael J. McDermott to Patrick Pearse, 4 April 1910, Pearse Papers, NLI.

[311] Report on St Enda's School. *The Report of the Commissioners of Intermediate Education for the Year 1910,* 'Mathematics, Algebra, Middle Grade – Mr Feely.'

[312] *Ibid.* 'History and Geography, Preparatory Grade, Mr McDonnell.'

[313] *Ibid.* 'Preparatory Grade – Mr Pearse.'

[314] Report on St Enda's College, *The Report of the Commissioners of Intermediate Education 1910.* 'Irish, Senior, Middle and Junior Grades – Mr Pearse'.

[315] Report on St Enda's College, *The Report of the Inspectors of Intermediate Education 1910.* 'Mathematics, Algebra, Preparatory Grade – Mr Pearse.'

[316] *Ibid.*

[317] *Ibid.* 'English, Middle Grade – Mr Pearse.' Oliver Goldsmith (1728–1774) poet and man of letters.

[318] *Ibid.* 'History and Geography – Mr Pearse.'

[319] *Ibid.* 'English.'

[320] *Ibid.*

[321] Pearse Patrick to Mrs Humphreys, 20 April 1910, Séamas O'Buachalla (ed.), *The Letters of P.H. Pearse.*

[322] Those who initially agreed to become members were: Joseph Dolan, Mary Hayden, John Henry, Mrs Stephen Gwynn, Shane Leslie and Séamas Mac Manus. All were Irish language revivalists and cultural nationalists.

[323] In August 1910, for example, Mrs Mauphill, informed Pearse that her son Patrick would not be enrolling at The Hermitage because his health was not 'equal to the increased distance he would have to go …' MS 21053 Mrs Mauphill to Patrick Pearse, 28 August 1910, Pearse Papers, NLI. The Mauphill family resided at 43, Grosvenor Square, Dublin 6, very close to Cullenswood House.

[324] Sighle Bairéid, interviewed by Proinsias O'Conluain 'This Man Had Kept a School', RTÉ, April 1979.

[325] Séan Sheridan, *What if the Dream Come True?*, p. 41. This was not the case. Pearse recorded in an official document that the 'Distance of School from Railway Station' was '1 mile from Rathfarnham Tram'. See MS 21087 Pearse Papers, NLI. At the period in question the number 17 tram served Rathfarnham Village and Pearse's estimate of 1 mile was rather less than accurate!

[326] 'The beautiful and historic demesne known as The Hermitage, Rathfarnham has been secured as its future home. The grounds include 50 acres of delightful woodland and pasturage with garden orchard, playing fields, tennis court, etc. They are watered by a busy stream and contain a picturesque island-studded lake, spacious study hall, library, laboratories, art room, classrooms, gymnasium, refectory and dormitories are in the course of equipment …' *The Irish Times,* 3 September 1910. *The Irish Times* appears in the list of unpaid creditors forwarded to Pearse in June 1912. The sum of £18 10s was outstanding and remained unpaid at the time of his death.

[327] George Gavan Duffy (1882–1951), son of Sir Charles Gavan Duffy, founder of *The Nation.* George Gavan Duffy was a supporter of the Gaelic

League and a close friend of Pearse. As a solicitor, he was well placed to assist Pearse in the task of setting up the school.

[328] Alex Wilson was a prominent Belfast accountant. He was a supporter of the Gaelic League, contributed generously to St Enda's and advised Pearse on financial matters between 1911 and 1916. Dolan's personal investments in the school were not reimbursed until January 1930, when he received a payment of £600 from Mrs Margaret Pearse. MS 21090 (2) Joseph Dolan to Mrs Margaret Pearse, 22 January 1930, Pearse Papers, NLI.

[329] MS 21053 Patrick Pearse to Gertrude Bloomer, 13 October 1911, Pearse Papers, NLI.

[330] *Ibid.* The financial position of St Ita's had deteriorated rapidly since Pearse had rented The Hermitage. Only in January 1911 he had written to his friend Mrs Margaret Hutton that St Ita's was 'practically free from debt.' MS 8617 Patrick Pearse to Mrs Margaret Hutton, 21 January 1911, Pearse Papers, NLI. For details of the accounts of St Ita's for 1911 see Accounts of St Ita's School 1911, MS. 21088 (5), Pearse Papers, NLI.

[331] See MS 21053 Letters from Clery's & Co., Dublin, to Patrick Pearse: 13 October 1910, 3 March 1911, 20 March 1911, Pearse Papers, NLI.

[332] See MS 21092–3 Gill & Sons, Publishers, to Patrick Pearse, 29 September 1911, Pearse Papers, NLI.

[333] A record of subscriptions to St Enda's at May 1911 shows the following donations (in pounds): Margaret Hutton 50, Mrs Bulfin 1, 'Jos' Bulfin 1, Michael Smithwick 1, Mrs Gywnn 25, J.J. Reddin 10, J.B. Dowling 10, Douglas Hyde 5, Agnes O'Farrelly 2, Edward Martyn 1, Sir Bertram Windle (2 shares), Alex Wilson (100 shares) Michael Smithwick (10 shares). Bulfin, Gywnn and Reddin had children enrolled at St Enda's. See 'Sums Subscribed to St Enda's 1910', MS 5051 Pearse Papers, NLI.

[334] Seán T. O'Ceallaigh was a member of the Gaelic League, the IRB and a founder member of Sinn Fein. He had been manager of *An Claid-heamh Soluis* in 1903 and was appointed general secretary of the Gaelic League in 1915. He was a close fiend of Pearse and supported his work at St Enda's where his brothers Micheál and Maitiú were enrolled.

[335] Patrick Pearse to Mary Maguire 31 May 1912, cited in *Comhair*, November 1975.

[336] MS 21053 Patrick Pearse to Gertrude Bloomer, 13 June 1912, Pearse Papers, NLI.

[337] See MS 21053 (7–13) Boland's Flour Mills to Patrick Pearse, 24 March 1910, 5 May 1910, 2 June 1910, Pearse Papers, NLI.

[338] MS 5051 Patrick Pearse to Alex Wilson, 23 June 1912, Pearse Papers, NLI. See also MS 7879 Patrick Pearse to George F.H. Berkeley, 23 November 1910, Letters and Papers of George F.H. Berkeley, NLI. Louise Gavan Duffy was the sister of George Gavan Duffy and later opened her own school, Scoil Idé, on the site of the original St Ita's at Oakley Road.

[339] See MS 5051 'Memorandum regarding Scoil Éanna Accounts', Alex Wilson, (n.d.) 1912, Pearse Papers, NLI.

[340] MS 5051 Patrick Pearse to Alex Wilson, 23 June 1912, Pearse Papers, NLI. St Ita's was also owed £75 in outstanding fees.

[341] Patrick Pearse to Gertrude Bloomer 30 July 1912, Pearse Papers, NLI. On Easter Sunday 1916 Pearse sent Gertrude Bloomer a cheque for £5. See Patrick Pearse to Gertrude Bloomer, 12 March 1916, Pearse Papers, NLI.

[342] Bulmer Hobson gaelic activist, Vice-President of Sinn Féin in 1907, founder and editor of *Irish Freedom* in 1910 and Secretary of the Irish Volunteers in 1913.

[343] Joseph Mc Garrity (1874–1940) leading figure in *Clan-na-Gael*, an American organisation that raised funds for the IRB. Mc Garrity gave generous support to St Enda's and was closely connected with the plans for the Easter Rising.

[344] *Gaelic American*, 7 March 1914.

[345] See Patrick Pearse to J. McGarrity, 1 April 1914, Séamas O'Buachalla (ed.), *The Letters of P.H Pearse.*

[346] Fragment (n.d. 1914). Pearse Collection, Pearse Museum, KGA.

[347] Patrick Pearse to John Kilgallon, 14 May 1914, Pearse Collection, Pearse Museum KGA.

[348] Pearse delivered the oration on Robert Emmet in New York, 2 March 1914 and the second oration, again in New York, one week later. These were carried in the press in Ireland.

[349] 'Redmonites' was the term popularly applied to followers of John Redmond (1856–1918), leader of the Irish Parliamentary Party in 1900. Redmond committed the Irish Volunteers to supporting the British in the First World War.

[350] Patrick Pearse to Joseph McGarrity, 19 October 1914, Séamas O'Buachalla (ed.), *The Letters of P.H. Pearse*.

[351] This view was echoed by Desmond Ryan who opined that 'had the war not intervened, he [Pearse] would have cleared St Enda's of every penny of debt.' See 'The Man Called Pearse', in Desmond Ryan (ed.), *The Complete Works of P.H. Pearse, St Enda's and Its Founder*, p. 209.

[352] MS 9081 Patrick Pearse to Gertrude Bloomer 4 December 1914, Pearse Papers, NLI.

[353] *Ibid.*

[354] *Ibid.*

[355] *Ibid.*

[356] Boland's Ltd to Patrick Pearse, 15 December 1912, cited in Ruth Dudley Edwards, *Patrick Pearse: The Triumph of Failure*, p. 150.

[357] Patrick Pearse to unidentified correspondent 18 May 1914, Pearse Collection, Pearse Museum, KGA. In October 1914 Pearse appealed 'against assessment of Income Tax' claiming lack of income. He argued that the school 'is run at a loss' but also that he '[kept] no books.' On the contrary, the Pearse Papers contain detailed accounts for St Enda's. Patrick Pearse to unidentified correspondent, 9 October 1914, Pearse Collection, Pearse Museum, KGA & Pearse Papers, NLI, *passim*.

[358] *Ibid.* Pearse concluded another letter (October 1914) in characteristically defiant tone: 'I have no asset except a suit of clothes, a uniform, a rifle, and a sword.' Pearse to Inspector of Taxes, 9 October 1914, Pearse Collection, Pearse Museum, KGA.

[359] Alfred Dennis, 'A Memory of P.H. Pearse', *Capuchin Annual* (1941).

[360] See Patrick Pearse to J. McGarrity, 2 September 1915, Séamas O'Buachalla (ed.), *The Letters of P.H. Pearse*.

[361] Others who had contributed significant amounts were: Joseph Dolan (£1100), Séamas Mac Manus (£350), Mrs Clarke (£300) and Louise Gavan Duffy (£100).

[362] Patrick Pearse to Joseph McGarrity, 2 September 1915 Séamas O'Buachalla (ed.), *The Letters of P.H. Pearse.*

[363] *Ibid.*

[364] *Ibid.*

[365] MS 21087 Attendance Register for Drawing Classes 1 August 1915 – 31 July 1916, Pearse Papers, NLI.

[366] See *St Enda's Attendance Book 1915-1916* (copy) MS 3497 NLI.

[367] In June 1916 Mary Hayden wrote to Mrs Pearse advising her that Dr Coffey, a supporter of St Enda's and president of University College Dublin (1909–1941) was already anxious 'not to further identify the College (St Enda's) with the Rising.' MS 210–59 Mary Hayden to Mrs Margaret Pearse, 11 June 1916 Pearse Papers, NLI.

[368] See MS 5050 Daniel. C. Maher, Solicitor, to Joseph Holloway, June 1916, Holloway Papers, NLI. A letter dated 24 April (Easter Monday) 1916 was posted to Pearse by the Office of the Inspector of Taxes demanding payment of 'all taxes due'. See MS 21053 (16) H. Harrison to Patrick Pearse, 24 April 1916, Pearse Papers, NLI.

[369] Margaret Pearse to An Taoiseach Eamon De Valera, 13 October 1941, File S 9045A Nat. Arch.

[370] Scrapbook of press cuttings, MS 32695/ 1 (3) NLI.

[371] See 'A Memory of P.H. Pearse', Alfred Dennis, *Capuchin Annual* (1941).

[372] 'By Way of Comment', *An Macaomh*, Vol. II. No. 2. May 1913.

[373] See Court Martial Statement of Patrick Pearse, 2 May 1916 (copy) Pearse Papers, NLI.

[374] *An Camán*, February 1932, p. 13.

[375] 'From a Hermitage' (June, 1915), 'Peace and the Gael' (December, 1915), 'Ghosts' (Christmas 1915), 'The Separatist Idea' (1 February, 1916),

'The Spiritual Nation' (13 February 1916), 'The Sovereign People' (31 March, 1916).

[376] Patrick Pearse, The Story of A Success, I – Beginnings, in Desmond Ryan (ed.), *The Complete Works of P.H. Pearse, St Enda's and its Founder*, p. 3.

[377] *Ibid.*

[378] *Ibid.*, p. 6.

[379] 'By Way of Comment', *An Macaomh*, Vol. I, No. 1, Midsummer 1909.

[380] *Ibid.*

[381] *The Nation*, 21 March 1909 review by the novelist William Patrick Ryan (1867–1942) father of Desmond Ryan. While working in London he was involved with the Southwark Literary Club and the Irish Literary Society, editor of the *Irish Peasant* from 1905 (later *The Peasant* and finally the *Irish Nation*) and published a number of plays and books on socialist themes. He was author of *The Irish Literary Revival* (1894), *The Pope's Green Island* (1912) and *The Irish Labour Movement* (1919).

[382] *Ibid.*

[383] *Ibid.*

[384] *Sinn Fein,* 27 March 1909.

[385] 'By Way of Comment', *An Macaomh*, Vol. II, No. 3, Christmas 1910.

[386] Cited in Ruth Dudley Edwards, *Patrick Pearse, The Triumph of Failure*, p. 335.

[387] Desmond Ryan (ed.), *The Complete Works of P.H. Pearse, St Enda's and its Founder*, V – A Retrospect, p. 90. The placing of storytelling beside Religious Instruction is noteworthy in the light of a later remark by Ryan. Writing in 1957 he opined that Pearse's 'ideal Irishman would have been Cúchulainn baptised.' The close identification between models of sacrifice, such as Christ and Cúchulainn, became a dominant aspect of Pearse's thinking from about 1914. See Desmond Ryan 'Pearse, St Enda's and The Hound of Ulster', *Threshold*, Vol. I, No. 3, p. 58 (The Lyric Players Theatre, Belfast, 1957).

[388] 'By Way of Comment', *An Macaomh*, Vol. I. No. 1. Midsummer 1909. In the Programme for *The Coming of Fionn*, performed at St Enda's in March 1909, Pearse recalled the following anecdote; 'A little pupil of whom I asked the other day why a St Enda's boy should never tell a lie replied: 'Because the Fianna never told a lie.' I had to explain that we had a higher precept and example than even those of the Fianna ...' Programme for *The Coming of Fionn*, St Enda's School, 20–22 March 1909, NLI.

[389] 'Celtic' heroes such Cúchulainn were the subject of folklore collections by prominent cultural revivalists such as Lady Gregory, Douglas Hyde and T.W. Rollerston.

[390] 'By Way of Comment', *An Macaomh*, Vol. I, No. 1, Midsummer 1909.

[391] 'By Way of Comment', *An Macaomh*, Vol. II, No. 3, Christmas 1910.

[392] See Desmond Ryan (ed.), *The Complete Works of P.H. Pearse, Plays Poems Stories*.

[393] See *Ibid.*, p. 57 (the Play comprises only one Act).

[394] *Ibid.*, p. 59.

[395] *Ibid.*

[396] Desmond Ryan, *Remembering Sion*, p. 119.

[397] 'By Way of Comment', *An Macaomh*, Vol. I, No. 1, Midsummer 1909.

[398] 'By Way of Comment.' *An Macaomh*, Vol. II, No. 2, May 1913.

[399] *Ibid.*

[400] *Ibid.* Pearse records only that he retold the dream to 'my boys at a school meeting ...' There is no other record of the event and the listeners are unknown. As the dream had occurred some 'four' years previously and Pearse recorded this incident in 1913, the listeners must have been schoolboys rather than past pupils. The custom of past pupils (many of whom were active in nationalist circles and in the Easter Rising) returning to board at the school did not begin until the school was re-located to The Hermitage.

[401] *Ibid.*

[402] *Ibid.*

[403] *Ibid.*

[404] *Ibid.*

[405] *Ibid.*

[406] *Ibid.*

[407] 'By Way of Comment', *An Macaomh*, Vol. II, No. 3, Christmas 1910. It is worth noting that the 'true thing' is not specified. The emphasis is upon the nobility of a cause, rather than the cause itself.

[408] See 'By Way of Comment', *An Macaomh*, Vol. II, No. 2, May 1913.

[409] *Ibid.*

[410] *Ibid.*

[411] See *Prospectus of Scoil Éanna (1909)*.

[412] *Ibid.*

[413] 'By Way of Comment', *An Macaomh*, Vol. II, No. 3, Christmas 1910.

[414] 'Religious Training', *Prospectus of Scoil Éanna (1909)*.

[415] *An Scoláire*, Vol. I, No. 6, 18 May 1916.

[416] See *An Scoláire* Vol. I, No. 9, 7 June 1913, p. 2.

[417] Griffith & O'Grady (eds), *Curious Journey*, recollection of Joseph Sweeney, pp. 38–9. An unidentified visitor to the Pearse Museum recollected that as a child he heard the noise of these small explosives. Recollection of Brian Crowley, Archivist, Pearse Museum. December 2004.

[418] See Donagh MacDonagh, *P.H. Pearse*, p. 5. NLI MS 33 694/G. Liam Mellows (1892–1922) IRB member and founding member of Irish Volunteers, combatant in Easter Rising, member of IRA, Sinn Féin TD for Galway in 1921, executed December 1922. Regarding the involvement of Liam Mellows at St Enda's see C. Desmond Greaves, *Liam Mellows and the Irish Revolution*, pp. 80–3 & p. 311. Seán Heuston, nationalist, participant in Easter Rising, executed May 1916.

[419] See Frank Robbins, *Under the Starry Plough*, p. 52. The Irish Citizen Army was constituted by James Larkin to protect striking workers during general strike in Dublin (1913).

[420] Eugene Cronin to Theresa Howard (n.d.) Pearse Collection, Pearse Museum, KGA.

[421] See Ella Young, *Flowering Dusk*, p. 112 & 'A Memory of P.H. Pearse' Alfred Dennis, *Capuchin Annual*, 1941. Lord Edward Fitzgerald (1763–98) notable leader of the United Irishmen; arrested and mortally wounded in May 1798.

[422] See 'By Way of Comment', *An Macaomh*, Vol. II, No. 2, May 1913.

[423] 'By Way of Comment', *An Macaomh* Vol. II, No. 3, Christmas 1910.

[424] *Ibid.*

[425] *Ibid.*

[426] See *Dublin Review*, Spring 1923. Desmond Ryan later wrote that 'Denis Gwynn's total lack of humour, political prepossessions and post-war disillusion colour his otherwise living portrait of Pearse ...' See Desmond Ryan, *Remembering Sion*, p. 161. In 1931 Gywnn recalled Pearse's 'colossal egoism' and remarked that 'he came to see and live the day that was to come when he himself was to lead a rebellion in Dublin in the tradition of Robert Emmet's rising in 1803.' See Denis Gwynn, *The Life and Death of Roger Casement*, p. 395.

[427] See Joe Good, *Enchanted By Dreams, the Journal of a Revolutionary*, p. 21. Nor were all the insurgents beyond school going age. See Griffith and O'Grady (eds), *Curious Journey,* p. 57.

[428] Griffith and O'Grady (eds), *Curious Journey*, recollection of Joseph Sweeney, p. 38.

[429] See Sean O'Mahony, *Frongoch, University of Revolution*, p. 114.

[430] Mrs Margaret Pearse (oral recording), The Pearse Museum.

[431] See Frank Fahy, *Memories of the Brothers Pearse*, p. 17.

[432] The name David Sears appears on the list of those garrisoned at the South Dublin Union, but it is not known if this is the same Sears who attended St Enda's and was a member of the Brothers Pearse Commoration Committee (1917). Lists of those who participated in the Rising appear in John O'Connor, *The 1916 Proclamation*. It is likely that Patrick Touhy, who was a First Class (the equivalent of Leaving Certificate

Year) pupil in 1908–9, also participated as the name appears on the list of those who were garrisoned at the General Post Office. O'Connor, however, does not include Touhy among the members 'E' Company 4th Batt alias who were stationed with Pearse at the GPO. See Patrick Pearse to Mrs Pearse, 26 April 1916, in Séamas O'Buachalla (ed.), *The Letters of P.H. Pearse*. See also Sean O'Mahony, *Frongoch University of Revolution*, p. 114. Again, it is possible that Peter O'Connor, whose name appears on the list of those garrisoned at the General Post Office, is the same person who was enrolled in the Second Class (equivalent to Fifth Year) at St Enda's School in 1908–9.

[433] See Louis N. Le Roux, *Patrick H. Pearse*, Desmond Ryan (trans.), p. 176.

[434] Patrick Pearse to Mrs Pearse, 26 April 1916, Séamas O'Buachalla (ed.), *The Letters of P.H. Pearse*.

[435] *Ibid.*, Patrick Pearse to Mrs Pearse, 3 May 1916.

[436] Louis N. Le Roux, *Patrick H. Pearse*, Desmond Ryan (trans.), p. 120.

[437] *The Murder Machine*, 'Back To The Sagas.' Anne Devlin was Emmet's housemaid. She was tortured for information after his failed uprising and died shortly afterwards.

[438] See 'The Man Called Pearse', in Desmond Ryan (ed.), *The Complete Works of P.H. Pearse, St Enda's and its Founder*, p. 142.

[439] *Minutes of the Commissioners of National Education in Ireland*, 27 July 1916, p. 20.

[440] F.W. Pim, *The Sinn Féin Rising: A Narrative and Some Reflection*, p. 17.

[441] *Eighty-Second Report of the Commissioners of National Education in Ireland for 1915-16*, [8372] (H.C., 1917).

[442] Bernard MacLaverty, *Cal* (Belfast, 1984) cited Declan Kiberd, *Inventing Ireland: The Literature of Modern Ireland*, p. 213.

[443] *The Murder Machine*, 'The Murder Machine.'

[444] Henry Giroux, *Schooling for Democracy*, p. 35.

[445] See *The Murder Machine*, 'Back to the Sagas.'

[446] Henry Giroux, *Schooling for Democracy*, p. 81.

[447] *Ibid.*

[448] *Ibid.*

[449] *Ibid.*, See also Henry Giroux, *Theory and Resistance, a Pedagogy for the Opposition*, p. 36.

[450] *Ibid.*

[451] *Ibid.*

Five

The Murder Machine: Schooling as Resistance

THE MURDER MACHINE: PEARSE'S CRITIQUE OF EDUCATION IN IRELAND

Pearse rejected British governance in Ireland and viewed its admin-istration of education there as unacceptable. In *The Murder Machine* he recalled spending 'the greater part of [his] life in immediate contemplation of the most grotesque and horrible of the English inventions for the debasement of Ireland ... their education system'.[1] It was, he concluded, 'an even filthier thing' than a one-time penal proposal for the castration of Catholic clerics.[2] There was, he argued, 'no education system in Ireland' rather 'the simulacrum' of one.[3] The English were 'too wise a people to attempt to educate the Irish ... as well expect them to arm us' he added.[4] This remark, while almost an aside, is by no means insignificant. Pearse believed schooling had been used to regulate a long colonised people but also recognised in it the means of their liberation. He pointedly equated education and intel-lectual liberation with political freedom. Drawing upon an analogy of Eoin McNeill, he compared education in Ireland with that vouched to the slave class in ancient society.[5] While the children of the free were taught 'all noble and goodly things' to make them 'strong and proud and valiant', all such 'dangerous knowledge' was withheld from slaves.[6] The object of such systems was not to make them good men, but 'good slaves'.[7] A similar system, he argued, operated in Ireland. Certain 'slaves' acted as 'jailors' over ordinary 'slaves' who laboured in 'dingy places called schools'.[8] These 'higher slaves' were trained in buildings called 'colleges and universities'.[9] The system was effective because it was a relentless type of automation, an 'immensely powerful engine'.[10] Its codes and regulations restricted innovation, each carrying out 'mysterious and long-drawn out processes of shaping and moulding'.[11] The process was unending, obeying 'immutable' and 'predetermined' laws, 'devoid of understanding, of sympathy, of imagination'.[12] It was fed the 'raw human material' of Irish schoolchildren and what it could not 'refashion after regulation pattern' it ejected 'with all the likeness of its former self crushed from it, a bruised and shapeless thing, thereafter accounted waste'.[13]

Education in Ireland was based upon the assumption of Ireland's place within the Empire, the system was an inversion; schools in Ireland taught children to deny their nation:

> I deny the spirituality of my nation; I deny the lineage of my blood; I deny my rights and responsibilities. This Nego is their Credo, this evil their good … to invent such a system of teaching and to persuade us that it is an education system, an Irish education system to be defended by Irishmen against attack, is the most wonderful thing that the English have accomplished in Ireland, and the most wicked.[14]

An obligatory curriculum 'imposed by an external authority' upon each school-going child was 'the direct contrary of the root idea involved in education'.[15] Writing in December 1912, Pearse pointed to the '15,000' Intermediate Examination pupils 'pounding at a programme drawn up for them by certain persons sitting round a table in Hume Street. Precisely the same textbooks are being read currently, in every secondary school and college in Ireland. Two of Hawthorne's *Tanglewood Tales*, with a few poems in English, will constitute the whole literary pabulum of three-quarters of the pupils of the Irish secondary schools during this twelvemonths'.[16] The system, he complained, had 'damned more souls than the Drink Traffic or the White Slave Trade'.[17]

Pearse's views on national curricula are ignored to this day. Fifty years ago, and coincidently fifty years after Pearse penned this criticism, the research group Tuairim-London argued in their report on Irish education that 'the nation which imposes uniform curricular on all its schools is the exception rather than the rule. No group of children is identical and no syllabus perfect and even the best syllabuses should be used only as guides.'[18]

SCHOOLING AS PROTEST

Throughout history there have been those who rejected formal State education, choosing instead to create institutions outside the mainstream, modern adherents of 'home schooling' are among the inheritors of this tradition. Founders such as Pearse establish schools in opposition to prevailing systems which they believe to be unacceptable for political, social or educational reasons. These radical reformers reject the view of schooling as a process of socialisation and share the belief that harm is done to children and the wider community due to the 'structures, values and techniques of mainstream schooling'.[19] The nature of their opposition and the type of solutions they offer often differ greatly. The work undertaken by Pearse at St Enda's, for example, differs considerably from that of A.S. Neill at Summerhill School, England.[20] Nonetheless, both belong to the radical tradition – both created schools that were forms of dissent.

Radical theory may only retrospectively be ascribed to the work of Pearse and those in the late nineteenth and early twentieth century, who sought to challenge prevailing types of schooling. Thinkers such as Pearse and his contemporary Rabindranath Tagore belong to this tradition because each sought to contest the 'dominant ideologies and practices' of mainstream schools.[21] By conceiving of education as a political act, Pearse, in effect, practised what later became known as radical theory.

Giroux has repeatedly advanced this framework for understanding citizenship education and promoting the importance of democracy in education.[22] He holds that radical theory rests upon two assumptions. Firstly that there is a need for a 'language of critique, a questioning of presuppositions … radical educators, for example, criticise and indeed reject the notion that the primary purpose of public education is economic efficiency … they have the much more radical purpose of educating citizens … which is why the second assumption of radical education is a language of possibility, going beyond critique to elaborate a positive language of human empowerment'.[23] As Pearse employed the metaphor of 'machine' so Giroux warned against 'narrowing the scope of education so severely that schools become mere factories to train the work force'.[24] In order to resist these conceptions of education, Giroux recommended the development of a 'discourse of resistance', a way of speaking about education as an agent of change. Central to his concern is the question of the purpose of education: 'We have to ask what the purposes of education are, what kind of citizens we hope to produce?'[25] Like Pearse, his response is couched in the vocabulary of democracy, emancipation and empowerment. Giroux's modern critique makes Pearse's much earlier work at St Enda's immediately recognisable as stridently radical. He held schooling in Ireland to be an agent of cultural assimilation and a means of securing political compliance. He developed an understanding of school as an act of defiance, an arena in which instruments of assimilation such as curriculum, textbooks and syllabi could be challenged. His identification of schooling with the objectives of the language revival identifies Pearse's understanding of schooling as a form of 'cultural politics'.[26] The establishment of the student council, debating society and the emphasis upon pupil participation reflected his desire that pupils become 'critical thinkers', empowered 'to address social problems in order to transform existing political … inequalities'.[27] His conceptualisation of schooling as emancipatory was an exercise in the 'language of possibility' and at the boy republic of St Enda's he attempted to produce, in microcosm, what he hoped would characterise an independent Ireland. [28]

Another aspect of radical educational theory identifiable in Pearse's work is the relationship between school as an agent of transformation and other social movements. A number of the teaching staff at St Enda's were involved in political and cultural activities, including the Gaelic League and, more significantly, the IRB.[29] A youth branch of the Gaelic League, na Fianna Eireann, was established at the school. Involvement in these activities represents participation in the 'wider collective struggle' of the cultural nationalist movement.[30] The model of the teacher as activist is also relevant when discussing Pearse, whose work at St Enda's and on behalf of the Gaelic League were in fact complementary. Giroux describes this type of endeavour as making the political 'more pedagogical'.[31] Educators bring pedagogic skills to 'social groups and movements outside schools' that are addressing 'important social problems'.[32]

Central to notions of radical educational theory is the experience of democracy, and progressive educators tend to promote its exercise in schools, usually through pupil councils. In this way, democratic practices are learned through participation in the life of the school. This was advocated, for example, by Bertrand and Dora Russell (1894–1986) at Beacon Hill School.[33] Pupils should be inducted into the mores of democracy through encountering 'genuine problems of democracy at their level of maturity'[34] an experience most easily gained by participation in a student council such as that at St Enda's. The council had parallels in the English public school system but at St Enda's, Pearse envisaged a more consultative role for the pupils. In this he attempted to provided a 'democratic culture in which pupils (were) encouraged to resolve ... problems through ... collective decision making'[35] thus anticipating the modern development of citizenship education and the role schooling could play in promoting the 'the evolution of a more democratic social order'.[36] The inspectors who visited St Enda's in 1908 noted, for example, that the school debating society was the first they had encountered.

Freire's conception of the teacher as 'transformative intellectual'[37] and his insistence upon their professional freedom was much earlier identified by Pearse who argued, for example, that teachers should have the freedom to choose texts, design syllabi, influence curricula and chose methodologies.[38] Freire explained that to 'talk about teachers as intellectuals is to say that they should have an active role in shaping the curriculum ... shaping school policy, defining educational philosophies'.[39] Referring to the 'question of text' he enquired: 'Who authorizes them, who produces them?' and what is the 'range of meanings' they 'make available or legitimise?'[40] Again, the process of education as transformative may mean the identification of 'disqualified knowledges' and their reinstatement in the life of the school.[41] To secure political ends, policy makers may purposely omit these 'knowledges'. It can be argued, for example, that the omission of Irish from the National School programme in 1831 was an ideological decision. The absence of Irish represented a silence which implied that the vernacular was worthless. Pearse held that schoolchildren received a sanctioned version of the past that emphasised the identity of Ireland within the British Empire and that the separateness of cultures and the narrative of conflict and dissent were ignored; students had, in other words, become 'ideologically and materially' incorporated into the dominant culture.[42] They had heard only one version of their story. Pearse cited the absurdity of English-only speaking inspectors visiting Irish-speaking children in schools in *Gaeltacht* areas (encounters that can only be described metaphorically as silences) arguing, in effect, that Irish schooling had been constructed on what Giroux later called 'omissions'.[43] C.S. Andrew's recollection that as a child he knew nothing of Cúchulainn testifies to such a 'silence'. Pearse understood the critical relationship between what was offered and withheld in schools, and that as long as Irish education was controlled from Westminster, 'silences and omissions' that facilitated cultural assimilation and political compliance would characterise Irish schooling.[44]

PEARSE AND SCHOOLING

Pearse's writings on schooling initially focused on the role of the language and nationalism in education. Yet early articles such as 'The Children' (1904), while primarily concerned with Gaelic League activities for children, shed light on his understanding of childhood.[45] 'Modern Ireland', he claimed, did not interest itself 'as it should in the wellbeing, the happiness, the thoughts and doings of its children'.[46] Children needed tales, songs, drama, toys, sweets and such like.[47] Irish children did not get 'enough of these' while their parents could afford 'tobacco and drink'.[48] Even in 'philistine England' children were 'thoughtfully looked after', while in America and on the continent 'the brightening of child life' was carried 'almost to a mania'.[49] He therefore called on League branches to organise Feisanna and dramatic plays where toys, rather than the customary 'dry-as-dust' book, should be offered as prizes'.[50] Schools might hold singing and dancing competitions, followed by a magic lantern show where children should be treated to tea, cakes and fruit, rather than the usual 'stale bun and tin mug of ginger beer'.[51] Pearse believed that as few adults as possible should be present at these events to allow children free time with their peers.

The article demonstrates an enlightened understanding of childhood and was informed by his developing sense of the purpose of schooling, the aim of which he wrote, in 1904, was 'not the imparting of knowledge, but the training of the child to be a perfect man or woman'.[52] This thought appears throughout Pearse's writings where he repeatedly insists that the main aim of schooling is 'bringing up a child'. It was this belief in the importance of the process that provoked him to such fury over the unrepresentative nature of the various Boards of Education, qualification for which should be 'competency to direct the administration of education, and not the possession of particular political or religious beliefs'.[53] Pearse, therefore, considered that schooling was related to moral development. It had to do with the formation of people who were responsible and prepared to contribute to the enhancement of society, by transforming their pupils, schools transformed society; a neat inversion of the nineteenth-century British colonial project.

Because the National and Intermediate Systems lacked, what Pearse called, 'freedom for the individual', Ireland had 'no education system' only 'an elaborate machinery for teaching persons certain subjects'.[54] A 'compulsory programme imposed by an external authority upon every child in the country' was 'the direct contrary of the root idea involved in education'.[55] Conformity underpinned the 'machine', every school having to 'conform' to a 'type'.[56] For Pearse, it was anathema that all children preparing for examinations should be obliged to use the same textbooks, regardless of ability. Pressure to prepare pupils meant that schools were unprepared to venture outside the fixed syllabus. The teacher who sought to give pupils a broader experience of litera-ture, for example, did so 'at his peril' and, while pupils might benefit, the endeavour would 'reduce his results fees'.[57] At St Enda's, each pupil was encouraged to select the subjects he believed best suited his require-ments and abilities.[58] Parents, guardians and staff contributed to the decision, but no pupil was 'forced into a grove of study for which he evinced no special talent or native inclination'.[59]

Another striking feature of Pearse's thought was his conviction of the importance of the natural environment in schooling. He strove to help children develop a regard for the natural environment and, always predisposed to finding practical ways to enhance learning, suggested that they collect seashells, wild plants and so forth to display in the classroom. This collection could be constantly renewed and used by the teacher in giving lessons in language, history and geography. Where possible, schools should create small gardens where children could learn to plant and cultivate flowers and vegetables.[60] While 'to the youngsters it is all play', they were in fact learning the skills of horticulture, order, cleanliness and economy.[61] Such a project would also help develop their powers of observation, teach them how to keep records and assume responsibility. For Pearse, only poor resources or lack of teacher commitment limited the possibilities. Indeed, access to the rural environment played an important part in Pearse's decision to move to The Hermitage. He believed that observation of the natural world should lead to a better understanding of the fundamental certainties of life, the co-existence of beauty with harshness and death.[62]

Pearse and his brother William were fond of animals. Their sister, Margaret, remembered that they were filled with 'righteous indignation' when confronted with cruelty and it appears that it was the only conduct that provoked anger in Pearse.[63] This attitude clearly influenced the boys and nature study formed 'one of the favourite subjects at Scoil Éanna'.[64] The school diary for Christmas 1910 recorded that one boy had provided a shelter in the dormitory to a carrier pigeon caught in poor weather while another boy had nursed a lame magpie. These were typical incidents.[65] Pearse successfully made such behaviour part of school life.[66] Along with the school garden, the pupils tended the animals on the school farm the milk from which was sold locally.[67] The pupils also regularly visited the National History Museum and Botanical Gardens in Dublin.

Pearse held empathetic views upon the significance of the personality of the teacher. He should also be a 'tolerant and genial friend' and pupils should feel comfortable in approaching him on any subject 'not foreign to the office of teacher'.[68] He should not remain aloof from anything that was of interest to his pupils: 'The teacher of the primary school should care a good deal for marbles and leap-frog; the secondary teacher should be an enthusiast on football and hurley'.[69] Pearse encouraged teachers to familiarise themselves with pupils' enthusiasms and chat about them 'in French if French is being taught, in German if German is being taught, in Irish if Irish is being taught'.[70]

A good teacher could make the school day 'infinitely interesting to the youngest or the most thoughtless child'.[71] A teacher who did not 'know or love' his work would remain ineffective, regardless of the most inspiring programmes. Teachers should be honourable and idealistic; their character, ideals, sympathies and enthusiasms were the most important aspect of any school.[72] Further, if science and art were taught by 'scientists and artists, and not merely persons with certificates' then the teaching would be 'inspirational'.[73] Pearse could not have poets and writers as his teachers but he invited them to St Enda's: 'Nearly everyone whose name stands for high thought or achievement in any sphere of wholesome endeavour,' he wrote in 1909, 'will address our boys in their Study Hall'.[74] Indeed, the pupils of St Enda's were treated to a succession of distinguished speakers. Apart from notables such as Lady Gregory (1852–1932), Roger Casement (1864–1916), W.B. Yeats (1865–1939), Maud Gonne (1866–1953) and Padraig Colum (1881–1972), many others gave lectures including botanists, historians and linguists.[75]

As Pearse's views on education developed so did his conception of the good teacher, the noblest of whom lives in intimate contact 'with a beautiful life'.[76] By making his own life 'a thing of grace and beauty' the teacher has the happiness of seeing 'successive generations of good men or women grow up around him'.[77] The vocabulary reflects an almost mystical conception and in October 1908, one month after opening St Enda's, he wrote in *An Claidheamh Soluis* that 'with the exception of the clergymen, no one has a higher calling than the teacher'.[78]

Pearse overestimated the importance of the personality of the teacher because he believed that an emotional engagement between teacher and pupil was essential to teaching. Equally, until he gained some experience of school life at St Enda's, he was unable to disentangle the personality of the teacher from its importance to the language revival. He demanded that teachers actively support the revival and foster a spirit of patriotism in their pupils[79] and while berating them as 'obstacles' to the Bilingual Programme[80] he also called for freedom for the 'individual teacher'.[81] Indeed, Pearse is most inconsistent when writing about teachers. On the one hand he called for freedom to allow them select texts, teach as they saw fit, devise individual syllabi and so on while being adamant that they support the language revival, even at the risk of jeopardising extra salary payments. His identification of language revivalism with the teaching body led him to complain in 1907, that very few delegates at the INTO Annual Congress had made speeches in Irish; 'The teachers of Ireland,' he wrote, had not yet 'nailed the colours of the Irish Nation to their masthead' and were 'wont to regard themselves as the civil servants of a foreign power'.[82] He also complained that they too often drew attention to grievances about pay and conditions, although he was prepared to ask teachers to support the language movement at any cost. He conceded, for example, that many teachers viewed the Bilingual Programme with timidity and that its implementation would make extra demands on their time. Yet he insisted that 'all good teaching' made 'large demands on the time ... and energy and patience of the teacher'.[83] The programme would, eventually, 'vastly lighten the burden of work both for teachers and pupils, making it easier to teach all subjects'.[84] Irish should not be avoided on the grounds of difficulty or because it did not pay.[85] It was synonymous with national identity and teachers were duty bound to teach it just as they must teach the 'other subjects which form the essential portions of the education of an Irish child'.[86] Though teachers could earn fees for teaching Irish as an extra subject, Pearse insisted that they had 'no right to demand ... special remuneration for teaching this subject more than for any other teaching subject which is within the minimum school day of four hours'.[87] Three years previously, Pearse had complained of the poor levels of teacher pay.[88] He condemned 'the starvation policy of the British Treasury with regard to Irish primary education' and complained that 'cheapness' was 'the chief recommendation for a secondary teacher in Ireland'[89] yet was prepared to call on them to teach Irish without pay if necessary. Despite the difficulties associated with poor remuneration, uncertain tenure, the pressure of inspection and State examinations, Pearse insisted that teachers were duty bound to assist in the language revival and instil a spirit of patriotism in their pupils.[90]

Teachers had other duties. According to Pearse the formation of the child's character was central to 'true' education.[91] This involved the inculcation of virtues such as 'manliness, purity and reverence'.[92] The 'whole life of a teacher should be a sermon to his pupils'.[93] However, Pearse singled out patriotism as the one virtue every teacher had a 'special duty' to teach, and was anxious to identify love of country with love of parents, 'for duty to country is paramount to duty to parents'.[94] Each child 'had a fundamental right' to be taught that Ireland was his 'mother' and that he had a 'duty to know her, to love her, [and] work for her'.[95] The explicit inculcation of patriotism, he noted, was common in European, British and American schools.[96] The methods for inculcating national pride were characteristically practical. Teachers should organise visits to local sites of interest, nature trips should be made so that local fauna and flora might be studied and children should familiarise themselves with the history of their locality.

Pearse had high expectations. The teacher should be of 'fine character and lofty ideal', 'warmly Irish in sympathy' and 'a worker for Ireland'.[97] He expected much from them because they were the point of contact with the next generation.[98] But he cautioned against jingoism. The teacher's patriotism should be 'generous and wholesome' and not an act of propaganda.[99] Children should be taught to take their Irish identity for granted and understand that their allegiance to Ireland was above 'every other secular person, institution, or conception'.[100]

Ultimately, Pearse settled upon the model of fosterer to represent the ideal teacher. His understanding of the teacher/fosterer was similar to the modern understanding of the teacher as acting in *loco parentis* although, characteristically, he self-mockingly joked about 'how blue Dr Hyde, Mr Yeats and Mr MacNeill would look if their friends informed them that they were about to send their children to be fostered'.[101] Yet the notion was underpinned by a serious conception of the relationship between teacher and pupil. Pearse based his model upon a practice that originated in ancient Gaelic society. The laws governing fosterage were complicated but, given Pearse's regular use of Dublin's National Library, it is possible that he was familiar with the custom in some detail. The Ancient Laws of Ireland (Seanchus Mór) had been published in Dublin in 1869 and a 1901 edition of the Laws by Robert Atkinson, was held at the St Enda's library.[102]

Fosterage entailed the short-term adoption of children, usually between noble families, so that the child might learn the arts of oratory, tribal law, rhetoric and military skills. Usually it served to ensure peace between powerful families or tribes (tuath).[103] The child became the surrogate child of the fosterer and the latter became a substitute parent, assuming both the responsibility and rewards of that position. The analogy suited Pearse's developing understanding of the teacher's role which he saw as connected with fostering the 'elements of character already present' in the child.[104] This was 'exactly the function of the teacher … to foster that which is native in the soul of his pupils, striving to bring its inborn excellence to ripeness'.[105] Indeed, 'among the Gaels', the word for teacher was the same as that denoting 'fostering'.[106] The world of the Gaelic sagas and, in particular, the Boy Corps of Eamhain Macha, the boyhood home of the Ulster warrior Cúchulainn, presented Pearse with a symbolic antidote to the 'murder machine'.[107] This world of fostered boys, drilled in the arts of discourse, law and war, provided an obvious analogy for St Enda's. The Corps was a type of school and its members wedded to the notion of sacrifice and honour. It was a Gaelic model and therefore could act as the antidote to English schoolbook heroes such as Wellington and Nelson.[108] The closeness of the Boy Corps to nature and the meshing of their physical, moral and intellectual training reflected the type of educational experience Pearse wished to provide at The Hermitage. Their self-governing code of honour represented a type of micro-democracy, the type he attempted to establish at St Enda's. The Boy Corps was mythological and Pearse understood it to be so, yet he wrote that 'all these things were designed with a largeness of view foreign to the little minds that devise our modern makeshifs for education'.[109] He advocated the myth of the Boy Corps as the antidote of the 'myth' of the Irish child as citizen of the Empire – an untruth that denied the fundamental attributes of nationhood such as language and self-government: if the Battle of Waterloo had been won on the playing fields of Eton, independence would be won on the hurling fields of St Enda's.[110] Pearse would thus subvert the colonisers myth in order to forge a new national identity.

If teachers were to fulfil a role like that of the fosterer then only the most deserving should be recruited. The Boy Corps provided the model for a new system of schooling to replace that which tolerated as teachers 'the rejected of all other professions, rather than demanding for so priest-like an office the highest souls and the noblest intellects of the race'.[111] Allowing for hyperbole, this comment testifies to the ongoing change in Pearse's appreciation of the teaching task. Undoubtedly his view was much influenced by his work with the pupils at St Enda's, yet the following illustrates how his appreciation had developed:

> One's life in a school is a perpetual adventure, an adventure among souls and minds; each child is a mystery, and if the plucking out of the heart of so many mysteries is fraught with much in labour and anxiety, there are compensations richer than have ever rewarded any voyagers among treasure islands in tropic seas'.[112]

As Pearse gained more experience of teaching, his perception of the profession modified. In a lecture delivered at the Mansion House, Dublin, in December 1912, he spoke of the teacher as fosterer but also introduced the figure of 'the Master' – a personality around which a community of learning evolved.[113] The historical models Pearse cited were Christ and the Disciples ('a sort of school') and the early Irish monastic communities of St Enda of Aran and Colmcille.[114] Again, he turned to the example of the Middle Ages when 'everywhere little groups of persons (clustered) around some beloved teacher' and in this way 'learned not only the humanities but all gracious and useful crafts'.[115] Hence, there had been no need for 'State art schools' or 'State technical schools' because apprentices learned from master craftsmen.[116] Pearse was drawn to this 'personal element' in learning.[117] No child should be 'merely a unit in a school … but in some intimate personal way the pupil of a teacher'.[118] While the personality of the teacher should in no way hinder the development of the pupil he should, nonetheless, be 'an inspiration and an example'.[119]

While Pearse was often critical of the teaching profession he believed that it had an important role and in 1913 outlined his vision for the profession in an independent Ireland. An Irish government should appoint a Minster in charge of a Department of Education. This department should ensure that all teachers were employees of the State, adequately remunerated, provided with security of tenure, at liberty to pursue promotion and provided with suitable pensions.[120] Teachers should be given a greater voice in the content and operation of the education system, indeed teachers 'would be the system' and the Inspectorate would be drawn from their ranks while 'promoted teachers' staffed the training colleges.[121] Pearse's offerings on the role of the teacher in an independent Ireland were not comprehensive and he admitted that he had 'little' to say of 'organisation'.[122] Rather, he offered an overview that reflected an enlightened and empathetic understanding that demonstrates how his view had developed since the early 1900s. But his insistence that teachers had a duty to encourage patriotism is problematic.

NATIONALISM AND EDUCATION

There was a close relationship between Pearse's nationalism and his thinking on education. Apart from the language question, Pearse hoped to see schools become national in tone and atmosphere. The exact nature of his wish is difficult to define because it depended upon his belief, and that of the wider Irish Ireland movement, that the country and its schools were anglicised, copying English customs and neglecting those they perceived as intrinsically Irish. Revivalists wished to see an end to foreign games such as soccer, imported dances and fashions and turn instead to past-times deemed inherently Irish.

The school syllabus at the beginning of the twentieth century allowed few significant concessions to social and political differences between Irish and English children. C.S. Andrews described Dublin as 'totally anglicised' and recalled being taken to a:

> review in the Castle to celebrate the King's birthday … thousands turned up to see it … Dublin was an English city … soccer football was the game talked of and played everywhere … and it was, at that time, purely an English game … in cricket we followed the fortunes of Surrey and Kent.[123]

Andrews recalled that:

> Our nursery rhymes were English and we knew all about Dick Whittington, Robin Hood and Alice in Wonderland, but we'd never heard of Fionn or Cúchulainn. Portraits of the King and Queen were often on display in shop windows … at school in Dominick Street … Irish was never mentioned.'[124] Andrews 'never read anything at all about Ireland at this time', rather, he read 'Coral Island … and Chips'.[125]

Roger Casement recalled that at Belfast Ballymena Academy, he was taught 'nothing about Ireland … I don't think the word was ever mentioned in a single class of the school'.[126] In 1941, Alfred Dennis recalled that the Dublin in which Pearse 'lived his passionate years' was intellectually divided between 'English liberalism' and 'the glamour' of revolutionary movements.[127] In 1955, Maire Nic Shuibhlaigh opined that the Irish Theatre, established by Edward Martyn in 1914, foundered because audiences 'were still being catered for by English stock companies and cheap British variety troupes.'[128]

Pearse's support of the cultural revival was sincere and broad ranging. He was anxious to see it take hold in schools and understood that if the movement were to maintain its momentum it must appeal to the next generation. This is why, in spite of much opposition within the Gaelic League, he supported the Irish Government Bill of 1907, as it would allow local councils to gain a significant degree of control over schools.[129] The Irishising of the schools was the first step on the path to a national renaissance.[130] If he could convince them to support the Irish Ireland movement, children would begin to think of themselves as citizens of an Irish nation and, when adults, might take practical steps to secure that nationhood: 'The children must be brought to feel that they are Irish children; that this is Ireland; and they are destined to become citizens of an Irish Nation'.[131] Consequently, nationalism was a key factor in his educational thinking.

In 1904, Pearse wrote that 'bad education is at the root of all national decadence'.[132] By 'bad education' he meant that which was not 'Irish' in tone and spirit. The National System was a 'pillar of foreignism', one which 'in ideal and practice spells Anglicisation'.[133] The system had 'deliberately eliminated the national factor' to the extent that the Irish were unaware that that they were 'slaves'.[134] Hence Pearse had launched his editorship of *An Claidheamh Soluis* by committing the Gaelic League to the 'intellectual independence' of Ireland.[135] As early as 1903 he supported a suggestion in the *Gaelic Journal* that an Irish-only school be established in one of the *Gaeltacht* areas. He added that such a school, and others like it, would necessarily 'withdraw the pupils from the existing National Schools'.[136] In effect, he advocated the establishment of a network of Irish-only schools in opposition to the National System, funded and managed by 'Irish Irelanders'.[137]

The American system provided an attractive model. There, the process of fostering patriotism began in elementary school through the singing of national songs and honouring the flag. This impressed Pearse and he pointed out that what informed schooling in America, was not the need to 'cram' children with information, rather, to prepare them for responsible citizenship.[138] He was also struck by the apparent classlessness of the American schoolroom. Education was provided free of charge by the State for children of all social backgrounds. Vast State expenditure, innovative methodology and the emphasis on patriotism, struck him as the antithesis of the education system in Ireland, which he characterised as a 'shackling of the mind'.[139]

The type of nationalism Pearse was advocating at this period (1904) was conservative and focused on children acquiring knowledge of the history, geography and botany of Ireland.[140] This should be approached in a practical way: 'Far more effective than the mere didactic preaching of patriotism,' he wrote, 'would be well-directed efforts to bring the children into some direct relation with the country they inhabit – its natural beauty, its wild living things, its rocks, its rivers, its ruins. Saturday excursions should be made to the scenes of famous fights, the sites of famous dúns or churches'.[141]

In America a wide range of activities were undertaken in elementary schools. Libraries, museums and gardens were encouraged and small school farms and vegetable plots were created so children could learn the basics of horticulture and animal husbandry. While these had obvious practical value, Pearse believed that they also helped children feel part of their community and encouraged a sense of belonging. The inculcation of national pride was, he argued, a feature of education in every 'enlightened country'.[142] In Denmark, for example, 'old Danish folksongs are sung in schools, in Belgium the children are taught the Battle of Waterloo was a Flemish victory … in America schoolchildren salute the American flag as they pass to their desks'.[143] Irish children should be encouraged to feel that they are Irish and owe their 'allegiance and their love to that Nation'.[144] While he insisted on the use of Irish as the chief means of achieving this, he also suggested that 'foreign games which actively compete with Irish games should be prohibited'[145] and by 1907 he was insisting that the 'Irishising' of the schools was more important than 'any mere subject' including Irish.[146] Rather, the first duty of the schools should be the 'breeding, for the weal of Ireland, of a race of patriots'.[147] In confusing the purpose of school with a 'duty' to breed 'a race of patriots' Pearse made a grave error; he confused intellectual liberation with political liberation and in doing so ceased to think educationally. A truly liberal education would allow pupils to embrace or reject patriotism based solely upon its merits; anything else is tantamount to indoctrination.

In 1908, *An Claidheamh Soluis* reproduced a circular from Coiste an Oideachais, the education committee of the Gaelic League, stressing the importance of 'teaching' patriotism. Pearse supported this and highlighted the German government's insistence on the duty of schools to 'foster an ardent spirit of true patriotism in the young'.[148] Irish schoolchildren should be 'fired' by tales of nationalist heroes such as Sarsfield, taught to recite stirring ballads and 'constantly reminded' of their separateness from England.[149] Teachers should stress that it was 'a disgrace and a badge of slavery for a race to use the language of any other in preference to its own'.[150] He supported the call for the schools to assist in the 'transition from Anglicisation' and the Committee's suggestion that schools hold a Feis on St Patrick's Day each year, at which prizes would be awarded for dance, song and story-telling. At this event a 'discourse on love of Ireland and everything Irish' should be given and the need to speak Irish, play Irish games and buy Irish products encouraged.[151] Finally, children should be 'warned against Anglicisation in all shapes and forms'.[152]

Pearse's views were not dissimilar to many of his generation.[153] Eveleen Nicolls, for example, was an enthusiastic Gaelic League supporter. She drowned in the summer of 1909 while visiting the *Gaeltacht* area around Dingle, Co. Kerry, and after Pearse's execution it was suggested that they had been romantically attached.[154] Her essay, 'Nationality in Irish Education' (1910), was a typical revivalist tract.[155] Like Pearse, she argued that the education system in Ireland was designed to 'keep from Irish children all knowledge of the past of their nation … a colourless and un-national thing' that actively attempted to frustrate the bond between the child and 'his country'.[156] Nicolls held that, because successive generations were educated in this way, Ireland's folk heritage had been jeopardised. Her concern was widely shared by revivalists such as Lady Gregory, W.B. Yeats, T.R. Rollerston and Douglas Hyde, some of whom had made collections of folklore especially along the west and southern seaboards.[157] Patriotism in schools was a popular topic among revivalists at this period. A contributor to the *Irish Educational Review* insisted that education was concerned with responsibility to the State; indeed, ultimately it was a process of induction into the nation. A boy in an English school 'learned' what it was to be an English boy, a member of the English nation, aware of its customs, aspirations and attendant responsibilities; this was the same for a French, German or Irish schoolboy. Nationalism in education, the writer contended, was not subversive rather it was customary and unavoidable.[158]

The literature of the Revival is replete with calls for a more nationalist atmosphere in schools. It was continually argued that a comprehensive course in Irish history be introduced in National and intermediate schools and the language employed in these essays and articles is often similar to that used by Pearse. Writing in 1908, Revd Andrew Murphy, for example, called for teachers of history to develop in pupils 'a love of their native land, pride in her glories' and the inculcation of a 'sprit of patriotism'.[159] John Redmond complained that education and over-taxation were two means by which Ireland had been 'annihilated'.[160] Others believed that the education system appeared to have no purpose other than Anglicisation and Bulmer Hobson complained that 'in education … English control is everywhere'.[161]

The reluctance of the schools to embrace cultural nationalism was a perennial source of frustration to revivalists and private intermediate schools in particular were frequently attacked for their lack of enthu-siasm. Commentators complained that while having administrative and curricular freedom not enjoyed by the National Schools they continued 'to be anglophile'.[162] In these schools, Ireland's 'language and native literature were ignored, her history unstudied and Irish art, science and music treated as things unknown'.[163] They acted as if Irish had no existence 'outside books'.[164]

Nationalist publications such as *The Leader*, *An Claidheamh Soluis* and *Sinn Féin* encouraged parents to send their children to schools that would provide a less Anglo-centric culture than that purport-edly offered by the traditionally exclusive schools, such as Clongowes Wood and Blackrock College, although their connection with nation-alism is, in fact, striking. [165] D.P. Moran sneeringly referred to these schools as offering 'respectability', the distained preserve of 'Castle-Catholics'.[166] Thomas Davis had earlier criticised them for offering only 'the things' that are 'least worth learning'.[167] When Pearse set out to 'challenge the whole existing education system of Ireland' he was referring to the schooling that these institutions provided – an 'English' education but in 'Irish' schools.[168] These schools, he held, embraced and perpetuated the anglicising programme of Britain in Ireland, providing the administrators for the colonial project, both here and abroad.

These criticisms were not unfounded. A number of Irish schools had strong connections with the British Armed Forces as demonstrated, in particular, by the involvement of past pupils in the First World War in particular. Indeed, this relationship has been neglected in Irish educa-tional history generally. Several past pupils of Blackrock College died in the war, and it was believed that another, Walther Cronin, invented the depth charger that proved so devastating to German U-Boats.[169] Past pupils of Clongowes Wood College, Thomas Esmonde and Thomas

Crean were awarded the Victoria Cross in the Crimean and Boer Wars respectively. John Vincent was also awarded the Victoria Cross for bravery at Guillemont in September 1916.

It is, therefore, not surprising that Pearse (although he could never know the full extent of past pupils involvement in the First World War) and others should consider these schools as bastions of Britain in Ireland. Writing three years after Pearse's execution, Stephen Gwynn complained that typically in these schools 'there must be no appeal to Irish patriotism … Irish history may not be taught as a subject, and, until lately, anything bearing on it, however remotely, was taboo'.[170]

After the establishment of St Enda's in 1908, Pearse's attacks upon the system became more politically charged. 'An Irish school,' he wrote, 'must be permeated through and through by Irish culture, the repository of which [was] the language.'[171] By 1910, his earlier adherence to cultural nationalism was beginning to give way to a more strident republicanism. Symbolically the change was represented in his confession that, whereas at Cullenswood House he used to speak to the boys of the deeds of Cúchulainn, at The Hermitage his thoughts had turned to Robert Emmet – from mythical symbol to revolutionary martyr.[172]

Writing in January 1910, Pearse argued that while not every British undertaking in Ireland had been designed to 'injure our welfare', there could be no doubt concerning the 'evils' of the educational system.[173] It was 'cunningly designed to destroy our nationality', its authors did not teach contempt for Irish language, history or culture; by simply ignoring them they had 'attained the desired result quiet as effectually'.[174] The antidote was a potent strain of nationalism and in his speech at the Mansion House, Dublin, in 1912 Pearse insisted that nationalism was among 'the most powerful of educational resources'.[175] Irish education had failed because it had ignored 'the nationalist factor'.[176] Irish nationalism, he held, undaunted by 'Cromwell … the Penal Laws … and the horrors of '98' had almost succumbed to 'three-quarters of a century's education'.[177]

This more radical tone reflected the shift in Pearse's political position and as he drifted toward military separatism he offered a new vision for an education authority in an independent Ireland. Significantly, however, he assured his readers that his scheme presupposed 'the getting rid not only of the British Treasury' the 'master of everything in Ireland' but also of 'the British connection'.[178]

Notes:

[1] *The Murder Machine*, 'The Broad Arrow.'

[2] *Ibid.*

[3] *Ibid.*

[4] *Ibid.*

[5] Eoin MacNeill (1867–1945) nationalist, historian and professor of early Irish history at University College Dublin. He was Commander in Chief of the Irish Volunteers (founded November 1913), supporter of the 1921 Treaty and Minister for Education in the Free State. MacNeill's two sons attended St Enda's School.

[6] *The Murder Machine*, 'The Broad Arrow.'

[7] *Ibid.*

[8] *Ibid.*

[9] *Ibid.*

[10] *The Murder Machine*, 'The Murder Machine.'

[11] *Ibid.*

[12] *Ibid.*

[13] *Ibid.*

[14] *The Murder Machine*, 'I Deny'.

[15] *The Murder Machine*, 'Of Freedom in Education.'

[16] *Ibid.*

[17] *The Murder Machine*, 'When We Are Free.'

[18] Tuarim-London Research Group, *Irish Education*, p. 25.

[19] See Allen Graubard, *Free the Children, Radical Reform and the Free School Movement*, p. 7.

[20] A.S. Neill, educational reformer and founder of Summerhill School, England.

[21] Rabindranath Tagore, Nobel Laureate, cultural nationalist and school founder. Henry Giroux, *Theory and Resistance in Education, a Pedagogy for the Opposition*, p. 115.

[22] See Henry Giroux, *Boarder Crossings, Cultural Workers and the Politics of Education*, Part I. Interview: The Hope of Radical Education.

[23] *Ibid.*, p. 10.

[24] *Ibid.*, p. 11. Elsewhere Giroux quotes Aronowitz who spoke of the effect of schooling at the service of the marketplace: 'Human thinking becomes mechanized and the mind corresponds to the machine – a technicized, segmented, and degraded instrument that has lost its capacity for critical thought, especially its ability to imagine another way of life.' Cited in Henry Giroux, *Theory and Resistance in Education, a Pedagogy for the Opposition*, p. 121.

[25] Henry Giroux, *Border Crossings, Cultural Workers and the Politics of Education*, p. 12.

[26] Henry Giroux, *Schooling for Democracy, Critical Pedagogy in the Modern Age*, p. 9.

[27] *Ibid.* For Pearse inequalities resided in the constitutional political domain and its repercussions for schooling, rather than in the arena of social injustice.

[28] Peter McLaren, *Critical Pedagogy and Predatory Culture*, p. 32.

[29] See Chapter Five.

[30] Henry Giroux, *Schooling For Democracy*, p. 33.

[31] *Ibid.*, p. 35.

[32] *Ibid.*

[33] Bertrand Russell, mathematician and philosopher. Dora Black (later Russell), feminist writer and political activist. The Russell's founded Beacon Hill School, see Chapter Five.

[34] Jesse Newlon, 'Democracy or Super-patriotism?' *The Social Frontier*, April 1941, p. 210, cited in Giroux, *Schooling for Democracy*, p. 43.

[35] Wilfred Carr and Anthony Hartnett, *Education and the Struggle for Democracy, the Politics of Educational Ideas*, p. 63.

[36] *Ibid.*

[37] Paulo Freire, *Boarder Crossings, Critical Pedagogy and Cultural Power*, p. 15.

[38] See *The Murder Machine*, 'When We Are Free.'

[39] Paulo Friere, *Boarder Crossings, Critical Pedagogy and Cultural Power*, p. 15.

[40] *Ibid.*, p. 154. See *The Murder Machine*, 'When We Are Free.'

[41] Michel Foucault, 'Two Lectures', in C. Gordon (ed. & trans.) *Power/Knowledge: Selected Interviews and Other Writings 1972-77*, p. 83.

[42] Henry Giroux, *Theory and Resistance in Education, Pedagogy for the Opposition*, p. 38.

[43] Henry Giroux, *Schooling for Democracy, Critical Pedagogy in the Modern Age*, p. 100. See Pearse's 1905 essay, 'Education in the West of Ireland' *Guth na Bliadhna*, reproduced in O'Buachalla, *P.H. Pearse, a Significant Irish Educationalist.*

[44] 'Pedagogy is always related to power. In fact educational theories, like any philosophy, are ideologies that have an intimate relation to questions of power.' Henry Giroux, *Border Crossings, Cultural Workers and the Politics of Education*, p. 15.

[45] See 'The Children', *An Claidheamh Soluis*, 26 November 1904, p. 6.

[46] *Ibid.*

[47] *Ibid.*

[48] *Ibid.*

[49] *Ibid.* Pearse was also struck by the democratic nature of the pupil-teacher relationship in American schools. See 'A National Education', *An Claidheamh Soluis*, 16 April 1904, p. 6.

[50] *Feiseanna* are Irish dancing and music competitions. 'The Children', *An Claidheamh Soluis*, 26 November 1904, p. 6.

[51] *Ibid.*

[52] 'The Philosophy of Education', *An Claidheamh Soluis*, 12 November 1904, p. 6.

[53] 'An Irish Education Board', *An Claidheamh Soluis*, 1 December 1906, p. 7.

[54]   *The Murder Machine*, 'Master and Disciples.'

[55]   *The Murder Machine*, 'Freedom in Education.'

[56]   *Ibid.*

[57]   *Ibid.*

[58]   On freedom in schooling see *The Murder Machine*, 'Freedom in Education.'

[59]   *The Prospectus of Scoil Éanna (1909)*, Selection of Course.

[60]   *The Prospectus of Scoil Éanna (1909)* offered to each pupil who 'so desires' a plot of ground, which he is at liberty to plan out and cultivate according to his own taste … under skilled direction.' See 'Nature Study and Physical Science.'

[61]   'The Philosophy of Education', *An Claidheamh Soluis*, 12 November 1904, p. 6.

[62]   *Ibid.*

[63]   Desmond Ryan recollected that Pearse would 'tell us with pride that he had never lost his temper since the school had started, and this was strictly true …' See Desmond Ryan, The Man Called Pearse, *The Complete Works of P.H. Pearse*, p. 201.

[64]   *An Macaomh*, Vol. I. No. 2. Christmas 1909, p. 52.

[65]   See *An Macaomh*, Vol. II, No. 3, Christmas 1910, p. 76, 'October 5th' and p. 78, 'November 7th'.

[66]   Yet a letter from Eugene Cronin, a pupil of St Enda's since 1914, relates how he and a friend had gone 'torching' and 'killed a thrush and a blackbird.' This letter was written after Pearse's death. Eugene Cronin to Theresa Cronin (Aunt Theresa) 16 January 1917, Pearse Collection, Pearse Museum, KGA.

[67]   See *St Enda's Roll Book 1908-9*, entry for 25 September 1908, Pearse Museum, Rathfarnham.

[68]   *Ibid.*

[69]   *Ibid.*

[70]   *Ibid.*

[71] See 'Irish Schools As They Are and As They Ought To Be', *An Claidheamh Soluis*, 19 November 1904, p. 6.

[72] 'Live Teaching in the Secondary School', *An Claidheamh Soluis*, 6 January 1906, p. 6.

[73] See *The Murder Machine*, 'Back to the Sagas.' These remarks were initially made in a speech at the Mansion House, Dublin in December 1912.

[74] 'By Way of Comment, *An Macaomh*, Vol. I, No. 2, Christmas 1909.

[75] See, for example, *An Macaomh*, Vol. I. No. 2. Christmas, 1909, p. 52, Miss Helen Laird on Plant Life.' On the persons who visited the school see *An Macaomh*, Vol. I, No. I, Midsummer 1908, p. 86. Padraic Colum, dramatist, novelist and folklorist. Maud Gonne, political activist, founder of *Inghinidhe na hEireann* (Daughters of Ireland) in Dublin in 1900 and *Bean na hEireann* (Women of Ireland) a journal espousing military separatism (1908), supported the anti-treaty forces during the Irish Civil War.

[76] 'The Formation of Character', *An Claidheamh Soluis*, 26 January 1907, p. 7.

[77] *Ibid.*

[78] 'The Teaching Profession', *An Claidheamh Soluis*, 3 October 1908, p. 10.

[79] 'The systematic inculcation of patriotism is part of the school *regime* of every enlightened country', 'The Philosophy of Education', *An Claidheamh Soluis*, 12 November 1904, p. 6.

[80] 'The New Coiste Gnótha: Its Work', *An Claidheamh Soluis*, 9 May 1903, p. 5.

[81] 'Freedom … for the individual teacher to impart something of his own personality to his work, to bring his own peculiar gift to the service of his pupils, to be, in short, a teacher, a master, one having an intimate and permanent relationship with his pupils, and not a mere part of the educational machine …' 'Education Under Home Rule', a lecture delivered in the Mansion House 11 December 1909, *An Claidheamh Soluis* 4 January 1913, 11 January 1913, 18 January 1913, 15 February 1913, 22 February 1913, 1 March 1913.

[82] 'The Teachers', *An Claidheamh Soluis*, 13 April 1907, p. 7.

[83] 'The Bilingual Programme', *An Claidheamh Soluis*, 24 September 1904, p. 6.

[84] *Ibid.*

[85] 'About the Intermediate', *An Claidheamh Soluis*, 9 December 1905, p. 6.

[86] 'Should We Demand Fees For Irish As An Ordinary', *An Claidheamh Soluis*, 28 March 1908, p 9.

[87] *Ibid.*

[88] 'The British Treasury and Ireland', *An Claidheamh Soluis*, 25 February 1905, p. 6. See also 'The Starvation Policy', *An Claidheamh Soluis*, 2 February 1907, p. 7.

[89] *Ibid.*

[90] An intermediate teachers salary during the period 1900–1910 was approximately £120 for men and £80 for women.

[91] 'The Philosophy of Education', *An Claidheamh Soluis,* 12 November 1904, p. 6.

[92] *Ibid.*

[93] *Ibid.*

[94] *Ibid.*

[95] *Ibid.*

[96] *Ibid.*

[97] The Secondary School, *An Claidheamh Soluis*, 25 November 1905, p. 6.

[98] *Ibid.* '… he must realise the awfulness and the responsibility of his position as one into whose hands it is given to mould for good or ill the characters of future Irish citizens.'

[99] *Ibid.*

[100] *Ibid.*

[101] *Ibid.* Douglas Hyde (1860–1949) Irish language scholar, president of the Gaelic League and first President of Ireland.

[102] Robert Atkinson, *Ancient Laws of Ireland*, Vol. VI (n.p. Dublin 1901). The Pearse Museum.

[103] See Dillon & Chadwick, *The Celtic Realms*, p. 129.

[104] 'By Way of Comment', *An Macaomh*, Vol. I, No. 2, December 1909.

[105] *Ibid.*

[106] *Ibid*. See also *The Murder Machine*, 'An Ideal in Education.' 'To the old Irish the teacher was *aite*, 'fosterer' the pupil was *dalta*, 'foster-child', the system was *aiteachas*, 'fosterage'.

[107] *Eamhain Macha*, the mythological home of Meave, Queen of Ulster and her consort Conchobar, and location of the foster home where the warrior Cúchulainn and his friend Ferdia, as children and members of the fostered group or Crops, were taught the military arts. The legendary site is identified with Navan Fort, close to Armagh.

[108] For emphasis on British Imperial history in syllabi and examinations see, for example, Intermediate Education Board for Ireland, *Rules and Programme of Examinations For 1907*, Accounts and Papers (27) Vol. XCI. p. 41 & p. 47. See also Intermediate Education Board for Ireland, Examinations, 1906, History and Geography, MS 21087 Pearse Papers, NLI.

[109] By Way of Comment, *An Macaomh*, Vol. I. No. 2. December 1909. Shaw correctly pointed out that in relation to Celtic Ireland 'of the education of boys or of anyone else we know virtually nothing.' See Francis Shaw, 'The Canon of Irish History – A Challenge', *Studies*, Vol. LXI (1972), p. 131.

[110] 'I am certain that when it comes to a question of Ireland winning battles, her main reliance must be on her hurlers. To your camans, O boys of Banba!' 'By Way of Comment', *An Macaomh*, Vol. I, No. 2, December 1909. This sentiment was echoed in *An Scoláire*, the school magazine of St Enda's some years later. A pupil, lamenting the state of hurling as compared with the school's earlier years wrote; 'What was it urged those brave boys whose place you have taken to fight their battles … it was because they dreamt themselves as patriots leading mighty hosts to free their native land.' See 'The Old Order Changeth', *An Scoláire*, Vol. I, No. II, p. 3. 20 March 1913.

[111] *The Murder Machine*, 'Back to the Sagas.' The comment reflects those of Comenius who held that 'educators of men must be the most select of all', Comenius, *Pampaedia*, p. 136.

[112] The Murder Machine, 'Back to the Sagas.'

[113] 'Education under Home Rule', *An Claidheamh Soluis*, 11 January 1913, p, 6.

[114] *Ibid*.

[115] *Ibid.*

[116] *Ibid.*

[117] *Ibid.*

[118] *Ibid.*

[119] *The Murder Machine*, 'Of Freedom in Education.'

[120] See *The Murder Machine*, 'When We Are Free.'

[121] *Ibid.*

[122] *Ibid.*

[123] C.S. Andrews, *Dublin Made Me*, p. 42. Dublin Castle, seat of British administration in Ireland.

[124] *Ibid.*

[125] 'Todd Andrews in conversation with Pádraig Ó'Rathallaigh', RTÉ, November 1947.

[126] Cited in Geoffrey de C. Parminter, *Roger Casement*, p. 34. Roger Casement (1864–1816) highlighted the cruelties associated with commercial mining in the Belgian Congo and South America. He was a member of the Gaelic League and executed for his involvement in the Easter Rising.

[127] See Alfred Dennis, 'A Memory of P.H. Pearse', p. 259, *Capuchin Annual*, December 1941.

[128] Maire Nic Shuibhlaigh, *The Splendid Years*, p. 152. On the influence of 'petty-bourgeois (English) culture' on late nineteenth century Dublin see also, Michael Tierney, *A Classicist's Outlook*, p. 174.

[129] See 'The Bill', *An Claidheamh Soluis*, 18 May 1907, p. 7.

[130] 'Irishise' was a verb Pearse used to describe the process whereby a schools was imbued with an Irish 'tone'. For example where pupils would be exposed to Irish history, songs and folklore and the Irish language would be used in ordinary conversation.

[131] ''The Secondary School', *An Claidheamh Soluis*, 25 November 1905, p. 6.

[132] 'Irish Education', *An Claidheamh Soluis*, 28 May 1904, p. 6.

[133] 'The Primary Schools', *An Claidheamh Soluis*, 20 August 1904, p. 51.

[134] *The Murder Machine.* 'Back to the Sagas.'

[135] 'The Issue At Stake', *An Claidheamh Soluis*, 14 March 1903, p. 4.

[136] 'The New Coiste Gnótha: Its Work', *An Claidheamh Soluis*, 9 May 1903, p. 5. The word 'National' is couched in inverted brackets to denote Pearse's contention that the system was, in fact, not national as it catered only for children whose vernacular was English.

[137] *Ibid.*

[138] See 'A National Education', *An Claidheamh Soluis*, 16 April 1904, p. 6.

[139] See 'Irish Education', *An Claidheamh Soluis*, 28 May 1904, p. 6.

[140] On the early nature of early cultural nationalism see Brian Murphy, 'Father Peter Yorke's 'Turning of the Tide' (1890): The Strictly Cultural Nationalism of the Early Gaelic League', *Eire-Ireland*, Vol. 23 (1988). See also Declan Kiberd 'Uprising', *Inventing Ireland, the Literature of the Modern Nation*.

[141] 'The Philosophy of Education', *An Claidheamh Soluis*, 12 November 1904, p. 6.

[142] *Ibid.*

[143] *Ibid.*

[144] 'The Secondary School', *An Claidheamh Soluis*, 25 November 1905, p. 6.

[145] *Ibid.*

[146] 'The Duty of the Schools', *An Claidheamh Soluis*, 7 September 1907, p. 7.

[147] *Ibid.*

[148] See 'The Schools', *An Claidheamh Soluis*, 7 March 1908, p. 9.

[149] *Ibid.*

[150] *Ibid.*

[151] *Ibid.*

[152] *Ibid.*

[153] Differences between revivalists were frequently played out in the pages of *An Claidheamh Soluis* and *The Leader*. But the development of Pearse's cultural nationalism into a more militant and separatist strain was typical of many. For a discussion of the relationship between cultural and separatist nationalism see John Hutchinson, 'The Gaelic Revival (c. 1890–1921): Its Socio–Political Articulation in *The Dynamics of Cultural Nationalism*.

[154] See Le Roux, *Patrick H. Pearse*, p. 39, Thomás O'Crohan *The Islandman*, p. 197. Ruth Dudley Edwards *Patrick Pearse, the Triumph of Failure*, pp. 124–6, Micheál O'Dubhshláine. *Oighean Uasal ó Phríomhchathair Eireann & A Dark Day on the Blaskets*. Writing in 1970 Padraig Ó'Snodaigh commented that 'according to some people' William Pearse and Mabel Gorman 'became deeply attached. If this was so his love was as ill fated as his brother's for Eibhlín' Padraig Ó'Snodaigh, 'Willie Pearse: Artist', *Leabhrán Cuimhreacháin Aran Fhoilsiú ar Ocáid Bronnadh Eochar Scoil Éanna are Uachtarán na hEireann, Eamonn De Valera*, 23 April 1970. On Mabel Gorman see Chapter Four.

[155] Eveleen Nicolls, *Nationality in Irish Education*.

[156] *Ibid.*, p. 4.

[157] Lady Augusta Gregory (1851–1932) folklorist, dramatist and nationalist. William Butler Yeats (1865–1939) dramatist and poet.

[158] See Wilfred O'Kane, 'Educational Advantages of a Language Revival', *The Irish Educational Review*, Vol. II, No. I, p. 114, October 1908.

[159] Revd Andrew Murphy, 'History in the National Schools', The Irish Educational Review, Vol. II, No. I, p. 114, October 1908.

[160] J.E. Redmond, *Some Arguments for Home Rule: Being a Series of Speeches Delivered in the Autumn of 1907 by J.E. Redmond*, p. 2.

[161] See Revd M. O'Riordan, *Catholicity and Progress in Ireland*. Bulmer Hobson, *Defensive Warfare: A Handbook for Irish Nationalists*, p. 10.

[162] Thomas O'Flannghaile, *For the Tongue of the Gael*, p. 11.

[163] *Ibid.*

[164] Máire Ní Murchadha, 'The Educational Value of the Gaelic Revival', *The Irish Educational Review*, Vol. I, No. I (1907) p. 161.

[165] See Senia Paseta, *Before the Revolution*, p. 37. Clongowes College, Co. Kildare and Blackrock College, Co. Dublin were both private boarding schools for boys. It is interesting to note, nonetheless, how many revival luminaries came from such schools. Both John Redmond and Thomas Kettle were past pupils of Clongowes Wood College, Eamon De Velara of Blackrock College and P.D. Moran had been educated at Castleknock College, a similarly middle-class private boys school. Michael Cusack, founding member of the Gaelic Athletic Association had taught in Blackrock College and Clongowes Wood College. Eoin MacNeill enrolled his sons in Belvedere College, before moving them to St Enda's. Both Cathal Bruagh and Joseph Plunkett, executed leaders of the Easter Rising, were past pupils of Belvedere.

[166] Moran was founder and editor of the nationalist newspaper *The Leader* (1900) and author of *The Philosophy of Irish Ireland* (1905).

[167] Cited in Arthur Griffith (ed.), *Thomas Davis, the Thinker and Teacher*, p. 169.

[168] See St Enda's, *An Craobh Ruadh*, I. 1 May 1913. According to D.P. Moran these colleges offered 'A sound *English* education' to 'the *Irish* nation' (emphasis in original), *The Leader*, 1 September 1900.

[169] See Sean P. Farragher CSSp *Blackrock College 1860-1995*, p. 160.

[170] Stephen Gwynn, *Irish Books and Irish People*, p. 75. Ms. Máire Bruagh recollected that upon returning from England to teach in the Ursaline convent school in Cork city in the years preceding 1916, her aunt Máire Nic Shuibhlaigh received complaints from parents that the tone of her lessons was 'too Irish'. Máire Bruagh interviewed by author 2003.

[171] 'By Way of Comment', *An Macaomh*, Vol. I, No. I, Midsummer 1909.

[172] 'I am not sure whether it is symptomatic of some development within me ... or comes naturally from the associations that cling about these old stones and trees, that, whereas at Cullenswood House I spoke oftenest to our boys of Cúchulainn ... I have been speaking to them oftenest here of Robert Emmet and the last stand. Cúchulainn was our greatest inspiration at Cullenswood; Robert Emmet has been our greatest inspiration here.' 'By Way of Comment', *An Macaomh*, Vol. II, No. 3, Christmas 1910.

[173] 'The School and the Nation', *An Claidheamh Soluis*, 1 January 1910, p. 9.

[174] *Ibid.*

[175] 'Education Under Home Rule', *An Claidheamh Soluis*, 22 February 1913, p. 6.

[176] *Ibid.*

[177] *Ibid.*

[178] *Irish Review*, June 1914.

Six

Why Pearse Matters

As editor of *An Claidheamh Soluis*, Pearse was central to the Gaelic League's success in introducing Irish into schools during the late nineteenth and early twentieth centuries. Reflection upon the ways in which Irish was most effectively taught led him to consider the activity of schooling and teaching in the wider context, and while his initial understanding of teaching was limited by his hopes for the language revival, his experience at St Enda's led to a more generous conceptualisation. His examination of bilingual teaching in Belgium and the series of articles subsequently published in *An Claidheamh Soluis* revealed his developing ability to think rigorously about teaching.[1]

The success of the language revival in schools was mirrored by the campaign for Irish as compulsory for matriculation to the NUI, although Pearse's grasp of the function of university education in the wider cultural, intellectual and economic life of a country appear limited. Employing the standard rhetoric of the revival movement he insisted that the new university must 'inculcate lofty national ideals' and 'educate the people' on 'national lines'.[2] Yet this does not necessarily reflect a narrow vision. Pearse was not an uncultured man, but, as editor of *An Claidheamh Soluis*, he was charged with representing the wishes of the Gaelic League. His views upon the wider role of the NUI are not recorded.

His assertion that Irish was 'essential to the liberal education of an Irishman' was patently untrue, but in recognising the potential implications of obligatory Irish for school curricula Pearse helped secure the language at intermediate level and in doing so bequeathed a permanent legacy to the Irish educational system;[3] an achievement described by Michael Tierney as 'thoroughly justified and healthy'.[4]

THE CHARISMATIC TEACHER

Pearse's view of teachers and the teaching task changed noticeably between 1903 and 1909. The rhetoric employed in *The Singer*: 'I felt it proud and wondrous to be a teacher'[5] reflects his conviction that to teach represented a way of life rather than simply an occupation and his belief that teachers should strive to identify and empathise with their pupils' interests and personality is echoed in the works of later educational thinkers.[6] The work of Christopher Clark, for example, indicates that children recognise a teacher's willingness 'to learn who [they] are and what [they] love' as a characteristic of the 'good teacher'.[7]

But Pearse's understanding of the teacher is incomplete and problematic. He advocated the teacher as a 'charismatic' figure – the type beloved of Hollywood, robustly independent, often operating outside, or in opposition to, school tradition and custom.[8] Such a figure is reluctant to employ traditional management strategies, textbooks and resources, relying instead upon intuition, reciprocated respect and novelty.[9] He is characteristically 'unprepared'.[10] Indeed the very considerable amount of manuscript material left by Pearse does not contain preparatory notes or jottings for a single lesson.[11] The charismatic practitioner is typically 'over-reliant upon personality and tends to eschew utilising established teaching methodologies'.[12] While the existence of such personalities may help resist definitions of the teaching task as little more than the sum of competencies that assist 'performativity'[13] the emphasis upon personality may 'mystify' teaching, presenting it, ultimately, as an art, unattainable by those not pre-possessed of the suitable personality.[14] Good teaching, in other words, does not simply happen, any more than safe landings; it is the result of many factors and does not simply emerge 'from the identity and integrity' of the teacher'.[15]

Pearse excluded opportunities for growth in teaching and infers that it is a natural endowment; that those who are most effective are simply possessed of the 'right stuff'.[16] While he wrote of the teaching life as 'fascinating' and richly rewarding he did not outline what these rewards might be.[17] His private and public writings convey little sense of teaching as a professional undertaking, concerned, in some part, with helping children to master disciplines. In Pearse's world the classroom is not presented as an arena where the teacher can find intellectual fulfilment. His is defined in terms of what gratification can be offered to the pupils and Pearse is silent on any scenario that might allow for a silent, subject-centred engagement. Within his schema the teacher is autonomous, an individual whose strength of personality, rather than depth of knowledge or aptitude for teaching, will ensure his success.

This conception does not allow for uncertainty, which so often leads to critical reflection and improvement. It precludes the usual developments teachers undergo and takes as its starting point the understanding of the pupil-teacher relationship as a type of fosterage without allowing for the possibility that such an emotional commitment might be unattainable or undesirable by either teacher or pupil.[18] While always insisting that pupils should be free to develop, it appears to deny the teacher the freedom to do likewise. For Pearse, the ideal teacher must conform to a conception which, arguably, demands attributes of character which are not necessarily prerequisites for good teaching. This is not to suggest that his view of the teacher was not sincere or even worthy but in overemphasising how the teacher could facilitate the development of the pupil, Pearse, in effect, disregarded or ignored the intellectual and emotional needs of the teacher as private citizen and public professional.

These observations also shed light upon the staff Pearse employed at St Enda's. While evidently committed to the notion of the teacher as charismatic, Pearse not only seems to have failed to find such individuals for his school, but on the contrary employed characters that were remembered as mundane and workmanlike. Only MacDonagh is remembered with enthusiasm. The members of the Pearse family were convenient employees and even though Willie was evidently committed to the school his teaching appears to have been uninspired. Comments made by the inspectors, particularly Ensor, regarding the accomplishments of some of the teachers are difficult to reconcile with Pearse's hopes for a model school. The high turnover of staff reflects uncertainty at the school and Pearse's inability to provide long-term employment. It seems, ultimately, that his criterion for the selection of teachers was their commitment to the ideals of cultural nationalism, rather than teaching expertise. While the immediate aftermath of the Rising meant that it was difficult for Mrs Pearse to continue the school, it is striking that she had to continue the project almost single-handedly. Had Pearse been concerned to build up a body of teachers committed not only to the cultural aspirations of St Enda's but also to it as a site for learning, then the school might have fared better in the 1920s and '30s. The ambivalence of government in this period implies that, in wider circles, St Enda's was considered inoperable without Pearse. Given the commitment of successive administrations to the cultural and linguistic revival, the iconic status of the Pearse brothers and the symbolic significance of St Enda's, it is telling that it failed to become established in the new State. This failure had its origins in Pearse's inability to meaningfully distinguish between schooling as furthering ideology and schooling as fostering learning.

ST ENDA'S – A NOBLE FAILURE?

At St Enda's, Pearse attempted to convert his pedagogical design into actual classroom practice, but despite the rhetoric of progressivism, day-to-day teaching at the school was quite conventional and, in many ways, conformist. He often employed teachers on the basis of their Irish-Ireland sympathies rather than their espousal of any innovative teaching methods. School reports emphasise academic progress and reveal an ordinariness that was at odds with the pronouncements of the school prospectus of 1909, where it was stated that prizes would not be awarded on the basis examination results 'but on good conduct and progress' and that courses were 'framed with a view to capturing' the 'imagination' of pupils.[19] Indeed, there is evidence that Pearse followed the customary practice of ranking pupils according to their examina-tion results. A 1914 report card for Eugene Cronin ranked him sixth in his class.[20]

Nonetheless, Pearse evidently provided a welcome and attractive learning environment at St Enda's. His efforts to adorn the school with paintings and sculpture, to promote the creation of a substantial library, his understanding of the homesickness experienced by boarding pupils and efforts to offset them by 'treats', his willingness to operate the school upon the understanding that trust should lead to self-governance and his relentless insistence that the talents, dispositions and aspirations of the child should be central to the educative process, resulted in the creation of a congenial and stimulating school environment; a view shared by the inspectors. The pupil magazine allowed the boys freedom to poke gentle fun at each other and occasionally their teachers. It acted as a testing ground for their literary and artistic pretensions and allowed them to artiulcate their support or objection to aspects of school life in a considered and formal manner that had to withstand the scrutiny of publication.

Contact between St Ita's and St Enda's reveals Pearse's concern that pupils be afforded time and space for a type of social interaction quite uncommon for the period. The visits by Gaelic League luminaries, such as Douglas Hyde and Eoin MacNeill, coupled with those by figures such as Countess Markievicz and Roger Casement, exposed the pupils to the most prominent nationalist thinkers in early twentieth-century Ireland. In this way, Pearse physically located his pupils at the heart of Gaelic Revival discourse – surely an exciting place to be in the first decade of twentieth-century Ireland.

The influence of nationalism at the school is difficult to measure. Certainly, the contemporaneous cultural milieu and the influence of family and friends must be considered when assessing the decision by past pupils of St Enda's to become involved in the Easter Rising. Indeed, in promoting patriotism, Pearse reflected a wider social and cultural agenda. The *Suggestions for Schools* published in England in 1905, proposed that the 'broad facts' of the evolution of the British Empire 'ought to form a stirring theme full of interest to every young citizen'.[21] The authors of the contemporaneous *Suggestive Handbook of Practical School Method* noted that 'love of country' or 'patriotism' were 'noble sentiments and the human race is better, happier, and nobler by their cultivation ... patriotism causes the heart to beat high at our country's glorious past and the pricelessness of our inheritance'.[22] A pamphlet on the 'Teaching of Patriotism', published in Dublin in 1916, noted that 'the feeling will come only as the result of the idea pervading the whole school ... every subject can be made to serve the same end', continuing, 'it is clear that the early school days, when character is malleable, are the seasons for receiving ideas of patriotism and for responding to the cause of self-sacrifice'.[23] By no means was Pearse a lone voice; he was typical of his time, if not less militaristic and partisan than many others.

Desmond Ryan argued that to read the story of St Enda's as a 'pastoral idyll' that began 'beneath Rathmines elms' and ended in a 'fiery epic beneath the burning ruins of the Dublin Post Office' was unjust and untrue[24] while Ruth Dudley Edwards has insisted that Pearse was 'not training revolutionaries'.[25] The inculcation of patriotism at St Enda's was not untypical in schools of the period and a dominant feature of pre-First World War British and Irish society. In 1934, Shane Leslie noted that Pearse meant to 'Irish sentiment' what Rupert Brooke had meant 'to the British'.[26] The importance of this cannot be overemphasised. Modern historians have accused Pearse of unduly influencing his pupils and cite the involvement of past pupils in the Rising as evidence. But this is to ignore of the type of patriotic rhetoric popular at the time, particularly in England, a type that led many thousands to their death in the First World War. Peter Parker observes in his fascinating *The Old Lie: The Great War and the Public School Ethos* that it 'was not militarism as such that we find in the schools of the nineteenth century, but an espousal of values which promoted local and national patriotism: house, school, country, in that order.'[27] In 1910, Shrewsbury School debated and carried the motion that warfare was 'essential to the welfare of the human race';[28] at Westminster School in 1914 a motion was carried that 'it will be disastrous to the World when Arbitration takes the place of War'.[29] Before St Enda's was founded, the majority of English schools had established Officers' Training Corps supported by the War Office. The great heroes of ancient Greece and the medieval knights of the Arthurian legends were held up to boys in British Public schools as models of self-sacrifice in the same way Pearse lionised Cúchulainn. As late as 1928 Dr Cyril Norwood, headmaster of Marlborough and later Harrow, wrote that what 'has happened in the course of the last hundred years is that the old ideals have been recaptured. The ideal of chivalry which inspired the knighthood of medieval days, the ideal of service ... '[30] but Norwood was writing after the war; Pearse, like so many other headmasters of English and Irish schools, had no knowledge of the appalling horror, for them it was easy to speak to their boys of 'playing the game' and to condemn them in hindsight is to afford ourselves a luxury they did not have.

The British Army occupied The Hermitage between 1916–17, forcing Mrs Pearse to relocate the school to Cullenswood House. St Enda's was reopened again in Rathfarnham in 1917 and Mrs Pearse bought the property in the early 1920s.[31] The challenge of operating the school after 1922 was considerable. Enrolment was small and Mrs Pearse had difficulty retaining teachers and securing funding. One of many letters sent to the Department of Education on her behalf in the 1930s argued that, as it was the aim of the government to 'gaelicise education', it would 'seem a pity to allow the school founded by the past president of the Irish Republic to go out of existence for the sake of the trifling support needed to make it permanent'.[32] But public and political support was conspicuously lacking and Mrs Pearse faced increasing financial difficulty. Her supporters repeatedly petitioned for government help as pupil numbers dwindled. In July 1932, the Private Secretary to President De Valera informed Mrs Pearse that the administration could not see how the school could continue to operate at a loss, adding that it had 'occurred to the President that the best line of approach … might be by way of utilising St Enda's as a University Hostel … or Preparatory College'.[33]

The indifference of De Valera's administration was reflected in the educational policy of all future governments. The child-centred pedagogy of Pearse, indeed the European phenomenon that had been embraced by the Revised Programme for National Schools in 1900, did not inform policy in independent Ireland. The sound pedagogy of bilingualism was jettisoned in favour of a policy of complete restoration in which the Irish language became a 'potent force'[34], acquiring 'mystical', almost 'magical properties'.[35] Irish language policy, however, lacked the creativity and common sense of Pearse's vision.

THE LEGACY OF PATRICK PEARSE

Pearse's proposals for education in an independent Ireland were far from comprehensive and he admitted to having little to say of 'organisation' or 'mere machinery'.[36] He did, however, recommend the creation of one Department of Education, having limited administrative authority, under a single minister.[37] Schools should be granted autonomy in the 'details of their programmes' and teachers should be the system's 'centre of gravity', indeed they, rather than 'clerks', would 'be the system'.[38] The inspectorate would be selected from the teaching body, promoted teachers would become teacher educators and teacher education would be brought into 'close touch with the universities'.[39] Schools should be 'well equipped' and award prizes for individually designed programmes. In keeping with the thought of many radical school founders 'manual work' would form part of the life of every school and each member of the 'child republic' would contribute to the selection of 'their own laws and leaders'.[40] Notably, the formal encouragement of student councils in Ireland only appeared in the Education Act of 1998.[41] Manual work, in the sense that Pearse intended, has not become a part of a comprehensive educative experience for Irish schoolchildren. Pearse's insistence upon the central role of the teaching body reflects his developing understanding of the teaching task and anticipated the consultative culture that now exists between teachers and the State. He submitted these observations to indicate 'the general spirit' of how education could be 'recreated' and they must be considered in this context.[42] They reflect a serious commitment to thinking about educational provision, a task to which Pearse 'dedicated the greater part of [his] life'.[43]

Pearse's educational thought was ignored by the new Irish government in 1922 and by successive administrations as 'educational policy was subsumed by the plan for reviving the Irish language'.[44] As J.J. Lee noted: 'It cannot be said that his ideas have failed in modern Ireland. They have never been seriously tried.'[45]

Perhaps Pearse's most tangible legacy is represented by the existence of a small number of schools that trace their origin directly to his work at St Enda's and St Ita's. James O'Byrne founded Árd Scoil Éanna (St Enda's High School) in Dublin, in the late 1930s. O'Byrne had worked in a number of schools, including Clongowes Wood and Belvedere College, before taking a position at St Enda's in 1921. When the school closed in 1935 he secured a post at CBS Westland Row, which William and Patrick Pearse had attended as boys. In 1939 he established Árd Scoil Éanna in the new suburb of Crumlin, assisted by Ms Margaret Pearse, who lent school furniture from St Enda's and taught religion until permanent staff were recruited, including James Fisher, a colleague from St Enda's. Irish was important in the life of the school but it was not the language of instruction. Like St Enda's the school was lay Catholic and the youth movement na Fianna and the

Gaelic League held meetings at Árd Scoil Éanna, as they had done at
St Enda's. O'Byrne retired as headmaster in 1956 but the management
of the school remains within his family.

While influenced by Pearse's educational work, O'Byrne had wider
social concerns: 'For Pearse, education was political because it was
colonial, for O'Byrne it was political because it was not accessible'.[46]
This reflected O'Byrne's commitment to the social policy of *Sinn Féin*
but also the explicitly political nature of his interest in schooling. He was
anxious that, like St Enda's, the school should have a 'family atmosphere'
and that 'character formation' should be its principle task.[47] As a private
lay Catholic secondary school, unconnected with the parish structures
and situated in a new suburb of Dublin, Árd Scoil Éanna was an innovative establishment. Such schools were often employed as templates for
similarly innovative institutions, and Conan Cannon visited O'Byrne on
a number of occasions before opening Sandymount High School, a lay
co-educational school in South Dublin.[48] Árd Scoil Éanna presently
operates with an enrolment of about 150 students.

The Irish nationalist Louise Gavan Duffy had unsuccessfully offered
to lease St Ita's in 1912 and later founded Scoil Bhríde in her own
home on St Stephen's Green in 1917. The school was later moved
to Pembroke Road and then Earlsfort Terrace, where it was utilised
by trainee teachers connected with the Education Department of
University College Dublin. Finally Ms Margaret Pearse provided
a permanent location on a site adjacent to Cullenswood House in
the mid-1960s. The son of C.S. (Todd) Andrews, Niall Andrews, and
the historian Owen Dudley Edwards, father of Pearse's biographer,
attended the school as children. In the 1920s the school was renowned
for its emphasis on sport, drama and pageantry. Louise Gavan Duffy
was much influenced by Pearse's political credo and was an active
political campaigner.[49] The school holds the legacy of Pearse as 'part of
its identity' and operates today as a primary school with an enrolment
of 330 pupils.[50]

Although bequeathed to the State by Ms Margaret Pearse,
Cullenswood House fell into disrepair in the 1970s. In 1987 a committee
was established to raise funds for its restoration and in 1996 a group
of parents proposed establishing a gaelscoil on the premises. They
undertook to lease Cullenswood House and opened Lios na nÓg there
in December 1997.

Lios na nÓg is a unilingual school, practising 'full immersion' in the Irish language for all pupils.[51] The school staff and parents 'respect' the legacy of Pearse and there is an annual school visit to the Pearse Museum at The Hermitage.[52] Notably, a grandniece of Brian Seoighe presently teaches at the school. Enrolment at Lios na nÓg has increased from twenty-one pupils in 1997 to more than 200, the school employs eight staff and operates an Irish-language playschool. The school holds Irish classes for adults and has plans to become a cultural and artistic centre.[53] The establishment and success of Lios na nÓg demonstrates the powerful influence of Pearse's educational work and perhaps represents the most appropriate acknowledgment of his legacy.

Pearse's educational thought was firmly embedded within late nineteenth and early twentieth-century child-centred discourse. Notions of learning as a process of 'growth',[54] the centrality of the child in schooling, the dislike of rote learning, corporal punishment and terminal examinations, the insistence upon 'freedom'[55] and enlightened conceptualisation of the teacher-pupil relationship belong to the European legacy of Rousseau, Pestalozzi and Froebel and Pearse's espousal of these is neither pioneering or original. His pedagogical thought cannot be considered innovative because it reflects or re-articulates concepts that were already part of the common discourse. The Revised Programme for National Schools (1900) for example, embraced and promoted an enlightened and child-centred agenda for primary schooling. Before any part of *The Murder Machine* was penned (1912–14) the *Report of the Intermediate Board for Ireland* (1911) noted that the payment of grants on the basis of yearly examinations 'cannot be said to be educationally sound'.[56] The Report also noted that, 'as written examinations cannot properly and fully test the efficiency of any one school or the teaching capacities of the staff, it is clear that they cannot be regarded as a true test of the relative efficiency of schools, especially when the schools, as is the case in Ireland, are of such different types, with varying objects and aims.'[57]

Pearse's description of the system as an automation that 'compresses and re-moulds'[58] to a 'regulation pattern',[59] his plea for 'freedom' for 'Irish education' to 'grow on … natural lines' and his damning of the system to 'promote competitive examinations in the under-world' reflect the tone, imagery and vocabulary of this report. [60] This is not to say that Pearse was consciously derivative, but that his educational thinking reflected enlightened views that were evolving at the time. The position that Pearse was a significant pedagogical thinker is not sustainable. His pedagogical thought, while enlightened, forward-looking and revealing a noble conceptualisation of the educative endeavour, was not innovative or original.

Pearse's significance as an educational thinker lies instead in the domain of radical education although his unwillingness to acknowledge the benefits that resulted from widespread primary provision in the nineteenth century resulted in a skewed rendering of history. Indeed, his familiarity with the development of education in Ireland is uncertain as he fails to provide historic instances, beyond the anecdotal, to support his critique of the system and this diminishes the impact of his argument generally. In Pearse's version of schooling in Ireland, fact too readily becomes subservient to the need to persuade, leading to an imbalanced and incomplete picture. He was silent on The Commission on Manual and Practical Instruction (Belmore Commission) and its impact upon the Revised Programme of 1900; he failed to point to the significance of that Programme or of the Dale and Stephens Report of 1905 and appears unaware that the vocabulary he often employs to describe the type of schooling he is advocating is resonant of that used in the reports of the National and Intermediate Commissioners. *The Murder Machine* fails to take account of the enlightened discourse around educational policy in Ireland in the first two decades of the twentieth century and Pearse's failure or unwillingness to acknowledge this leaves his wider critique weakened and imbalanced.

However, Pearse's identification of schooling in Ireland as associated with a colonial mindset is not unconvincing. The period before 1831 was marked by recurrent educational initiatives designed to make Ireland Protestant and English speaking. While the establishment of the National System was a welcome development it was conceived at a time characterised by agitation for reform. Wider social events, changes in understandings regarding educational and democratic participation, in other words, acted as compelling forces in the decision to establish the National School System in Ireland.[61] It was not a voluntary act of benevolence.

By the early 1900s, cultural nationalists were able to effect significant changes in an education system they perceived as culturally hostile, including increases in the number of pupils studying Irish, the introduction of the Bilingual Programme and Irish as an obligatory

matriculation subject for entrance to the National University of
Ireland. Pearse argued that the curriculum, textbooks and examination
content – the means and ends of schooling in Ireland – were in fact
indifferent to Irish culture, history, literature, language and nationalist aspirations and that by its omissions and content reinforced and
transmitted the assumption of political union with Great Britain as
unproblematic. This, coupled with his equally prescient realisation that
this curricular colonialism could be confronted and inverted within
the school, the structure that had historically acted as its vehicle of
transmission, represents an early and explicitly political conceptualisation of schooling as a potentially defiant and transformative jesture.
His argument that the assimilative nature of the curriculum represented
an act of political absorption was among the earliest contributions to
the discourse concerning the relationship between curriculum and
power. He insisted that, what Giroux terms the 'cultural script' of
curriculum content could be challenged and rewritten.[62]

The radical nature of St Enda's was never in question. Indeed the
decision to establish a lay Catholic school in Ireland in 1908 was itself
a radical gesture and reflected Pearse's preparedness from the outset to
move outside the traditional terrain of educational provision. In establishing St Enda's as a place where he could instigate this process, Pearse
represents the 'transformative intellectual', those educators Giroux
defines as preparing their students for cultural or political emancipation.[63] Pearse argued that, as the provision of education did not lie in
the hands of an elected Irish Parliament operating in a independent
state, it did not reflect the democratically articulated needs and concerns
of a sovereign people. His insistence that the English were 'too wise a
people … to educate us' has to be considered against the backdrop of an
Anglocentric curriculum which he and many of his generation considered to be part of the greater 'machine' of political domination. St Enda's
therefore, offered a model of defiance; it was established in order that
change might be effected. Pearse's insistence upon freedom included
what Freire described as the possibility to give 'direction to history'.[64]
According to Freire, revolutionary educators must anticipate the new
society they wish to initiate, they must take risks.[65] Radical reform
cannot be achieved by mere innovations in teaching methods; instead,
education must be 'revolutionized'.[66] Seventy years previously Pearse
had insisted: 'Let us therefore not talk of reform, or of reconstruction.

You cannot reform that which is not'.[67] St Enda's, therefore, was to be an exemplary and radical alternative; its founding principles were political defiance and social transformation.

In recognising that schooling could act as a 'weapon'[68] in displacing or altering the political equilibrium, Pearse and a small number of early twentieth-century radical school founders identified a potential of empowerment not articulated again until the advent of modern radical education theory in the late 1960s. The identification of education as contested terrain, and the creation of a school as a model of defiance, establish Pearse as an important, innovative and original thinker and locate him firmly within the radical education tradition. Hence his work remains relevant, not only for educational historians but also for those with an interest in the operation of democracy and dissent. If Pearse has a legacy, therefore, it is as a founding father of the pedagogy of protest.

Much of what Pearse advocated is now part of contemporary educational discourse: the acquisition of language by emphasising oral rather than written competence, the increased democratic participation of pupils in schooling, the benefits of creative teaching methodologies, the role of universities in initial teacher education and the recognition of the right of women to full access to higher education, the emphasis upon individual pupil needs and the unsuitability of a wholly academic curriculum for all, the need for more imaginative forms of evaluation and assessment at primary and secondary level, the importance of the physical environment in enhancing pupils enjoyment of school and the conceptualisation of the learner as participant in the process of learning, rather than simply a recipient. Pearse's identification of schooling and curriculum as contested terrains pre-dates that of later commentators, such as Freire, and has been overlooked by commentators.

Finally, the passage of time has done much to lessen the impact of his radical proposals concerning the curriculum in early twentieth-century Ireland. In 1906, for example, the intermediate history examinations contained the following questions: 'How did the Whigs and Tories of Queen Anne's reign differ … ?', 'Give as fully as you can an account of the British surrender at Saratoga or at Yorktown', 'Give a brief account of Farifax's campaign in Kent and Essex during the Second Civil War', 'Distinguish three Dukes of Norfolk during the Tudor period, and write a short account of two of them'.[69] The cultural and political assumptions that informed these examination questions were deeply rooted and it is against this reality that Pearse's project should be measured. He re-imagined the curriculum so that Irish history, literature and language would be taken for granted and their place in contemporary schooling has its origins in the work of cultural revivalists, such as Pearse and Hyde.

Ultimately, Pearse's contribution was his insistence that an education system could only be considered valuable when it had its origins in, and reflected the concerns of, the society that fashioned it. A system imposed from outside, regardless of its merit, was incomplete because it could not claim to reflect the aspirations of those for whom it was intended. In this, Pearse reflected the wider social and political developments of early twentieth-century Europe concerning the operation of genuine democracy, nationhood and the colonial project.

Notes

[1] These articles, published under the title 'Belgium and its Schools', appeared in *An Claidheamh Soluis* in two series from August 1905 to September 1906 (series one) and from September 1906 to March 1907 (series two).

[2] 'The New University: Irish Essential for Matriculation,' *An Claidheamh Soluis*, 22 August 1908, p. 8.

[3] 'Irish as an Essential: The Why and the Wherefore', *An Claidheamh Soluis*, 19 December 1908, p. 9.

[4] Martin Tierney (ed.), Michael Tierney, *A Classicist's Outlook*, p. 176.

[5] 'The Singer', *The Complete Works of P.H. Pearse, Plays, Poems, Stories*.

[6] On the notion of teaching as a way of living see Pádraig Hogan, 'Teaching and Learning as a Way of Life', *Journal of Philosophy of Education*, Vol. 37, No. 2 (2003).

[7] Christopher M. Clark, *Thoughtful Teaching*, p. 15.

[8] See Alex More, *The Good Teacher: Dominant discourses in Teaching and Teacher Education*, p. 53.

[9] *Ibid.*, pp. 55–7.

[10] *Ibid.*, p. 55.

[11] The Murder Machine, 'Back to the Sagas.'

[12] Alex More, *The Good Teacher: Dominant Discourses in Teaching and Teacher Education*, p. 68.

[13] See Pádraig Hogan, 'Teaching and Learning as a Way of Life', *Journal of Philosophy of Education*, Vol. 37, No. 2 (2003), p 215.

[14] Alex More, *The Good Teacher: Dominant Discourses in Teaching and Teacher Education*, p. 69.

[15] See Parker J. Palmer, *The Courage to Teach: Exploring the Inner Landscape of a Teachers Life*, p. 10

[16] Mitchell and Weber, *Reinventing Ourselves as Teachers: Private and Social Acts of Memory and Imagination*, p. 183.

[17] 'By Way of Comment', *An Macaomh*, Vol. I. No. 2. December 1909.

[18] The concept, as Pearse understood, has deep-seated historic antecedents. See, for example, George Steiner, *Lessons of the Master*, p. 34.

[19] *Prospectus of Scoil Éanna, (1909)* Pearse Papers, NLI.

[20] School report card on Eugene Cronin for school year 1913–14, 22 June 1914, Pearse Collection, Pearse Museum.

[21] See R.D. Bramwell, *Elementary School Work, 1900–1925*.

[22] See R.J.W. Selleck, *The New Education, 1870-1914*, p. 248.

[23] May C. Starkie, *What is Patriotism, the Teaching of Patriotism* (n.p. Dublin, 1916).

[24] Desmond Ryan, 'A Retrospect', *St Enda's and its Founder, the Complete Works of P.H. Pearse*, p. 89.

[25] Ruth Dudley Edwards, *Patrick Pearse, the Triumph of Failure*, p. 143.

[26] Shane Leslie, *The Passing Chapter*, p. 24.

[27] Peter Parker, the *Old Lie: The Great War and the Public School Ethos*, p. 56.

[28] *Ibid.*, p. 61.

[29] *Ibid.*, p. 62.

[30] *Ibid.*, p. 105.

[31] The Hermitage was closed by the British Army during the Easter Rising and Mrs Margaret Pearse later sought compensation for loss of earnings and damage to the buildings, see MS 21059 (illegible) Donald, (Dublin County Council) to Mrs Margaret Pearse, 6 February 1919, Pearse Papers, NLI.

[32] Clan Éanna to the Department of Education, May 1932, National Archive (S9045B).

[33] Private Secretary to the President to Mrs Margaret Pearse, July 1932, Nat. Arch. (S9045B).

[34] John Coolahan, *Irish Education: Its History and Structure*, p. 38.

[35] D. Akenson, *A Mirror to Kathleen's Face*, p. 35.

[36] *The Murder Machine*, 'When We Are Free.'

[37] *Ibid.*

[38] *Ibid.*

[39] *Ibid.* It should be noted that, with the exception of the Irish language, this is the first explicit admission by Pearse of the importance of teacher education.

[40] *Ibid.*

[41] *Education Act* 1998, 'Miscellaneous'.

[42] *The Murder Machine*, 'When We Are Free.'

[43] *Ibid.* 'The Broad Arrow.'

[44] D. Akenson, *A Mirror to Kathleen's Face*, p. 26.

[45] J.J. Lee, 'In Search of Patrick Pearse', in Máirín Dhonnchadha and Theo Dorgan (eds), *Revising the Rising*, p. 138.

[46] Réiltín McCall, great-granddaughter of James O'Byrne, interviewed by author, 2004.

[47] Eileen O'Byrne, daughter of James O'Byrne, interviewed by author, 2004.

[48] Oral recollection of Eileen O'Byrne. Sandymount High was founded in 1947 and closed in 1999.

[49] The present principal of Scoil Bhríde, Iseult Ní Chléirigh, recalled that her great-aunt was 'let go' from her post in a 'convent school on St Stephen's Green' when discovered to have taken part in a political demonstration (C. 1919–20). She was subsequently re-employed by Louise Gavan Duffy. Iseult Ní Chléirigh interviewed by author, 2004.

[50] Iseult Ní Chléirigh interviewed by author, 2004.

[51] Áine Ní Fhíthigh (principal) interviewed by author, 2004.

[52] *Ibid.*

[53] Similar events are held at the Pearse Museum, at The Hermitage.

[54] See *The Murder Machine*, 'The Murder Machine.'

[55] *Ibid.* 'Of Freedom in Education.'

[56] *Report of the Intermediate Education Board for Ireland, 1911*, [Cd. 6317] (H.C., 1912), xx.

[57] *Ibid.*, xxi.

[58] *The Murder Machine*, 'The Murder Machine.'

[59] *Ibid.*

[60] *Ibid.* 'Of Freedom in Education.'

[61] This argument is developed in B. Walsh, 'Teacher Education in Ireland', *Education Research and Perspectives*, Vol. 33, No. 2 (2006).

[62] Henry Giroux, *Border Crossings: Cultural Workers and the Politics of Education*, p. 82.

[63] Henry Giroux, *Schooling For Democracy, passim.*

[64] Paulo Freire and Antonio Faundez, *Learning to Question, a Pedagogy of Liberation*, p. 77.

[65] *Ibid.*

[66] *Ibid.*

[67] *The Murder Machine*, 'I Deny.'

[68] Harold Silver, *English Education and the Radicals*, 1730–1850, p. 15.

[69] Intermediate Examinations Board of Ireland, History and Geography examinations (various, June 1906) NLI, MS 21087.

Bibliography

SYNOPSIS

I. Manuscript Material. National Library of Ireland

George F.H Berkeley Letters and Papers
Con Colbert Papers
Mary Hayden Diaries
Bulmer Hobson Papers
Joseph Holloway Diaries
Count Joseph Plunkett Papers
Thomas MacDonagh Papers
Eoin MacNeill Papers
Pearse Papers: Documents; Letters of James Pearse, Mrs Margaret Pearse, Ms Margaret Pearse, Patrick Pearse, William Pearse, Mary Brigid Pearse. Accounts & Miscellaneous items / correspondence pertaining to St Enda's school
Prospectus of Scoil Éanna, 1909
Prospectus of Scoil Éanna, 1911–12
Prospectus of Scoil Éanna 1931
Prospectus of Scoil Íde, 1910–1
St Enda's Roll Book 1908–9
St Enda's Roll Book 1915–16
Minute Books of the Gaelic League
Pearse / Cronin correspondence. Pearse Collection, Pearse Museum, Kilmainham Goal Archives.
Miscellaneous items. Pearse Museum, the Hermitage, Rathfarnham
Correspondence of Mrs Margaret Pearse and Government, National Archives, Dublin.
Archive Documents, miscellaneous items, Scoil Bhríde, Dublin
The Alexandrian, Alexandra College, Library

II. Published Primary Source Material. Parliamentary Proceedings: Reports and Commissions, Ireland and Britain 1825-1932

The First Report of the Irish Education Inquiry 1825, [400]
The Second Report of the Irish Education Inquiry 1826–27, [12]
The Third Report of the Irish Education Enquiry 1826–27, [13]
The Fourth Report of the Irish Education Enquiry 1826–27, [89]
The Fifth Report of the Irish Education Inquiry 1826–27, [441]
The Sixth Report of the Irish Education Enquiry 1826–27, [442]
The Seventh Report of the Irish Education Inquiry 1826–7, [443]
The Eighth Report of the Irish Education Inquiry 1826–27, [509]
The Eighth Report of the Irish Education Inquiry 1826–27, [509]
The Ninth Report of the Irish Education Inquiry 1826–27, [516]

ii. Reports of the Commissioners of National Education (Ireland)

Second Report by the Commissioners of National Education, 1835, [300]
   (H.C., 1835)

Third Report by the Commissioners of National Education, 1836, [44] (H.C., 1836)

Fourth Report by the Commissioners of National Education, 1837, [110]
   (H.C.,1837–38)

Fifth Report by the Commissioners of National Education, 1838, [160] (H.C., 1839)

Sixth Report by the Commissioners of National Education, 1839, [246] (H.C., 1840)

Seventh Report by the Commissioners of National Education, 1840, [353]
   (H.C., 1842)

Eighth Report by the Commissioners of National Education, 1841, [398]
   (H.C., 1842)

Ninth Report by the Commissioners of National Education, 1842, [471]
   (H.C., 1843)

Tenth Report by the Commissioners of National Education, 1843, [569]
   (H.C., 1844)

Eleventh Report by the Commissioners of National Education, 1844, [629]
   (H.C., 1845)

Twelfth Report by the Commissioners of National Education, 1845, [711]
   (H.C., 1846)

Thirteenth Report by the Commissioners of National Education, 1846, [832]
   (H.C., 1847)

Fourteenth Report by the Commissioners of National Education, 1847, [981]
   (H.C., 1847–48)

Fifteenth Report by the Commissioners of National Education, 1848, [1066]
   (H.C., 1849)

*Reports of the Commissioners of National Education from the years 1835–1848
   Inclusive*, [70] (H.C., 1851).

Eighteenth Report by the Commissioners of National Education, 1851, [1582]
   (H.C., 1852–3)

Nineteenth Report by the Commissioners of National Education, 1852, [1688]
   (H.C., 1852–3)

Twentieth Report by the Commissioners of National Education, 1853, [1834]
   (H.C., 1854)

Twenty-Third Report by the Commissioner of National Education, 1856, [2304]
   (H.C., 1857–8)

Twenty-Fourth Report by the Commissioners of National Education, 1857, [2456–1]
   (H.C., 1859)

Twenty-Fifth Report by the Commissioners of National Education, 1858, [2593]
   (H.C., 1859)

Twenty-Fifth Report by the Commissioners of National Education, 1858, [4193??] (H.C., 1859)

Twenty-Eighth Report by the Commissioners of National Education, 1861, [3026] (H.C., 1862)

Twenty-Ninth Report by the Commissioners of National Education, 1862, [3235] (H.C., 1863)

Thirtieth Report by the Commissioners of National Education, 1863, [3351] (H.C., 1864)

Thirty-First Report by the Commissioners of National Education, 1864, [3496] (H.C., 1865)

Thirty-Second Report by the Commissioners of National Education, 1865, [3713] (H.C., 1866)

Thirty-Fourth Report by the Commissioners of National Education, 1867, [4026] (H.C., 1877)

Thirty-Fifth Report by the Commissioners of National Education, 1868, [4193] (H.C., 1868–69)

Thirty-Sixth Report by the Commissioners of National Education, 1869, [C120] (H.C., 1870).

Thirty-Seventh Report by the Commissioners of National Education, 1870, [C 360] (H.C., 1871)

Seventy-First Report of the Commissioners of National Education 1904, [2567] (H.C., 1905)

Seventy-Second Report of the Commissioners of National Education, 1905–6, [3154] (H.C., 1906)

Seventy-Third Report of the Commissioners of National Education, 1906–7, [3699] (H.C., 1907)

Seventy-Fifth Report by the Commissioners of National Education, 1908–9, [5062] (H.C., 1910)

Seventy-Sixth Report of the Commissioners of National Education, 1909–10, [Cd. 5340] (H.C., 1910)

Appendix to the Seventy-Fifth Report of the Commissioners of National Education, 1908–9, [Cd.062] (H.C., 1910)

Appendix to the Seventy-Seventh Report of the Commissioners of National Education, 1910–11, [Cd. 6042] (H.C., 1911)

The Seventy-Eight Report of the Commissioners of National Education, 1911–1912, [6986] H.C. 1912

Appendix to the Seventy-Eight Report of the Commissioners of National Education, 1911–12, [7061] (H.C., 1912)

The Eighty-First Report of the Commissioners of National Education, 1914–15, [Cd. 8369] (H.C., 1916)

The Eighty-Sixth Report of the Commissioners of National Education, 1919–20, [Cmd. 1476] (H.C., 1920)

iii. Reports of the Commissioners of Intermediate Education (Ireland)

Report of the Intermediate Education Board, 1898, [C–9294] (H.C.,1899)

Report of the Intermediate Education Board, 1898, [C–9294] (H.C., 1899)

Report of the Intermediate Education Board, 1900, [Cd. 588] (H.C., 1901)

Report of the Intermediate Education Board, 1901, [Cd. 1092] (H.C. 1902)

Report of the Intermediate Education Board, 1902, [Cd.1670] (H.C., 1903)

Report of the Intermediate Education Board, 1903, [Cd. 2113] (H.C., 1904)

Report of the Intermediate Education Board, 1904, [Cd 2580] (H.C., 1905)

Report of the Intermediate Education Board, 1905, [Cd. 2944] (H.C., 1906)

Report of the Intermediate Education Board, 1906, [Cd. 3544] (H.C., 1907)

Report of the Intermediate Education Board, 1907, [Cd.4047] (H.C., 1908)

Report of the Intermediate Education Board, 1908, [Cd. 4707] (H.C., 1909)

Report of the Intermediate Education Board, 1909, [Cd. 5173] (H.C., 1910)

Report of the Intermediate Education Board, 1910, [Cd. 5768] (H.C., 1911)

Report of the Intermediate Education Board, 1911, [Cd. 6317] (H.C., 1912)

Report of the Intermediate Education Board, 1912, [Cd. 6893] (H.C., 1913)

Report of the Intermediate Education Board, 1913, [Cd. 7555] (H.C., 1914)

Report of the Intermediate Education Board, 1914, [Cd. 8008] (H.C., 1915)

Report of the Intermediate Education Board, 1915, [Cd. 8369] (H.C., 1916)

Report of the Intermediate Education Board, 1916, [Cd. 8603] (H.C., 1917)

Report of the Intermediate Education Board, 1917, [Cd. 8608] (H.C., 1918)

Report of the Intermediate Education Board, 1918, [Cmd. 323] (H.C., 1919)

Report of the Intermediate Education Board, 1919, [Cmd.1919] (H.C., 1920)

Report of the Intermediate Education Board, 1920, [Cmd. 1398] (H.C., 1921)

iv. Commissioned, Official and Institutional Reports

Hansard, Parliamentary Debates, 3rd Ser.,Vol.V. (1825) cols. 1257–1258

Hansard, Parliamentary Debates, 5th Ser.,Vol.VI (1831) cols. 1124–1305; 1287–1295

The Census of Ireland for the Year 1851, [582] (Dublin, 1855)

The Census of Ireland for the Year 1861, [3026] (H.C., 1862)

The Reports of the Presidents of the Queen's Colleges, Belfast, Cork and Galway for the Session 1849–1859: The Report of the President of Queen's College, Galway for the Academic Year of 1850–51 (HMSO; Dublin 1850)

Report of the Queen's Colleges Commission (Alex.Thom & Co. Ltd; Dublin, 1858)

Report of Her Majesty's Commissioners appointed to Inquire Into the Progress and Condition of the Queen's Colleges at Belfast, Cork and Galway (HMSO; Dublin, 1858)

Royal Commission of Inquiry on Primary Education (Ireland) 1870 Vol. I. Part I – X. Conclusions and Recommendations in the General Report [C 6] (H.C., 1870)

Royal Commission of Inquiry into Primary Education (Ireland) 1870 Vol. I. Part II. Part III Primary Schools [C 6a] (H.C., 1870)

Royal Commission of Inquiry into Primary Education (Ireland) 1870 Vol. II. Synopsis of Reports of Assistant Commissioners [C6–I] (H.C., 1870)

Royal Commission of Inquiry into Primary Education (Ireland) 1870 Vol. III. [C6–2] H.C. 1870

Royal Commission of Inquiry into Primary Education (Ireland) 1870 Vol. VIII, Containing Miscellaneous Papers and Returns furnished to the Commission. [C6–VII] (H.C., 1870)

The Report of the President of Queen's College, Cork, for the Academic Session 1880–81 (HMSO; Dublin, 1881)

The Report of the President of Queen's College, Galway, for the Academic Session 1881–82 (HMSO; Dublin, 1882)

Second Report of the Royal Commissioners on Technical Instruction 1884 Vol. I. Board of Education (HMSO; London, 1884)

Special Reports on Educational Subjects, 1896-7, [C. 8447] London, 1897.

Proofs of General and Special Reports of Inspectors' and Others: Prepared for Publication in the App., of the Commissioners' Annual Report for the Year 1895, Office of National Education, Dublin, 1897 [C 8925] (H.C., 1897)

Commission on Manual and Practical Instruction in Primary Schools under the Board of National Education in Ireland, 1897 [C 8383] (H.C., 1897)

Commission on Manual and Practical Instruction in Primary Schools under the Board of National Education in Ireland, First Report by the Commissioners 1898 [8383] (H.C., 1897)

Commission on Manual and Practical Instruction in Primary Schools under the Board of National Education, Final Report by the Commissioners 1897 [C. 8923] (H.C., 1898)

Revised Programme of Instruction in National Schools published in Appendix to the Annual Report by the Commissioners of National Education, 1902 [Cd 1890] (H.C., 1903)

Report by Mr F.H. Dale, His Majesty's Inspector of Schools, Board of Education on Primary Education in Ireland, 1904 [Cd 1981] (H.C., 1904)

Suggestions for the Consideration of Teachers and Others Concerned in the Work of Public Elementary Schools, Board of Education (HMSO; London, 1905)

Syllabuses [sic] of Experimental Science, Drawing, and Domestic Economy, Rules and
  Programmes of Examinations for 1907. Intermediate Education Board for Ireland.
  Accounts and Papers 27,Vol. XCI (HMSO; Dublin, 1906)
Royal Commission on Trinity College, Dublin, and the University of Dublin, First
  Report of the Commissioners, Dublin 1906 (HMSO; Dublin, 1907)
Royal Commission on Trinity College, Dublin, and the University of Dublin, Final
  Report of the Commissioners (Dublin, 1907)
Rules and Programme of Examinations For Intermediate Education Board for Ireland.
  Accounts and Papers 27,Vol. XCI (HMSO; Dublin, 1907)
Reports on Elementary Schools, 1852–82. (HMSO; London, 1908)
The National University of Ireland. Act of Parliament Charter and Statutes, X.
  The Senate. (HMSO; Dublin, 1908)
Dublin Commission Irish Universities Act, 1908. Report of Conferences with University
  Authorities and Representatives of Chambers of Commerce, Institutes of Architecture
  and Music, and other Persons, as to Provision for Technical, Commercial, and Other
  Studies in the National University of Ireland (Dublin, 1909)
The Montessori System. The Board of Education HMSO, London, 1912
Vice-Regal Committee of Enquiry Into Primary Education Ireland (HMSO;
  Dublin, 1918)
The Place of the Vernacular in Native Education (HMSO; London, 1925)
Reports of the President of University College, Dublin, 1908–1932 inclusive: The
  National University of Ireland Handbook, 1908–1932, Published for the Senate,
  NUI, at Sign of the Three Candles (Dublin, 1932)
Saorstát Éireann, Census of Population 1926, Vol.VIII (Irish Language; Dublin, 1932)

III. Policy Documents and Reports: 1922–1995 (Ireland)

National Programme of Primary Instruction, Issued by The National Programme
  Conference (Educational Company of Ireland; Dublin, 1922)
Irish Education (Tuarim-London Research Group; London, 1962)
Programme for Action in Education 1984–1987: laid by the Government before each House
  of the Oireachtas, January 1984 (Dublin Stationary Office, 1994)
Green Paper on Education: Education for a Changing World (Stationary Office, 1992)
Report on the National Education Convention. John Coolahan (ed.) / the Convention
  Secretariat. (The National Education Convention Secretariat; Dublin, 1994)
Charting our Education Future: White Paper on Education (Department of
  Education; Dublin Stationary Office, 1995)

IV. Pamphlets

Bryce, R. J., Principal of the Belfast Academy, 'Sketch for a plan for a system
  of National Education for Ireland including hints for the Improvement of
  Education in Scotland' (George Cowie *et al.*; London, 1828)

Buxton, Charles, 'A Survey of the System of National Education in Ireland', (John Murray; London 1835)

Cohalan, Revd Assistant Bishop of Cork, 'Trinity College: Its Income and Its Value to the Nation', (n.p. Dublin 1911)

Doyle, Revd Dr William, Archbishop of Dublin, 'Letters on the State of Education in Ireland: and on Bible Societies', addressed to a Friend in England by J.K.L. Dublin (n.p. 1825)

Walsh, Revd Dr William, Archbishop of Dublin, 'Bilingual Education' *Gaelic League* Pamphlet, No. 8 (Dublin, 1900)

Frazer Revd William, 'National Education: Reasons for the Rejection in Britain of the Irish System; A Brief Exposition for Christian Educationists' 2nd Edition (James Nesbit and Company; London 1861)

_____ 'The State of our Educational Enterprises, a Report of and examination into the Workings, Results and Tendencies of the Chief Public Experiments in Great Britain and Ireland' (Blackie and Son; Glasgow, 1858)

Giffard, John (ed.), 'Mr Orde's Plan of an Improved System of Education in Ireland: submitted to the House of Commons, April 12, 1787', Caldwell & Orde's Speeches 1785, 1787, Absentees 1783, 1798, the Crisis. *Union Pamphlets* 8, Dublin (n.d.)

Hobson, Bulmer, 'Defensive Warfare: A Handbook for Irish Nationalists', *Sinn Féin* (Belfast, 1909)

Hogan, Revd J.F. D.D., 'Irish Catholics and Trinity College' (Browne and Nolan; Dublin 1906)

'Irish in University Education: Evidence Given Before the Royal Commission on University Education', *Gaelic League* Pamphlets, No. 29 (Dublin, 1902)

Keane, Marcus, 'National Education and the Principles of Civil Government As Applicable Thereto' (George Herbert; Dublin, 1874)

MacNeill, Eoin, 'Irish in the National University of Ireland' (An Cló–Cumann Ltd; Dublin, 1909)

Maguire, John Francis, 'The Irish Education Question. The National System, Its Modifications and its Failure. Separate Education, Vindicated by its Necessity and its Advantages. The Case of the National Teachers'. Two speeches delivered in the House of Commons in 1860 and 1861 by John Francis Maguire, M.P. (n.p. Dublin, 1861)

Maynooth and the University Question, Evidence Before the Royal Commission, with an Introduction by Revd Dr O'Dea, Bishop of Clonfert (Browne and Nolan; Dublin, 1903)

Nicolls, Eveleen, 'Nationality in Irish Education', *Gaelic League* (Dublin, 1910)

Nulty, Revd T., Bishop of Meath, 'The Relations Existing Between Convent Schools and the System of Intermediate and Primary National Education' (Browne and Nolan; Dublin, 1884)

O'Curry, Eugene MRIA, lectures on the 'Manuscript Materials of Ancient Irish History', Delivered at the Catholic University of Ireland, during the Session of 1855–1856 (James Duffy; London & Dublin, 1861)

O'Donoghue, J., 'Letter to the Right Hon. Edward Cardwell, M.P., on the demand for a denominational system of Education in Ireland', Dublin, (n.p. 1860)

Orde, Thomas, 'Plan of an Improved System of Education in Ireland', Printed by W. Porter, (n.p. Dublin, 1777)

O'Riordan, Revd M., 'Catholicity and Progress in Ireland' (Kegan Paul, Trench, Turbner; London, 1905)

O'Sullivan, Mortimer D.D., 'Reasons for Declining To Be Connected with the System of National Education' (William Curry and Company; Dublin, 1841)

Pim F.W., 'The Sinn Féin Rising: A Narrative and Some Reflection', (n.p. Dublin, 1916)

Redmond, J.E., 'Some Arguments for Home Rule: Being a Series of Speeches Delivered in the Autumn of 1907', by J.E. Redmond (Sealy, Bryers and Walker; Dublin, 1908)

Starkie, May C., 'What is Patriotism, the Teaching of Patriotism', Dublin (n.p. 1916)

Starkie, W.J.M, 'The History of Irish Primary and Secondary Education During the Last Decade' (A. Thom & Co.; Dublin, 1911)

Wyse, Thomas, 'Educational Reform or the Necessity of a National System of Education' (Longman, Rees, Orme, Browne, Green & Longman; London, 1836)

V. Magazines

An Macaomh, Vol. I, No. 1, Midsummer 1909

An Macaomh, Vol. I, No. 2, Christmas 1909

An Macaomh, Vol. II, No. 3, Christmas 1910

An Macaomh, Vol. II, No. 2, May 1913

An Scoláire, Vol. I, No. 9, June 1913

An Scoláire, Vol. II, No. 2, May 1913

An Scoláire, Vol. I, No. 6, May 1916

An Scoláire Vol. I, No. 8 (n.d.)

An Scoláire, Vol. I, No. 9, June 1913

VI. Journals

An Camán, February & November 1932

The Galway Reader, Vol. I, No. 3, Winter 1948

Irish Ecclesiastical Record, Vol. IV, 1867

Irish Ecclesiastical Record, Vol. V, 1869

Irish Ecclesiastical Record, Vol. I, 1880

Irish Ecclesiastical Record, Vol. V, 1884

Irish Ecclesiastical Record, Vol. VI, 1885

Irish Ecclesiastical Record, Vol. VII, 1886

Irish Ecclesiastical Record, Vol. X, 1889

Irish Ecclesiastical Record, Vol. XI, 1890

Irish Ecclesiastical Record, Vol. XIII, 1892

Irish Ecclesiastical Record, Vol. XVIII, 1896

Irish Ecclesiastical Record, Vol. XXVI, 1909

Irish Educational Review, February 1911

Irish Review, June 1914

New Republic, September 1931

Quarterly Journal of Education, Vol. IX, No. XVIII, 1835

VII. Articles in Journals

Aldrich, Richard, 'The Three Duties of the Historian of Education', *History of Education*, Vol. 32, No. 2 (Taylor and Francis; UK, 2003)

Boland, Evan, 'Aspects of Patrick Pearse', *The Dublin Magazine*, No. 1, (New Square Publications Limited; Dublin, Spring 1966)

Buttimer, Cornelius G., 'Celtic and Irish in College, 1849–1944', *Journal of the Cork Historical and Archaeological Society*, Vol. XCIV, No. 253, January–December 1989 (Cork Historical and Archaeological Society, 1989)

Coleman, Michael, 'The Responses of American Indian Children and Irish Children to the School, 1850s–1920s: A Comparative Study in Cross–Cultural Education', *American Indian Quarterly*, Vol. 23, Nos. 3 & 4, Summer & Fall 1999
_____ 'Representations of American Indians and the Irish educational reports, 1850s–1920s', *Irish Historical Studies*, Vol. XXXIII, No. 129, May 2002

Corcoran, Revd Timothy, 'The Dublin Education Bill of 1787', *Irish Monthly*, August (Dublin, 1931)
_____ 'Financing the Kildare Place Schools', *Irish Monthly*, June (Dublin, 1932)

Dennis, Alfred, 'A Memory of P.H. Pearse', *Capuchin Annual*, Dublin December 1941

Donato, Rubén and Lazerson, Marvin, 'New Directions in American Educational History: Problems and Prospects', *Educational Researcher*, Vol. 29, No. 8 (2000)

Garvan, T., 'The Politics of Language and Literature in Pre-Independence Ireland', *Irish Political Studies*, Vol. 2, 1987 (Frank Cass; London, 1987)

Goodman, Joyce and Jane Martin, 'History of Education – Defining a Field', *History of Education*, Vol. 33, No. 1 (Taylor and Francis; UK 2004)

Higgins, Roisin & Ui Chollatain, Regina, 'The Life and After-Life of P.H. Pearse', *Irish Academic Press* (Dublin, 2009)

Hogan, Pádraig, 'Teaching and Learning as a Way of Life', *Journal of Philosophy of Education*, Vol. 37, No. 2 (Blackwell; Oxford, UK, 2003)

Horsman, Reginald, 'Origins of Racial Anglo–Saxonism in Great Britain Before 1850', *Journal of the History of Ideas*, Vol. xxxvil, No 3, July–September 1976 (Temple University; Philadelphia, 1976)

Hyland, Áine, 'The Treasury and Irish Education: 1850–1922: The Myth and the Reality', *Irish Educational Studies*, Vol. 3, No. 2 (1983)

Kilcullen James, 'Appreciation, Headmaster of St Enda's', Éire-Ireland, the Irish American Cultural Institute, Summer (1962)

Lee, J.J., 'In Search of Patrick Pearse', in Máirín Dhonnchadha and Theo Dorgan (eds), *Revising the Rising* (Field Day; Derry, 1991)

Lindsay, James, 'Irish Language Teaching: A Survey of Teacher Perceptions', *Irish Journal of Education*, Vol. ix, No. 2, (St Patrick's College, Drumcondra; Dublin, 1975)

Mahoney, Kathleen A., 'New Times, New Questions', *Educational Researcher*, Vol. 29, No. 8 (2000)

McCulloch, Gary and Watts, Ruth, 'Introduction: Theory, Methodology, and the History of Education', *History of Education*, Vol. 32, No. 2 (Taylor and Francis; UK, 2003)

MacDonagh Donagh, 'Thomas MacDonagh', *An Cosantoir*, Vol. V, No. 10 (Dublin; October, 1945)

MacGarry, Milo, 'Memories of Scoil Éanna', *Capuchin Annual* (Dublin, 1930)

Murphy, Brian, 'Father Peter Yorke's "Turning of the Tide" 1890: The Strictly Cultural Nationalism of the Early Gaelic League', *Eire–Ireland*, Vol. 23 (St Paul, Minn; Irish American Cultural Institute, 1988)

Nugent, Joseph, 'Patrick Pearse and Homosexual Panic', *NcNair Scholars' Journal*, Vol. 4 (University of California Press; Berkley, USA, 1996)

O'Braonáin, Cathóir, 'Poets of the Insurrection II – Patrick Pearse', *Studies*, September (1916)

O'Buachalla, Séamas, 'Educational Policy and the Role of the Irish Language form 1831–1981', *European Journal of Education*, Vol. 19, No. 1 (Dorchester-on-Thames Carfax Publishing; UK, 1984)

O'Callahan, Patrick, 'Irish in the Schools', *The Bell*, Vol. XIV, No. 1 (Dublin, April 1947)

O'Kane, Wilfred, 'Educational Advantages of a Language Revival', *The Irish Educational Review*, Vol. II, No. 1, October 1908 (Brown & Nolan; Dublin, 1908)

Pearse Commemoration Committee, Memories of the Brothers Pearse, Pearse Collection, Pearse Museum (n.p. Dublin, 1958–60)

Pearse, Margaret, 'Patrick and William Pearse', *Capuchin Annual* (Dublin; May 1943)

Pearse, Margaret, 'St Enda's', *Capuchin Annual* (Dublin, May 1941)

Pearse, Patrick,' Letter to Mary Maguire', *Comhair*, November (Dublin, 1975)

Quane, Michael, 'The Diocesan Schools 1570–1870', *Journal of the Cork Historical and Archaeological Society*, 2 ser., lxvi. January–June 1961

Reddin, Kenneth, 'A Man Called Pearse', *Studies*, June 1943

Ryan, Desmond, 'Pearse, St Enda's and the Hound of Ulster', *Threshold*, Vol. 1 No. 3, Summer 1957 (The Lyric Players Theatre; Belfast, 1957)

Shaw, Francis, 'The Canon of Irish History – A Challenge', *Studies*, Vol. LXI (1972)

Thornley, David, 'Patrick Pearse', *Studies*, Spring 1967

_____ 'Patrick Pearse and the Pearse Family', *Studies*, Autumn–Winter 1971

Walsh, Brendan, 'Teacher Education in Ireland', *Education and Perspectives*, Vol. 33, No 2 (Murdoch University; Australia, 2006)

Whitehead, Clive, 'The Medium of Instruction in British Colonial Education: a case of Cultural Imperialism or Enlightened Paternalism?', *History of Education*, Vol. 24, No.1 (Taylor and Francis; UK 1995)

Withers, Charles, 'Education and Anglicisation: the Policy of the SSPCK toward the Education of the Highlander, 1709–1825', *Scottish Studies*, No. 26 (University of Edinburgh Press / Tuckwell Press, Ltd; Edinburgh, 1982)

VIII. Newspapers

The Freeman's Journal: 4 January 1908; 2 January 1909; 8 February 1909

Irish Freedom, March 1913

The Gaelic American, 7 March 1914

Irish Independent, 14 April 2001

The Irish Nation: 16 January 1908; 23 January 1909

The Irish People: 3 October 1908; 2 December 1908; 26 December 1908; 9 January 1909; 6 February 1909; 19 December 1909

The Leader: 1 September 1900; 2 May 1908; 6 June 1908; 18 July 1908; 13 March 1909; 14 August 1909; 30 July 1910; 17 September 1910

The Nation, 21 March 1909

Sinn Fein, 9 January 1909; 30 Janusry 1909; 27 March 1909; 26 June 1909

Sunday Business Post, 15 April 2001

The Irish Times, 3 September 1908; 30 June 1909; 24 June 1909; 3 September 1910; 2 October 2002; 17 April 2004; 27 April 2004; 3 July 2004

The Sunday Times, 8 April 2001

IX. Student Periodicals

The Alexandrian, December 1901

The Alexandrian, June 1904

The Alexandrian, December 1904

The Alexandrian, June 1905

The Alexandrian, December 1905

The Alexandrian, June 1907

The Alexandra College Calendar (Hodges & Figgis Ltd; Dublin 1900–1910)

St Stephens, June 1901

St Stephens, December 1905

St Stephens, June 1909

X. Books

Akenson, Donald H. *The Irish Education Experiment, the National System of Education in the Nineteenth Century* (Routledge & Keegan Paul; London, 1970)

_____ *A Mirror to Kathleen's Face* (McGill-Queen's University Press; Montreal and London, 1975)

_____ *Small Differences, Irish Catholics and Irish Protestants 1815–192* (Gill and Macmillan/McGill–Queen's University Press; Montreal and Dublin, 1991)

Akenson, N., *Irish Education, a History of Educational Institutions* (Routledge & Keegan Paul; London, 1970)

Allen, J.W., *The Place of History in Education* (Blackwood; London, 1909)

Armstrong, H.E., *The Teaching of Scientific Method and other Papers on Education* (Macmillan; London, 1910)

Andrews, C.S., *Dublin Made Me* (Mercier Press; Dublin, 1979 and The Lilliput Press; Dublin, 2001)

Atkinson, Robert, *Ancient Laws of Ireland*, Vol. VI. (n.p. Dublin, 1901)

Balfour, Graham, *The Educational Systems of Great Britain and Ireland* (Clarendon Press; Oxford, 1898)

Ball, M. and James Fife (ed.), *The Celtic Languages* (Routledge; London, 1993)

Barrow, Robin and Alan Graubard, *Free the Children, Radical Reform and the Free School Movement* (Vintage Books; England, 1974)

Barrow, Robin, *Radical Education* (Martin Robinson; England, 1978)

Baum, Willa K., *Transcribing and Editing Oral History* (American Association for State and Local History; Tennessee, USA, 1977)

Bamford, T.W. (ed.), *Thomas Arnold on Education: A Selection of his Writings* (Cambridge University Press, 1970)

Barzun, Jacques, *Clio and the Doctors: Psycho-History Quanto-History* (Chicago Press; USA, 1993)

Beckett, J.C., *The Making of Modern Ireland* (Faber & Faber Ltd; London, 1981)

Best, Geoffrey, *Mid Victorian Britain 1851–75* (Fontana Press; London, 1979)

Bibby, Cyril (ed.), *T.H. Huxley on Education, a Selection from his Writings* (Cambridge University Press, 1971)

Birch, Revd P., *St Kieran's College, Kilkenny* (M.H. Gill and Son Ltd, Dublin, 1951)

Blewitt, Trevor, *The Modern School Handbook*m (Victor Gollancz Ltd London, 1934)

Booth, William, *In Darkest England and the Way Out* (C. Knight; London, 1970)
_____ *Life and Labour of the People of London* (Hutchinson; London, 1969)
Boyd, William and Edmund J. King, *The History of Western Education* (Adam and Charles Black; London, 1968)
Bradshaw, B., *The Dissolution of the Religious Orders in Ireland under Henry VIII* (Cambridge University Press, 1974)
Bramwell, R.D., *Elementary School Work, 1900–1925* (Thompson; London, 1927)
Briggs, Asa, *The Age of Improvement 1783–1786* (Longman; London, 1959)
Buddy, Cyril (ed.), *T.H. Huxley on Education* (Cambridge University Press, 1971)
Cardozo, Nancy Maud Gonne, Lucky *Eyes and a High Heart* (Bobbs Merrill; New York, 1978)
Carr, Wilfred and Anthony Hartnett, *Education and the Struggle for Democracy, the Politics of Educational Ideas* (Open University Press; United Kingdom, 1996)
Chambers, R.W., *Thomas More* (Jonathan Cape; London, 1935)
Chapman, Hester W., *The Last Tudor King, a Study of Edward VI* (Grey Arrow Books; London, 1961)
Clark, Christopher, *Thoughtful Teaching* (Cassell; London, 1995)
Clear, Caitriona, *Nuns in Nineteenth-Century Ireland* (Gill and Macmillan; Dublin, 1987)
Clifford, Angela (ed.), *'Godless Colleges' and Mixed Education in Ireland* (Athol Books; Belfast, 1922)
Coldrey, Barry M., *Faith and Fatherland, the Christian Brothers and the Development of Irish Nationalism, 1838–1921* (Gill and Macmillan; Dublin, 1988)
Colum, Mary, *Life and the Dream* (London; Macmillan & Co. Ltd, 1928 & 1945)
Cook, Pat, *Scéal Scoil Éanna* (Office of Public Works; Dublin, 1986)
Coolahan, John, *Irish Education: History and Structure* (Institute of Public Administration; Dublin, 1980)
Corcoran, Timothy, *State Policy in Irish Education, AD 1539–1816* (Fallon Brothers Ltd; Dublin, 1916)
_____ *Education Systems in Ireland from the Close of the Middle Ages* (Department of Education, University College; Dublin 1928)
Corish, Patrick J. (ed.), *A History of Irish Catholicism*, Vol. 3 (Gill and Son; Dublin & Sidney, 1968)
_____ *Maynooth College 1795–1995* (Gill and Macmillan; Dublin, 1994)
Costello, Peter, *Clongowes Wood: A History of Clongowes Wood College 1841–1989* (Gill and Macmillan, 1989)
Crowley, Tony, *The Politics of Language in Ireland 1366–1922* (Routledge; London, 1999)
_____ *The Politics of Discourse: The Standard Language Question in British Cultural Debates* (Macmillan Education Ltd; London, 1989)
Curtis, E., *A History of Ireland* (Bowen and Noble Ltd, 1909)

Curtis, S.J., *History of Education in Great Britain* (University Tutorial Press; London, 1948)

Daly, Martin, *Memories of the Dead* (The Powel Press; Dublin, 1916)

Davies, Norman, *Europe, a History* (Pimlico; UK, 1997)

Deane, Séamus, Celtic *Revivals, Essays in Modern Irish Literature* (Wake Forest University Press; Carolina, USA, 1995)

Dickens, A.G., *The English Reformation* (B.T. Batsford Ltd; London, 1968)

Dillon, M. & N. Chadwick, *The Celtic Realms* (Weidenfeld and Nicolson; London, 1972)

Donald, J., *Sentimental Education: Schooling, Popular Culture and the Regulation of Liberty* (Verso; London, 1992)

Dowling, Revd P.J., *The Hedge Schools of Ireland* (Mercier Press; Cork, 1968)

_____ *A History of Irish Education: A Study in Conflicting Loyalties* (Mercier Press; Cork, 1971)

Dunne, Joseph, 'What's the Good of Education?' in *The Routledge Falmer Reader in the Philosophy of Education*, Wilfred Carr (ed.) (Routledge; London, 2005)

Durcan, T.J., *History of Irish Education from 1800* (Dragon Books; Wales, 1972)

Durkaz, V.E., *The Decline of the Celtic Languages, a Study of Linguistic and Cultural Conflict in Scotland, Wales and Ireland from Reformation to the Twentieth Century* (John Donald Publishers, Ltd; Edinburgh, 1983)

Edwards, Ruth Dudley, *Patrick Pearse, the Triumph of Failure* (Poolbeg Press; Dublin, 1977)

Elizabeth, Countess of Fingall, *Seventy Years Young* (n.p. London, 1937)

Farragher CSSp, Sean P., *Blackrock College 1860–1995* (Paraclete Press, Dublin, 1995)

Fathers of the Society of Jesus, *A Page of Irish History* (Talbot Press; Dublin 1930)

Foley, Tadgh (ed.), *From Queen's College to National University, Essays on the Academic History of QCG/UCG/NUI Galway* (Four Courts Press; Dublin, 1999)

Foster R.F., *Modern Ireland, 1600–1972* (Penguin Press; England, 1988)

_____ *The Oxford History of Ireland* (Oxford University Press, 1992)

Foucault, Michel, *Power/Knowledge: Selected Interviews and Other Writings, 1927–1972*, (ed. and trans. G. Gordon) (Harvester Press; UK, 1980)

Freire, Paulo, *Pedagogy of the Oppressed* (Penguin Books, 1970)

Freire, Paulo and Antonio Faundez, *Learning to Question, a Pedagogy of Liberation* (WWC Publications; Geneva, 1988)

Froebel, Freidrich, *The Education of Man* (ed. & trans. W.N. Hailman) (D. Appleton and Company; New York, 1900)

Fuller, Timothy (ed.), *The Voice of Liberal Learning* (Yale University Press; USA, 1989)

Geyl, Pieter, *Napoleon, For and Against* (Yale University Press, New Haven; USA, 1949)

Giroux, Henry A., *Theory and Resistance in Education: A Pedagogy for the Opposition* (Heinemann Educational Books; London, 1983)

_____ *Schooling for Democracy: Critical Pedagogy in the Modern Age* (Routledge; London, 1989)

_____ *Border Crossings, Cultural Workers and the Politics of Education* (Routledge; London, 1992)

Glenavy, Lady Beatrice, *Today We Will Only Gossip* (Constable & Co. Ltd; London, 1964)

Good Joe, *Enchanted By Dreams: The Journal of a Revolutionary* (Brandon Books, 1996)

Gorst, H., *The Curse of Education* (Grant Richards; London, 1901)

Graubard, Allen, *Free The Children, Radical Reform and the Free School Movement* (Vintage Books; England, 1974)

Greaves, Desmond, *Liam Mellows and the Irish Revolution* (Lawrence and Wishart; London, 1971)

Green, A.J. (ed.), *Pestalozzi's Educational Writings* (Arnold; London, 1912)

_____ *Life and Work of Pestalozzi* (University Tutorial Press; London, 1913)

Griffith, Kenneth and Timothy O'Grady (ed.), *Curious Journey, An Oral History of Ireland's Unfinished Revolution* (Hutchinson; London, 1982)

Griffith Arthur (ed.), Thomas Davis, *The Thinker and Teacher* (M.H. Gill & Son; Dublin, 1916)

Gross, Beatrice and Ronald (eds.), *Radical School Reform* (Penguin Books; London, 1969)

Gwynn, Stephen, *Irish Books and Irish People* (Talbot Press Ltd; Dublin 1919)

_____ *Experiences of a Literary Man* (Thornton Butterworth Ltd; London, 1926)

Gwynn, Denis, *The Life and Death of Roger Casement* (Jonathan Cape; London, 1930)

_____ 'The Origins and Growth of University College, Cork', *University Review*, Jubilee Issue, Vol. II. 3 & 4, 1958 (Grant & Bolton; Dublin, 1958)

Hardy, J.G., *The Public School Phenomenon, 1597–1977* (Hodder & Soughton; London, 1977)

Hayden, Mary and George A. Mooney, *A Short History of the Irish People, Part II, From 1603 to Modern Times* (Educational Company of Ireland; New Edition, 1960)

Hindley, Reg, *The Death of the Irish Language – A Qualified Obituary* (Dáil Uí Chadhain; Dublin, 1991)

Hobsbawm, Eric, *The Age of Revolution 1789–1848* (Weidenfeld and Nicholson; Great Britain, 1962)

_____ *The Age of Capital, 1848–75* (Weidenfeld & Nicolson; London, 1975)

Holmes, Brian, *Educational Policy and the Mission Schools* (Routledge; London, 1967)

Holmes, E.G.A., *What Is and What Might Be* (Constable; London, 1912)

Horgan, John, *Parnell to Pearse* (Browne and Nolan Ltd / Richview Press; Dublin, 1949)

Hutchinson, John, *the Dynamics of Cultural Nationalism* (Allen & Unwin; London, 1987)

Huxley, T.H., *Science and Culture and Other Essays* (Macmillan; London, 1899)

Hyland, A. and K. Milne, *Irish Education Documents Volume I* (Church of Ireland College of Education; Dublin, 1987)

Irving, David, *Hitler's War* (Macmillan; London, 1983)

Jones, W.R., *Bilingualism in Welsh Education* (Cardiff University Press; Wales, 1966)

Skutnabb-Kangas, Tove, *Bilingualism or Not: The Education of Minorities* (Multilingual Matters; Clevedon, 1981)

Kelly, Adrian, *Compulsory Irish, Language and Education in Ireland 1870s–1970s* (Irish Academic Press; Dublin, 2002)

Ker, Ian, *John Henry Newman, a Biography* (Bristol Press; England 1991)

Kiberd, Declan, *Synge and the Irish Language* (Macmillan; London, 1993)

_____ *Inventing Ireland: The Literature of the Modern Nation*, Vintage (London; 1995)

Kockel, Ullrich, (ed.), *Landscape Heritage and Identity, Case Studies in Irish Ethnography* (Liverpool University Press, 1995)

Lawson, J. and Harold Silver, *A Social History of Education in England* (Methuen; London, 1973)

Lee Joseph, *The Modernisation of Irish Society, 1848–1918* (Gill & Macmillan; Dublin, 1973)

Lemon, M.C., *The Discipline of History and the History of Thought* (Routledge; England, 1995)

Leslie, Shane, *The Passing Chapter* (Charles Scribner and Sons; New York, 1934)

_____ *The Irish Issue in Its American Aspect* (T. Fischer Unwin; London, 1918)

Lewis, E. Glyn., *Bilingualism and Bilingual Education: A Comparative Study* (University of New Mexico Press; Albuquerque, 1980)

Londraville, Janis and Richard (eds.), *Too Long A Sacrifice: The Letters of Maud Gonne and John Quinn* (Associated University Press; London, 1999)

Louis N. Le Roux, *Patrick H. Pearse* (Phoenix Publishing Co. Ltd; Dublin, 1932)

MacBride, Anna (ed.), *Always Your Friend: The Gonne – Yeats Letters 1893–1938* (White, Norman, Jeffers, Hutchinson; London, 1992)

McCay, Hedley, *Padraic Pearse, A New Biography* (Mercier Press; Cork, 1966)

MacDonagh, Donagh, *P.H. Pearse* (n.d. n.p. Dublin)

MacManus, Antonia, *The Irish Hedge School and its Books* (Four Courts Press; Dublin, 2002)

Macnamara, John, *Bilingualism and Primary Education: A Study of Irish Experience* (Edinburgh University Press, 1966)

MacNunn, N., *A Path to Freedom in the Schools* (Bell; London, 1914)

Martin, F.X. (ed.), *Leaders and Men of the Easter Rising* (Methuen & Co. Ltd; London, 1967)

_____ *The Easter Rising 1916 and University College Dublin* (Browne and Nolan Ltd; Dublin, 1966)

Maurios, Andre, *A History of England* (Jonathan Cape; London, 1937)

Mangan, J.A. (ed.), *Benefits Bestowed? Education and British Imperialism* (Manchester University Press, 1988)

Maxwell, Constantia M.A., *Irish History from Contemporary Sources 1509–1610* (George Allen & Unwin; London, 1923)

McCartney, Donal, *UCD a National Idea, the History of University College, Dublin* (Gill and Macmillan, 1999)

McClelland, Alan, *English Roman Catholics and Higher Education 1830–1900* (Clarendon Press; Oxford, 1973)

McDonald, Walter, *Reminiscences of a Maynooth Professor* (Cape; London, 1925)

Meyer, Adolphe E., *Grandmasters of Educational Thought* (McGraw Hill Inc.; USA, 1975)

McLaren, Peter, *Critical Pedagogy and Predatory Culture, Oppositional Politics in a Postmodern Era* (Routledge; New York, 1995)

Millet, Benignus, O.M.F., *A History of Irish Catholicism* (Gill and Son Ltd; Dublin, 1968)

Milne, Kenneth, *The Irish Charter Schools 1730–1830* (Four Courts Press; Dublin 1997)

Mitchell, C. and S. Weber, *Reinventing Ourselves as Teachers: Private and Social Acts of Memory and Imagination* (Falmer; London 1996)

Montessori, Maria, *the Secret of Childhood* (trans. & ed., M.J. Costello. S.J.) (Ballantine Books; New York, 1991)

_____ *Dr Montessori's Own Handbook* (Schocken Books; New York, 1914)

Moran, Seán Farrell, *Patrick Pearse and the Politics of Redemption* (The Catholic University of America Press; Washington, USA, 1994)

More, Alex, *The Good Teacher: Dominant Discourses in Teaching and Teacher Education* (RoutledgeFalmer; London, 2004)

Morrisey, Thomas J.S.J., *Towards a National University: William Delaney 1835–1924 An Era of Initiative in Irish Education* (Wolfhound Press; Dublin, 1983)

Mulcahy, D.G. (ed.), *Irish Educational Policy: Process and Substance. Institute of Public Administration* (Dublin, 1989)

Murphy, Brian, *Patrick Pearse and the Lost Republican Ideal* (James Duffy; Dublin 1991)

Murphy, Daniel, *Comenius, a Reassessment of his Work* (Irish Academic Press; Dublin, 1995)

Murphy, James H. (ed.), *Nos Autem: Castleknock College and its Contribution* (Gill & MacMillan; Dublin 1996)

Murphy, John A., *The College: A History of Queen's / University College, Cork 1845–1995* (Cork University Press, 1995)

Neill, A.S., *Hearts Not Heads in the Schools* (Herbert Jenkins Ltd; London, 1945)

_____ *Summerhill, a Radical Approach to Education* (Victor Gollancz Ltd; London, 1962)

_____ *The Free Child* (Victor Gollancz; London, 1968)

Nicholson, Virginian, *Among the Bohemians: Experiments in Living 1900–1939* (Penguin Books; London, 2003)

Nicolls, Eveleen, *Nationality in Irish Education* (M.H. Gill and Son Ltd, 1910)

Ní Ghacháin, Mairéad, *Lúise Gabhánach Ní Dhufaigh agus Scoil Bhríde* (Johnswood Press, 1993)

NicShiubhlaigh, Maire, *The Splendid Years* (Duffy; Dublin, 1955)

Nowlan, K. and T.D. Williams (eds), *Ireland in the War Years and After, 1931–5* (Gill and Macmillan; Dublin, 1969)

Oakshott, Michael, *Rationalism in Politics and other Essays* (Macmillan; England, 1962)

_____ *On History and other Essays* (Basil Blackwell; Oxford, 1983)

O'Brien, Gerard (ed.), *Parliament, Politics and People, Essays in Eighteenth-Century Irish History* (Irish Academic Press, 1989)

O'Brien, R. Barry, *Studies in Irish History* (Oxford University Press, 1992)

O'Buachalla, Séamus (ed.), *The Letters of P.H. Pearse* (Colin Smythe Ltd; Buckinghamshire, UK, 1980)

_____ (ed.), *A Significant Irish Educationalist, the Educational Writings of P.H. Pearse* (Mercier Press; Dublin 1980)

_____ *Séamas Educational Policy in Twentieth Century Ireland* (Wolfhound Press; Dublin, 1988)

_____ (ed.), *An Piarsach sa Bheilg, P.H. Pearse in Belgium / P.H. Pearse in Belgie* (An Gúm; Dublin, 1998)

Ó'Catháin, Seán, *Secondary Education in Ireland* (Talbot Press; Dublin, 1951)

O'Connor, Anne and Susan Parkes, *Gladly Learn and Gladly Teach: A History of Alexandra College and School, Dublin, 1866–1966* (Blackwater; Tallaght, 1984)

O'Connor, Ulick, *The Troubles, Mandarin* (London, 1989)

_____ *The 1916 Proclamation* (Anvil Books; Dublin, 1986)

O'Connell, Maurice (ed.), *O'Connell, Education, Church and State* (IPA; Dublin, 1992)

O'Crohan, Thomás, *The Islandman* (Clarendon; Oxford, 1951)

O'Crohan, Seán, *A Day in our Life* (Oxford University Press, 1992)

O'Cuiv, Brian (ed.), *A View of the Irish Language* (Stationary Office; Dublin, 1969)

O'Donoghue, Thomas A., *Bilingual Education in Ireland, 1904–1922: The Case of the Bilingual Programme of Instruction*, Centre for Irish Studies Monograph Series, No. 1 (Murdoch University Press; Perth, Western Australia, 2000)

O'Dubhshláine, Micheál, *Oighean Uasal ó Phríomhchathair Eireann* (Brandon Press; Ireland, 1999)

_____ *A Dark Day on the Blaskets* (Brandon Press; Ireland, 2003)

Ó'Fearaíl, Padraig, *The Story of Conradh Na Gaeilge* (Clodhanna Teo; Dublin, 1975)

O'Flannghaile, Thomas, *For The Tongue of the Gael* (Sealy, Byrnes & Walker; Dublin, 1907)

O'Guiheen, Micheál, *A Pity Youth Does Not Last* (Oxford University Press, 1982)

O'Lúing, Seán, *Celtic Studies in Europe and Other Essays* (Geography
     Publications; Dublin, 2000)
O'Mahony, Sean, *Frongoch, University of Revolution* (FDR Teoranta; Dublin, 1987)
Ogilvie, Vincent, *The English Public School* (Batsford; London, 1957)
Ó'Riagáin, Pádraig, *Language Policy and Social Reproduction, Ireland 1893–1993*
     (Clarendon; Oxford, 1997)
Ó'Súilleabháin, Donnacha, *Cath na Gaeilge sa chórus Oideachais, 1893–1911*
     (Conradh na Gaeilge; Dublin, 1988)
Palmer, Parker J., *The Courage To Teach: Exploring the Inner Landscape of a
     Teacher's Life* (Jossey-Bass; San Francisco, USA, 1998)
Park, Joe, *Bertrand Russell on Education* (Allen and Unwin; London, 1964)
Peter Parker, *The Old Lie: The Great War and the Public School Ethos*
     (Hambeldon Continuum; UK, 1987)
Parminter, Geoffrey de C., *Roger Casement* (Barker; London, 1936)
Paseta, Senia, *Before the Revolution, Nationalism, Social Change and Ireland's
     Catholic Elite 1879–1922* (Cork University Press, 1999)
Pearse, Mary Brigid (ed.), *The Home Life of Pádraig Pearse* (Mercier Press; Cork 1979)
Pim, Frederic W., *The Sinn Féin Rising: A Narrative and some Reflections*
     (Hodges, Figgis & Co. Ltd; Dublin, 1916)
Porter, Raymond J., *P.H. Pearse* (Twayne Publishers; New York, 1973)
Plumb, J.H., *England in the Eighteenth Century* (Harmondsworth; Penguin Books, 1963)
Price, Glanville, *Languages in Britain & Ireland* (Blackwell Publishers; Oxford,
     England, 2000)
Pring, Richard, *Philosophy of Education: Aims, Theory, Common Sense and
     Research* (Continuum; London, 2004)
Beers-Quinn, David, *The Elizabethans and The Irish* (Cornell University Press;
     New York, 1966)
Robbins, Frank, *Under The Starry Plough* (Academy Press; Dublin, 1977)
Roberts, Gwyneth Tyson, *The Language of the Blue Books, the Perfect Instrument
     of Empire* (University of Wales Press; Cardiff, 1998)
Robson, Catherine, *Men in Wonderland: The Lost Girlhood of the Victorian
     Gentleman* (Princeton University Press, 2001)
Russell, Bertrand, *Why I Am Not A Christian* (Allen and Unwin; London, 1957)
Desmond Ryan, *Remembering Sion, a Chronicle of Storm and Calm* (Dublin, 1924)
_____ *The Complete Works of P.H. Pearse, St Enda's and its Founder* (Phoenix
     Press Publishing Co. Ltd; Dublin, Cork, Belfast, 1917)
_____ *The Complete Works of P.H. Pearse, Political Writings and Speeches*
     (Phoenix Press Publishing Co. Ltd; Dublin, Cork, Belfast, 1917)
_____ *The Complete Works of P.H. Pearse, Plays, Stories, Poems* (Phoenix Press
     Publishing Co. Ltd; Dublin, Cork, Belfast, 1917 & 1924)
_____ *The Pope's Green Island* (James Nesbit & Co. Ltd; London, 1912)

Santamaria, B.A., *Daniel Mannix, the Quality of Leadership* (Melbourne University Press; Carlton, Ashford, Middx., 1984)

Schenk, H.G., *the Mind of the European Romantics* (Constable; London, 1966)

Selleck, R.J.W., *the New Education, the English Background 1870–1914* (Sir Isaac Pitman & Sons Ltd; London, 1968)

Sheridan, Seán, *What if the Dream Come True?* (James Kelly, Dublin (n.d.))

Silver, Harold, *English Education and the Radicals, 1780–1850* (Routledge & Keegan Paul; London, 1975)

Simon, Brian, 'Can Education Change Society?' in *The RoutledgeFalmer Reader in History of Education*, Gary McCulloch (ed.) (Routledge, 2005)

Sisson, Elaine, *Pearse's Patriots, St Enda's and the Cult of Boyhood* (Cork University Press, 2004)

Skeffington, Andre Sheehy, *Skeff, the life of Owen Sheehy Skeffington 1909–1970* (Lilliput Press; Dublin 1991)

Skidelsky, Robert, *English Progressive Schools* (Penguin Books; England, 1969)

Stanley, R., *Life of Thomas Arnold* (D.D.B. Fellowes; London, 1845)

Steiner, George, *Lessons of the Master, the Charles Eliot Norton Lectures 2001–2002* (Harvard University Press; England, 2003)

Stone, Lawrence, *The Past and the Present Revisited* (Routledge; England, 1987)

Sugrue, Ciaran (ed.), *Curriculum and Ideology: Irish Experiences International Perspectives* (Liffey Press; Dublin, 2004)

Synge, J.M., *the Aran Islands* (Penguin Books; London, 1907)

Simon, Brian, *Education and the Labour Movement 1870–1918* (Lawrence & Wishart; London, 1965)

Tierney, Michael (ed.), *Struggle With Fortune* (Browne and Nolan; Dublin, 1954)

_____ *Eoin MacNeill, Scholar and Man of Action 1867–1945* (Clarendon Press; Oxford, 1980)

_____ (ed.), *Michael Tierney, a Classicist's Outlook* (Martin Tierney BL; Dublin, 2002)

Vinovskis, Maris A., *History and Educational Policymaking* (Yale University Press; New Haven, USA 1999)

Ward, Wilfred, *The Life of John Henry Cardinal Newman*, Vol. I. Longman's (Green & Co.; London, 1912)

Wardle, D., *English Popular Education 1780–1975* (Cambridge University Press; UK, 1976)

Webb, D.A and R.B. McDowell, *Trinity College, Dublin 1592–1952, An Academic History* (Cambridge University Press, 1982)

Webb, R.K., *Modern England, From the Eighteenth century to the Present* (Allen & Unwin; London, 1980)

Welch, Robert (ed.), *The Oxford Companion to Irish Literature* (Clarendon Press; Oxford, 1996)

White, J., *The Educational Ideas of Froebel* (University Tutorial Press; London, 1907)

Wiener, Leo (trans.), *Leo Tolstoy on Education* (University of Chicago Press, 1967)

Williams, D. (ed.), *the Irish Struggle* (Routledge & Keegan Paul; London, 1966)

Withers. C., *Gaelic in Scotland: The Geographical History of a Language* (Donald; Edinburgh, 1984)

Yeats, W.B., *Autobiographies* (Macmillan; London, 1955)

Young, Ella, *Flowering Dusk* (Longman's Green & Co.; New York 1945)

XI. Audio Archives and Audio Recordings

'Todd Andrews talks to Pádraig Ó'Rathallaigh' Radio Éireann, November 1947

Proinsias O'Conluain, 'This Man Kept a School', Radio Éireann, April 1979

Interview with Billy Moore (Liam Ó'Mordha), Pearse Museum, August 1992

Colm Porter, 'Silence Descends', Radio Éireann, January 2003

Rurí and Máire Bruagh (Nic Shuibhlaigh) interview by author, tape recording 15 October 2003

Réiltín McCall interviewed by author, 2004

Eileen O'Byrne interviewed by author, 2004

Iseult Ní Chléirigh interviewed by author, 2004

Áine Ní Fhíthigh interviewed by author, 2004

XII. Theses

Brosnahan, John, 'Education as an Instrumentum Regni in Tudor State Policy: Import and Result', M.A. in Education, (diss., University College Dublin, 1941)

Lane, Elizabeth, 'The Church Education Society for Ireland 1831–1871: An Examination of the Origins, Activities and Decline of the Church Education Society for Ireland', M.Ed. (diss., University College Dublin, 1990)

O'Sullivan, Dominic, 'Catholic Schooling in Mid–Victorian Ireland' M.Ed. (diss., University College Dublin, 1996)

_____ 'Catholic Schooling in Mid–Victorian Ireland', M.Ed. (diss., University College Dublin, 1996)

XIII. Conference Proceedings

Cooke, Patrick, 'P.H. Pearse: A Victorian Gael'. Paper presented at The Life and After–Life of P.H. Pearse, Interdisciplinary Conference, University College Dublin / Pearse Museum, Dublin, April 2006

Hyland, Áine, University College, Cork, 'Women in the Queen's Colleges and the National University of Ireland.' Paper presented to the History of Education Society (UK) Conference, Trinity College Dublin, November 2004

O'Malley, James, 'An Account of the Growth of the Lay Secondary Schools in Ireland, 1922–1970, the motives of lay founders, the demise of the

lay schools and the impact of lay education during that period.' Paper
presented to the History of Education Society (UK) Conference, Trinity
College Dublin, November 2004

Swindles, Julia, 'Pedagogy and Performance in Early Eighteenth Century
Britain'. Paper presented to the History of Education Society (UK)
Conference, Hommerton College, University of Cambridge, England,
December 2003

XIV. Miscellaneous Items

Hopkinson, Michael (ed.), *Frank Henderson's Easter Rising*, (Irish Narratives;
Cork University, 1998)

McMahon, Timothy (ed.), *Pádraig Ó Fathaigh's War of Independence: Recollections
of a Galway Gaelic Leaguer* (Irish Narratives; Cork University Press, 2000)

O'Snodaigh Pádraig, 'Willie Pearse: Artist', Leabhrán Cuimhneacháin
Aran, Fhoilsiú ar Ócáid Bronnadh Eochair Scoil Éanna ar
Uachtarán na hÉireann, Eamonn De Valera, 23 Aibreán 1970

If you enjoyed this book, you may also be interested in...

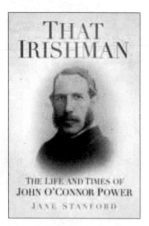

That Irishman
JANE STANFORD

The story of John O'Connor Power is the story of Ireland's struggle for nationhood itself. Born into poverty in Ballinasloe in 1846, O'Connor Power spent much of his childhood in the workhouse. From here he rose rapidly through the ranks of the Fenian Movement to become a leading member of the Supreme Council of the Irish Republican Brotherhood. In 1874 he was elected Member for Mayo to the British House of Commons where he was widely acknowledged to be one of the outstanding orators of his day. His speeches, both in Parliament and to the US House of Representatives, secured crucial concessions and support for the Irish cause.

978 1 84588 698 1

Quiet Revolutionaries
DR MARGARET Ó HÓGARTAIGH

This book examines the pivotal role Irish women played in the development of education, medicine and sport in one hundred years of change in their country and indeed the world in general. Ó hÓgartaigh examines the experiences of teachers and the medical approaches of a significant generation of doctors, and nurses' attempts to professionalise, both in Ireland and internationally. The challenges faced by women in other professions are also discussed, particularly the few dentists, pharmacists and veterinary surgeons. The origins of women's sport in Ireland are closely examined, as are the sporting careers of women, and the sporting restrictions in place in the 1930s, '40s, and '50s.

978 1 84588 696 7

Whose Past is it Anyway?
JUDE COLLINS

Ireland is on the cusp of what has become known as the 'Decade of Centenaries'. In this unique book, we gain an insight into three of these centenaries – the signing of the Ulster Covenant, the Easter Rising and the Battle of the Somme – from across the spectrum of political allegiances and perspectives. Including interviews with An Taoiseach Enda Kenny, Fr Brian D'Arcy, Niall O'Dowd and Roddy Doyle amongst many others, this collection of discussions touches upon the ethereal nature of our history, and the constantly shifting sands upon which we build our shared past.

978 1 84588 754 4

Visit our websites and discover thousands of other History Press books.

www.thehistorypress.ie
www.thehistorypress.co.uk